THE SHATTERED LENS

THE SHATTERED LENS

A WAR PHOTOGRAPHER'S TRUE STORY OF CAPTIVITY AND SURVIVAL IN SYRIA

JONATHAN ALPEYRIE

with Stash Luczkiw and Bonnie Timmermann

ATRIA BOOKS

New York   London   Toronto   Sydney   New Delhi

ATRIA
BOOKS

An Imprint of Simon & Schuster, Inc.
1230 Avenue of the Americas
New York, NY 10020

First Atria Books hardcover edition October 2017

ATRIA BOOKS and colophon are trademarks of Simon & Schuster, Inc.

For information about special discounts for bulk purchases, please contact Simon & Schuster Special Sales at 1-866-506-1949 or business@simonandschuster.com.

The Simon & Schuster Speakers Bureau can bring authors to your live event. For more information, or to book an event, contact the Simon & Schuster Speakers Bureau at 1-866-248-3049 or visit our website at www.simonspeakers.com.

Interior design by Amy Trombat

Manufactured in the United States of America

10 9 8 7 6 5 4 3 2 1

Library of Congress Cataloging-in-Publication Data
Names: Alpeyrie, Jonathan, author. | Luczkiw, Stash, co-author. | Timmermann, Bonnie, co-author.
Title: The shattered lens : a war photographer's true story of captivity and survival in Syria / Jonathan Alpeyrie with Stash Luczkiw and Bonnie Timmermann.
  Description: First Atria Books hardcover edition. | New York : Atria Books, 2017.
Identifiers: LCCN 2017016403 (print) | LCCN 2017027082 (ebook) | ISBN 9781501146541 (ebook) | ISBN 9781501146503 (hardback) | ISBN 9781501146534 (paperback)
Subjects: LCSH: Alpeyrie, Jonathan—Kidnapping, 2013. | Alpeyrie, Jonathan—Captivity, 2013. | Syria—History—Civil War, 2011—Biography. | Kidnapping—Syria—History—21st century. | Torture—Syria—History—21st century. | Survival—Syria—History—21st century. | Photojournalists—Biography. | War correspondents—Biography. | French Americans—Biography. | BISAC: BIOGRAPHY & AUTOBIOGRAPHY / Military. | BIOGRAPHY & AUTOBIOGRAPHY / Artists, Architects, Photographers. | BIOGRAPHY & AUTOBIOGRAPHY / Personal Memoirs.
Classification: LCC DS98.72.A47 (ebook) | LCC DS98.72.A47 A3 2017 (print) | DDC 956.9104/231092—dc23
LC record available at https://lccn.loc.gov/2017016403

ISBN 978-1-5011-4650-3
ISBN 978-1-5011-4654-1 (ebook)

I would like to dedicate the book to Bonnie Timmermann, who has made this possible from the beginning; to my mother, who has given me the strength in life; and to my father, who gave me the intellectual abilities to understand this world.

DISCLAIMER

As far as the limits and caprices of memory allow—especially in the fog of war and fear—this story is as true as it gets. I've taken liberties with many of the names in order to protect anyone still in harm's way and accommodate those who prefer not to advertise their actions or might still pose a danger to me. Some of the names I've simply forgotten or never knew.

BOOK 1

ENTER THE LEVANT

SOMETIMES YOU CAN SENSE when things are about to go terribly wrong. You get a premonition, a sign smacks you in the face. Some times there's a stirring in the marrow of your bones, a sort of queasiness in your soul, and you just know.

In the lead-up to the day when things went terribly wrong for me—April 29, 2013—I didn't have a clue about what was to come. It all seemed if not good, then at least business as usual in an unusual business. Maybe that Scud missile whistling in the distance over the Syrian border should have been taken as a warning. Or the account of those other journalists killed by government shelling. Or the rank taste of the bird I'd shot for lunch.

But I was too focused on the task at hand: to capture images of destruction and carnage. Because if I did my job well, I knew one of those images could serve as an icon of that particular confluence of events in history.

It wasn't that I thought I was immortal. Actually, I've always been cautious, probably too preoccupied with making sure that everything goes smoothly and safely. But of course, I'm always walking into bad situations. That's my job. I take pictures of people fighting. Not boxing matches, not street fights, but wars—armies and militias going at it with heavy weapons to alter the course of history. And at the risk of sounding arrogant, I've always felt like I could somehow make some good out of any bad situation. Maybe I was fooling myself. It's easy to make up all sorts of myths about yourself after the fact.

It was my third trip to the Syrian combat zone. The war had broken out in 2011 during the Arab Spring. The mythography around the war now offers us the image of a spark that had ignited the conflict: six kids in the southern city of Daraa arrested for writing antigovernment graffiti: "The people want the fall of the regime." They were tortured in prison, and Syrians all around the country started demonstrating against their dictatorial president, Bashar al-Assad, who tried to crush any dissent before it had a chance to fester. I personally doubt that any historical cause and effect is ever so clear-cut, but it does make for a moving story.

Bashar al-Assad, like his father Hafez before him, and like so many leaders in that part of the world, would not tolerate any opposition. Indeed, by all accounts both Assads were butchers. That so much of the population wanted something else—something better, kinder—was no surprise. The thornier issue was who wanted what—and why. My job was to go and see. In the purest sense, I was expected to serve as the world's eyes on the conflict.

THERE ARE TWO WAYS you can go into a field where human misery is your currency. Either you go in as a prism and refract the light, giving the subject a face and voice in the process, or you go in and feed off the light like a vampire feeding off blood. In the latter case the voice into which the light is translated turns into a scream. Usually the scream is more immediate, more effective than peering into a soul most don't even believe in. People have developed a need for images of horror.

But these are the last things you think about when you're there. Like any other job, the primary purpose is to get it done, get paid, and move on to the next task. I was working for Polaris Images, a photo agency. The heyday for conflict photographers was long gone—we were one of the first trades to get slammed by the digital revolution's bulldozer. I didn't start taking photos for a living until the early 2000s, so I was essentially part of the first "post-film" generation of photographers.

When you're competing not only with a host of local photographers, but also half the population—which now carry camera phones as prosthetic memories—you don't just need to be fast, you need to be professional. Without film to develop, everyone expects instant product. So you can spend all morning dodging mortar fire, then have to edit, caption and file photos in the afternoon and evening. If your agency gives you money to go somewhere, then that's good, you're ahead of the game. Otherwise you go on your own dime and send a steady stream of photos every day. Clients pick them out from a torrent of images updated continuously. It's worse than eat what you kill. More like scatter your chum and hope for the best.

YOU NEED TO TRAVEL light. Everything has to fit into a carry-on. No check-in baggage. Just before leaving for the front lines, I would ritualistically lay out my possessions on the bed, then pack them into my duffel bag.

This time Lebanon was my entry point. On my two previous trips to Syria I had come in from Turkey. Now I wanted to get closer to the fighting near Damascus.

Outside the window of my hotel room in Byblos I could see the Mediterranean Sea. A few waves lapped up against the sandy beach strewn with lounge chairs, but none of them big enough to surf. A day or two of beach might be nice after I got back safely, but I wasn't sure I'd get the chance. So I decided to go for a swim before I packed.

It was mid-April and the water was cold, but bearable. A very

Western-looking Lebanese family was relaxing in the lounge chairs: the father was working on his laptop and the mother was checking her phone, occasionally snapping a photo of her two boys, who would hide behind the lounge chairs, pointing their fingers like guns and shooting at each other with sound effects. When they started splashing in the waves, enacting some sort of amphibious assault, the mother went to the older boy, about ten, and had him take pictures of her knee-deep in the gentle waves. She spoke an Arabic peppered with English and French to her kids, and although she was wearing a bikini, she managed to cover herself up with a shawl when she posed for the photo.

I'd noticed the family the night before, in the lobby. The father ran some sort of export company. Byblos used to be an ancient Phoenician port. The Lebanese have trading in their blood—some Levantine strain in the DNA.

While he was snapping photos, the boy got sideswiped by an unexpected wave and the phone fell into the water. His mother got upset and scolded him in Arabic, tugging him by the ear. It was like an appendage of hers had fallen into an abyss, and while she was scolding him the phone got dragged out deeper than either she or her boys were willing to go.

I watched the mother's look of desperation and swam to where they were. Then I dove down and snatched the phone from what was only waist-deep water.

The mother thanked me profusely, as did the embarrassed boy, and she offered to buy me coffee. I turned it down because I had to pack.

The woman and her family were so polite and urbane, I thought. It was hard to imagine that just over the mountains, in Syria, they were shelling and massacring each other. But that's how it is in conflicts.

Back in my room I laid all my stuff out on the bed: three T-shirts; two long-sleeve thermal cotton shirts; an extra pair of jeans; four pairs of socks; four pairs of underwear, three of which had been hanging out on the balcony to dry; my still-wet Speedo trunks, which I wrapped in plastic; a bathroom kit full of toothpaste, toothbrush and floss, Band-

Aids and tourniquet; two Nikons, a D300 and a D100; my Mac Power-Book; a camera vest, and a heavy-duty ziplock bag of full of chargers, batteries and cables. I fit it all carefully into the duffel bag, making sure to maximize the limited amount of space, gave the room one more look-over, then threw on my light cotton jacket, ready to go.

FROM BYBLOS TO THE SYRIAN BORDER it was only about thirty miles as the crow flies. But because of the mountains I'd have to take a circuitous route. Most of my Lebanese contacts had come from a man named Robert Doueihy, a very sophisticated businessman from a prominent Maronite Christian family, whose forebears included some of modern Lebanon's luminaries. A close associate of the family was a man they called "the Doctor." He had a contact, a young Syrian man who worked as a smuggler, and this man had agreed to take me across the border into Syria. He was doing round-trips, carrying weapons and cash back and forth. The Doctor also had close contacts in Syria. I told him that I wanted to go into rebel-held territory north of Damascus. In the spring of 2013 rebels from the Free Syrian Army, a group of relatively moderate opposition fighters, controlled most of the area just over the Lebanese border as well as large parts of Homs and many suburbs of Damascus.

They first took me to Beirut, where we holed up in a safe house. My driver told me we were in Hezbollah territory. All Lebanese over a certain age still remembered the war that tore the city apart in the 1970s and '80s. I was born in 1979, so I was too young to remember. But one of my first political memories was the September 1986 wave of ter-rorist attacks in Paris, the city where I was born and raised until I was fourteen, when I moved to New York to live with my father. Every few days a bomb would explode in Paris. I learned that it had something to do with a place called Lebanon, with "that part of the world." So despite the return to normality, everyone in Beirut still seemed a bit edgy. The volatile mix of Hezbollah Shia, Sunni Muslims, and Christians, espe-cially with all the refugees from Syria, could explode at any moment.

And in fact there had already been several car bombs in Lebanon since hostilities had broken out next door.

As we were going through the downtown area our driver pointed to a street and said "Green Line," referring to the demarcation line between Muslim West Beirut and Christian East Beirut—a no-man's-land that had turned green during the war, overgrown with weeds, bushes, even trees, due to neglect.

On April 19 we left Beirut for Arsal, a town in Lebanon, close to the border. In 2012 Arsal had been attacked by Assad's forces, fanning fears that the conflict would engulf Lebanon as well. I sat in the backseat of a big pickup truck while an older gentleman, probably in his fifties and wearing a red keffiyeh, drove. The smuggler sat in the front passenger seat. We didn't say a word to each other during the whole two-hour drive.

We headed east toward the mountains, passing through the Bekaa Valley, then northeast to skirt the edge of Baalbek, a city known in ancient times as Heliopolis. I would have liked to stop and explore. When I was a teenager I wanted to be an archeologist—like Indiana Jones—and even took part in a few archeological digs: one in Spain when I was sixteen and two in France. I kept a book in which I collected photos of important ancient Roman sites. In fact, my first trip to Syria was in 2002, when I photographed various ruins there in order to add to that project. But I quickly realized that patiently sweeping aside layers of dirt to reveal artifacts buried in the earth could be deadly dull. So from there I turned to studying history, which became my major at the University of Chicago. Inevitably I was drawn to a more adrenaline-inducing path: examining history as it unfolds in real time.

Syria lay just over the mountains about six miles to the east. And history was unfolding there with a vengeance. Instead of photographing millennial ruins in a static state, as I had in 2002, my intention was to record the very process of a civilization's ruin. This process has always been complex and compelling. It sucked me and other combat reporters in like a vortex. And Syria in particular seemed to separate the professionals from the dilettantes. I couldn't wait to get over the border and be in the thick of it again. But I'd been there the year before and was also aware that the whole country was rapidly descending into hell.

SOMETIMES THE SHIFT BETWEEN normality and a war zone can be abrupt. In many cases you'll see a few checkpoints with armed soldiers to foreshadow the devastation ahead. Other times there's nothing but a sense of emptiness, a vacuum that begs to be filled with mayhem.

When we got to Arsal we had to drive through a few checkpoints, but they didn't stop us. By the evening we arrived at the old driver's house in a hilly area. They put me in the living room and laid a mattress on the ground for me. I'd been under the impression that they would smuggle me in that night, but they said no, you have to wait until the next day. I didn't meet anyone from the old man's family, I just slept there. My phone still had reception, so I sent a text to my father, who was in New York, to tell him I was safe and sound.

I woke up the next morning and waited. Three men had come to the house. One was half-British, half-Syrian; another was chubby with a red beard; and the third walked with the help of crutches because of polio. They had just come from the Battle of Al-Qusayr; at that time the city of Al-Qusayr was still controlled by rebel forces fighting the Assad government. The men had been trying to get into the city, but their car got targeted. They said it was very dangerous, they were getting hit by Grad missiles, which are Russian-made truck-mounted 122 mm multiple rocket launchers that hail ordnance indiscriminately on a vast area. (In Russian, *grad* means hail.) The bombing got very intense, but they managed to escape and regroup in that house.

Those men had been in Homs during the siege in February 2012, in the same house when Marie Colvin, the American journalist for the *Sunday Times*, was killed along with French photographer Rémi Ochlik. They described to me exactly what had happened: They had all been working out of the Homs press center, and apparently the Syrian government had picked up their satellite connection and shelled the area heavily with artillery. The man with crutches told me they got hit the first time and no one was killed; then, as they were waiting for another strike to come, they decided to get out of the building and go to another one. A group of them did, but Colvin and Ochlik refused—they thought it would be safer to stay put rather than risk moving through the streets. It was a mistake. The building was hit again; Colvin and Ochlik were killed. About seventeen rebels died trying to get the journalists out.

So I knew I was going into a dangerous area, but I didn't imagine it would be as bad as the Homs siege, where the whole city had been encircled.

My plan wasn't to go to Al-Qusayr, but rather to base myself farther south in Yabroud, which is only about fifty miles north of the Syrian capital. This would be safer than dodging grad missiles in a town that could fall any day to government and Hezbollah forces, I thought.

There was no way of knowing where the border was. Occasionally there was a checkpoint. At one of them, still in Lebanon, we were directed to pull over. A soldier wearing forest-green camouflage and white tennis shoes approached us and looked into the car. He leaned into the open window and cocked his head at me. The driver explained in Arabic who I was.

"Camera," the soldier said to me directly. "Show me your camera."

I did. He looked at it blankly and then pressed closer to the driver's ear, like he was about to kiss him. The driver mumbled something and opened the compartment between the two seats in the front of the pickup truck. In it there were stacks of hundred-dollar bills—tens of thousands of dollars, seemingly. He didn't pull any of them out, just showed them. I didn't understand what they were saying to each other in Arabic, but I could more or less get the drift. *We're messengers for the Doctor. This is money meant to keep the rebellion going.*

The soldier tapped the roof of the car, stood back, and waved us onward.

Not long after that, as we were picking up momentum on the road, a loud whistle broke over the sound of gravel crunching under our tires. On the horizon, in the valley, a missile whizzed by.

"Scud," the driver said, almost proudly. "From Bashar." As he pronounced Assad's name, he added a few words in Arabic, and one of them I recognized as some version of "dog."

I knew we were only a couple of miles from the border, but there was no sign of any demarcation. No signpost, no soldiers, only goods being ferried back and forth. And if I did see the Scud missile as a bad omen, I still had no clue that I myself might be considered one of these goods.

We drove for what seemed like hours over a dirt road cutting through dry, rolling hills into the Qalamoun Mountains. The smuggler sat shotgun and the older man drove. They weren't very friendly.

Suddenly the driver turned to me and said "Syria" as he pointed all around. I felt my heart drop a notch toward my stomach—thinking, *Oh shit, now I'm in Syria*. Then my phone lost all reception.

WE GOT TO YABROUD as it was getting dark. The small city of about twenty-five thousand people was in rebel-held territory and it had a large Christian population. Once we stopped, a few other men showed up and greeted me very cordially, as if I were a guest they'd been expecting for a long time. Then they put me back into the car and we drove deeper into town.

When we got out they led me into a storefront that must have been a dental lab. On the left, as you entered, there was a worktable where two young men in their twenties were making imprints and casts of false teeth, sculpting and polishing dentures. I'd never seen false teeth being made before. It was a mess, there was powder everywhere. It looked more like a cobbler's shop than a dental lab.

The men offered me some tea and hooked me up to the Internet connection. They introduced me to the man who owned the operation: he was bald on top with white hair sprouting out on the sides, and so small that I could literally see the top of his head. He wore little rectangular glasses. Like most people in that part of the Levant he was very fair-skinned; many of them even had blue eyes. He spoke some English and invited me into another room. I entered and the door closed quickly behind me.

This dental studio would serve as my office. On the right side there was the bathroom. Ahead was the staircase leading to the upper level, which had the Internet connection. Here I would sit with my computer every evening, connect to the outside world, and file my photos.

After I had spent about an hour watching a man delicately file a set of dentures from behind his thick glasses, a tall, lanky guy with dark, sharp, hawklike features showed up. "Hi, I'm Alfarook, I'm going to help you."

Alfarook was to be my fixer. A "fixer," in the trade of conflict journalism, is sort of a cross between a foster brother and Virgil leading Dante through the various circles of Inferno. He serves as translator and works his contacts to get you among the fighters. He can also be a driver and even provide you housing and food if necessary.

Working with a fixer requires a degree of trust that there is rarely enough time to develop. You have to make split-second decisions based on first impressions, past experience, intuition, or default. Alfarook, then, was my Virgil by default. My contacts in Lebanon, through the smuggler, had provided him for me, and I didn't even have to pay for his services. They just wanted to help the cause, they said: anything that would bring down the Assad government and establish a just rule in the country. Maybe the fact that I didn't have to pay the fixer should have rung alarms. But it didn't. In some situations you just have to accept kindness wholesale. Otherwise thinking about all the potential risks will paralyze you.

On the whole, my first impression of Alfarook was positive. He was a polite, smart, and reserved young man in his twenties. He seemed to believe in the cause and support the anti-Assad rebels in the Free Syrian Army. But he wasn't a fanatic. His English was quite good: he'd studied economics at Damascus University. So I asked him a few questions. Can we go see units on the front line? Can we go to hospitals or morgues? Can we go to areas that have been shelled recently? He said everything could be done, but I suspected he wasn't as gung ho about putting himself in danger as some other fixers I'd had in the past. He gave me a cell phone. I went upstairs, got online, and sent my father a message that I was safe. He never wanted to know too many details. "Just tell me you're okay," he always said.

FROM THE DENTAL-LAB-CUM-PRESS-CENTER, they drove me to a building about a half a mile away and showed me the apartment where I would be sleeping. It was big, clean, and fairly void of furniture. There were a couple of other people staying in the apartment building, so the smuggler warned me not to talk too much. Foreigners drew unwanted attention, and there could be informers anywhere. They gave me the key and said lock yourself in and don't make any noise.

I spent the first night sleeping in the smaller room, which was heated and had carpeting. All the other rooms just had tiles on the floor. The older man who drove and the smuggler shared the room with me. We woke up early that morning because Assad's forces were dropping bombs on the city—nothing particularly heavy, though. Everyone acted as if it were routine. The shelling would stop and then start again. We would look out the window and see a cloud of smoke rising, sometimes as close as a half a mile away.

Later in the day the two men drove off, back to Lebanon. I never saw them again.

In the mornings, as soon as I woke up, I'd call Alfarook with my new cell phone and he'd show up on his little 125 cc motorcycle. He'd take me around Yabroud to see areas in the aftermath of bombardment. Yabroud was important because it was strategically located near Al-Nabek, a slightly bigger city situated on the main Damascus–Homs highway, which was still under government control. If the rebels managed to cut off that highway, it would be a real blow. So of course the government regularly shelled Yabroud from Al-Nabek, which was less than five kilometers away. (I could walk five klicks in less than an hour.)

If we had to go farther out, such as when they bombed nearby villages, we took a cab, but those roads were very dangerous. Rebels drove in unmarked vehicles, so anything on the road was fair game. And some of the villages had only a few hundred people, so we'd be the only car in sight.

Although the attacks were nothing near as intense as the bombardment of Homs, random shells fell regularly on houses with civilians inside. There were always a few casualties next to the morgue or hospital. One time we got to a bombing site before any ambulances and there were a couple of dead people on the street. The civilians were clearly distraught, but you could also tell they were becoming inured to the carnage, walking past the casualties with their expression of outrage dimmed from repetition.

Alfarook took me to see a few refugee camps as well, which were usually located in schools. Most of the refugees were from Homs. On several occasions I spent some time with rebel units in the city, but apart from sporadic artillery shells and token bursts of machine gun fire, I didn't see any significant firefights.

It developed into a routine: shoot pictures all day and go to the dental lab in the evening. Upstairs in my little office I'd edit the shots and file anywhere from fifteen to twenty photos to my agency in New York: young men with guns, some looking more ready than others; snipers lying in wait behind walls with holes blown out of them; families in the throes of grief, their loved ones and homes mangled beyond recognition; whole families of refugees in a single schoolroom; wounded in the hospitals; cadavers at the morgue, awaiting burial. I'd make a selection, choose the images where I caught the light in a way that revealed some emotion or even a glimpse of truth. And with a few clicks of my trackpad they were in my agency's hard drive and out there for the world at large. Then I'd go back to my apartment and think about how to get better shots the next day.

One afternoon Alfarook took me along with his best friend, a stocky blond kid, to go hunting for food. They handed me a rifle. "Try this," Alfarook said. "It's like a camera. Point and shoot." I'd never been a gun person, apart from knowing a little about the history of military hardware, but either I was a natural, or just had beginner's luck, because I took aim at a little bird in a tree about seventy yards away, pulled the trigger, and it plopped to the ground. We ate it cooked over a barbecue with Alfarook's father at their country house, which had been damaged by shelling. Fortunately there was also goat meat and grilled tomatoes, because the tiny bird wasn't exactly delectable.

DURING THE WEEK SPENT in and around Yabroud, I kept telling Alfarook I wanted to see more action, a little closer to the front line. When it comes to photographing conflicts, the calculus is fairly simple: the closer you get, the better the shot. And the more heated the action, the more emotion you capture. It doesn't take a PhD. What's essential, though, is a monomaniacal focus on your objective and a willingness to put yourself in danger. Then comes the aesthetic aspect, which requires the ability to foresee action about to happen combined with an almost esoteric understanding of light and its properties.

We spent a few days with a unit and they took me with them to a sniper's nest, which was quite dangerous because it was on a rise overlooking the main road that connected Homs to Damascus and the government troops had to be vigilant about keeping their supply lines safe. There were about ten men in a bombed-out building; everything around it was destroyed. You looked out the window and you could see Al-Nabek a few miles away, which was mostly controlled by the government. And they were firing on us from over there.

Still, I wanted to go south. Alfarook didn't have any contacts there, but he said he would introduce me to another fixer-journalist who did. We went by motorcycle to pick him up at his building late at night. We climbed a staircase to a small, dark office in the back. There was a young man just sitting there, looking a little creepy as he sat slack-jawed in front of his laptop. He introduced himself. I sat down next to him on the couch and told him I wanted to see one of the units fighting closer to Damascus. "Okay, no problem," he said. "I have a good contact with that unit. I'll call him up and we'll organize everything."

He showed us pictures that he'd taken of the Syrian army. I asked if we could get that close. He said, "No problem." I couldn't remember his name, but as far as I was concerned he was Mr. No Problem. Can we get a car? "No problem." Can we get to the front line? "No problem." I probably could have asked him if it was possible to sneak into Bashar al-Assad's toilet and shave his balls while he was taking a crap, and he would have told me, "No problem." So we agreed. He said to come back tomorrow and we'd set something up with Alfarook.

In hindsight, I realize my alarm bells should have been ringing, but I was too bent on getting closer. I wanted to catch the expression on a soldier's face as he tries to come to terms with the gravity of his task, or maybe even catch a glint of truth in his eyes when he empties himself of all thought, absorbed in the frenzy of action, and becomes a single mote of dust swirling through the rubble of history.

TWO DAYS LATER ALFAROOK came in with his best friend Blondie's white pickup truck, and the four of us—me, Alfarook, Blondie, and No Problem—drove south an hour and a half from Yabroud toward Rankous, which was about thirty miles from Damascus, to a rebel unit holed up in a small village. I'd been in Syria a week by then and had already made arrangements to go back to Lebanon, from where I would catch a flight to Paris.

On the drive we stopped at a small town and parked the pickup in front of an abandoned villa. There were about ten soldiers there. We sat and had tea, everybody talking.

After a while the commander of the Free Syrian Army unit, Abu Faras, showed up in his camouflage uniform. He was a cordial, heavy-

set man with childlike eyes nesting between his beard and the keffiyeh wrapped around his head. We talked for about forty-five minutes
with Alfarook translating. He asked me where I was from. France, I said.
"Why do you want to take pictures of our unit?" I told him I just wanted
to get pictures of actual combat. I wanted to see the rebels fighting,
understand their cause better. He seemed to take my motivation at face
value, then went into a litany of crimes committed against the Syrian
people by the Assad family.

When Abu Faras finished talking, he excused himself to make a
phone call. He came back ten minutes later and said, "Okay, let's go."
I asked where we were going. "We can go to the front lines," he said.
"From there you will be close enough to see some of Bashar's army."

They decided to use Blondie's white pickup, although Blondie himself stayed at the villa. The commander took one soldier with him, but
they carried no weapons apart from Abu Faras's pistol.

I got in the back of the car and sat next to the new fixer, No Problem. Alfarook was driving, Abu Faras sat shotgun. Another soldier was
standing in the bed of the pickup, looking over the top.

After about fifteen minutes we came to a checkpoint. There was a
simple concrete structure with one opening and three walls, sort of like
a bus stop. An SUV was parked behind it. Two men emerged from the
concrete shelter wearing balaclavas and wielding AK-47s. They stopped
the car. Abu Faras opened the window. He told them calmly which unit
he belonged to, but they started shouting violently. They opened the
passenger-side door and dragged him out onto the ground.

That was when my mind switched from the calm hyperaware state
I usually fell into as I was approaching a front line to "Oh shit!" mode.
Everything shifted into slow motion, somewhat warped. *Now I'm in
trouble,* I thought to myself. Right away I felt a rush of pure fear pump-
ing through my chest and neck.

They opened the back door on the passenger side, grabbed my shirt,
and dragged me to the ground till I was planted on my knees. They did
the same to the soldier in the back and the fixer. Now we were all on our

knees, hands behind our necks. I looked up: two more men arrived at the scene; now there were four of them. They cuffed my hands behind my back and pulled my black T-shirt over my eyes so I couldn't see. I could feel the metal of a gun barrel pressed to the right side of my head. A split second later it poked my temple. Then the deafening bang.

All the noise around me was muffled in a liquid hum, and I thought, *This is what dying must sound like.* But in the ringing aftermath of the blast I realized I was still alive. I hadn't been shot. But I was in shock. A simple pistol fired next to my ear had practically effaced my will.

I looked through my T-shirt, which was somewhat threadbare, and saw Alfarook and No Problem on their knees to the right of the pickup, literally shaking with fear. Abu Faras and the soldier were behind me. The men in ski masks pulled their SUV around to the left side of the truck. They lifted me up and threw me in the back, behind the driver. I started worrying about all my gear, including my laptop, which was still in the white pickup truck. Then two of the men drove up in that same white pickup. I couldn't see Abu Faras or his soldier anymore. They put me in the SUV. The fat man who fired his pistol in my ear was in the driver's seat. Alfarook and No Problem were in the back with me. Riding shotgun there was a twitchy kid who looked somewhat psychotic. He kept his AK-47 trained on us.

As soon as they got in they made a U-turn and drove away very fast. I tried to lift my head up to see but the psycho kid hit me viciously upside the head with the butt of his rifle and I had to brace myself not to fall back unconscious. We drove for about five minutes. Then we stopped. They opened my side of the door and pulled me out gently so I wouldn't trip. The driver took me in front of the house. I was still covered and handcuffed, but I could see through the fabric of the shirt that I was in front of a door. There were two steps that led down to the house. I almost tripped, but he was holding me. He emptied my pockets and took everything: my phone, my wallet, my keys.

I could see that the two fixers were on their knees in front of the house, their heads also covered. Then two shots were fired. *I'm next,* I thought. They dragged me away from the door again and pushed me back into the car. Alfarook and No Problem were stuffed in, too. They hadn't been shot. But I could feel No Problem's leg trembling against mine. It seemed he was more terrified than I was. Then they all got back into the SUV and we drove away.

Within five minutes we came to another house. They threw us all on the floor with our hands tied behind our backs and blindfolded us with keffiyehs. The driver shouted a few things at me in Arabic, none of which I understood apart from the gist that I was in trouble. He seemed angry at the fact that I couldn't understand, so he roughed me up with a few pushes and smacks. Alfarook was too stunned to translate anything.

WE ALL LAY on the floor in a small room while the captors yelled at us, kicked us, stepped on our heads. From time to time one of them fired out the window, probably just to scare us. I was on my belly and shaking because it was getting cold. I could see Psycho, the kid with the AK-47, on the couch.

After about two hours my shoulder started hurting. So I told Alfarook to tell these fuckers to switch my cuffs from behind my back to the front. He tried to shush me, but I kept insisting, so he finally said something. The fat driver, whose name was Abu Talal, weighed the request with a grunt and agreed to switch the cuffs and turn me over, so now I could lie on my back with my hands crossed against my chest.

Night fell, and at one point they removed the two fixers' cuffs and let them walk out of the house. I was lying on my back and could see the entry door somewhat from under my blindfold. I saw their cheap made-in-China jeans. Then they walked out of my field of vision and I heard car doors open and close. I heard the ignition turn and the car driving away. I wasn't sure what to make of it. It might be good news for me.

Or maybe it wasn't good news. Maybe they were in on it.

Later that night the same men came back—minus the fixers—and offered me tomatoes and french fries. Because of the blindfold I couldn't see who was feeding me. Now they were gentle, trying to reassure me, saying it was all okay.

But I didn't buy it. *I'm fucked,* I thought. I imagined myself in the hands of some hooded figure in front of a camera, like in the videos from the Iraq War, and the knife sliding across my jugular, into my throat, the horrifying gurgles of blood gushing into my windpipe.

Then a few more minutes would pass, massaging my faculties of reason until I convinced myself that everything was merely the result of some miscommunication. And I believed that I could convince them, too. If only we could understand each other.

But suddenly that hope evaporated. I knew I was in trouble. No matter how much I tried to make sense of it—*this is all just a mistake . . . somehow it'll get resolved . . . this can't be happening to me*—I couldn't deny that it was *me* there, blindfolded, woozy with fear and fatigue, no clue as to what these men were muttering, what they meant with their guttural grunts, and I thought, *I'm fucked. I am truly fucked.*

THE DARK HOUSE

WHEN YOU SPEND HOURS, DAYS EVEN, handcuffed and blindfolded, surrounded by voices you don't understand apart from a tone and timbre that could easily be the prelude to more physical abuse and pain, serious questions inevitably crop up: *What did I do wrong to get into such a predicament? Have I been flirting with some sort of death wish? Playing chicken with myself in order to feel more alive?*

But these questions won't help when survival is the priority, so you sweep them away as fast as they come and archive them for when things get better. Because things have to get better. Any other attitude will get you lost in a bog of self-recrimination and doubt.

With survival the priority, I knew I had to keep my psychic forces intact. In order to do that I couldn't allow my fear to take me over. I couldn't succumb to self-pity. The first thing I needed to do was accept my situation, as bad as it was, and block out anything that might trigger feelings of attachment to anything outside of my new universe: no family, no friends, no people, places, or things that had become a part of me and were now inaccessible. I knew I wouldn't be able to do it perfectly, but I had to block it out as best I could.

IN THE DARK, with a keffiyeh covering my eyes and metal handcuffs digging into my wrists, I quickly came to know my captors by the sound of their voices, their steps through the house, the foul smell of their bodies and breath. Every once in a while I'd lean my head back and peek under the blindfold, or just push it up a few millimeters to get a look at them and verify whether my other senses were accurate.

Abu Talal was one of the men with the balaclavas who had grabbed us at the checkpoint, the one who had fired his pistol near my ear. He was the scariest of the crew. A hulking, fair-skinned man in his thirties with round, bearded face and blue eyes, he was the one who gave the orders to the younger men.

Ali was a serious bearded man in his early thirties, a devout Muslim who seemed to be dedicated to more than just the overthrow of Assad.

Then there was Psycho (I think his real name was Hakim, but to me he would always be Psycho), a wiry young eighteen-year-old with a sadistic streak and a lot to prove to his peers. This was the kid who had clocked me with the butt of his AK-47 in the SUV after we were cuffed.

My favorite was Mej. His real name was some version of Mahmoud, but since that was such a popular name in Islamic societies, they all had to be differentiated with other nicknames. About eighteen years old, he was short, stocky, and sported a mullet haircut, as if he'd grown up on late-eighties TV. He spoke only about ten words of English but was eager to communicate, interact and learn. He was the one who would feed me and he always let me go to the bathrooms, which were outside the house. He even loosened my handcuffs when I asked.

The foil of the group was another Mahmoud, a sixteen-year-old everyone called Baby Donkey because they thought he was an idiot. From my point of view, it seemed he was only there to spy on me. He would often linger behind the curtain and watch me to see if I did any-thing wrong, like try to lift my blindfold. None of the others liked him (an idiot comrade during combat can be a liability), so they would often take my side, and I'd steal cigarettes from him whenever I could.

DURING THE FIRST FEW HOURS and days of my captivity, I was haunted by the idea that someone had betrayed me. Could it have been my Leb-anese contacts? The Doctor? Most likely it was one of my fixers. Already in Syria I'd heard stories floating around of fixers selling out their cli-ents to kidnappers. But my first impression of Alfarook had been very positive. I'd made a conscious decision to trust him. More likely it was his friend, No Problem. But by the time I met him my judgment was too skewed by the prospect of getting closer to the action.

Since it was clear that the anti-Assad rebellion would only get sym-bolic gestures of assistance from the United States and other West-ern nations, they had to rely on other means of sustaining themselves financially. Jihad-friendly Salafi networks in Saudi Arabia and other Gulf states were one source. Kidnapping for ransom was another.

But from the way both Alfarook and his friend were trembling in the backseat of the car I could tell they were genuinely terrified. You can't fake that. If either of them was in on the kidnapping, then they weren't privy to the details, because the sheer chaos of the scene scared the shit out of them and they, too, were subjected to a mock execution.

Still, they were released that same evening. *Maybe I'll be released, too,* I kept thinking in those first few hours and days. There must have been a misunderstanding. If I could explain myself in Arabic they'd see that this was a big mistake. I was on their side. I was trying to get their point of view out to the world at large, which in turn would increase sympathy for them. But as soon as a thought like that gained traction in my head, Psycho or Abu Talal would come by and step on it just to let me know where I stood with them.

So there we were, in the middle of a bone-dry savanna on a clear night, looking up at the Milky Way's thick stripe stretching from one end of the sky to another. It was that time in the late evening when you're bathed with the purest form of happiness: that you made it through the day. And you just lie there—so tired it doesn't matter where you are, how hard the rocks are, or even what animals are watching you in the distance. All that matters is that you're alive and can experience the beauty of the earth and sky.

I had a thick sleeping bag that I used like a cushion to lie on top of. Behind me I had a tree to lean against if I wanted. But I lay on my back instead to look at the stars. At a certain point one of the men said something and I wanted to lift my head up to see who it was. I interlaced my fingers and brought my hands behind my head to pull it up. Then I felt something like a twig or a piece of wood prick me.

Within a few seconds I felt an incredible pain spread up my entire arm. My hand started cringing as all the muscles there contracted. I took my flashlight and covered it with my T-shirt before turning it on because I didn't want to give away our positions to the army. I shone the light on the ground and there was the culprit: a scorpion, about three inches long, a small one. The small ones, I later learned, were more dangerous because they didn't know how to inject the proper amount of venom; they shot too much. And this one was a cream-colored scorpion, the deadly kind.

I killed the scorpion with the flashlight, then stood up. The pain kept spreading and I knew I was in trouble. I went to see the commander and tried to explain. He wasn't sure what I was saying so we went back and I showed him the dead scorpion. The men's jaws dropped, and I knew it was not a good sign. The guy who spoke English translated a bit, saying, "We lose soldiers like this all the time. At least one dies every month." He basically said there was nothing they could do for me. Either your heart made it, or it stopped and you had a heart attack. Still, I thought: *This is not going to happen. I'm not going to die like that. I'll be fine.* And eventually I pulled through. The pain lasted for about two or three days. But just in my arm.

The next morning everyone was very impressed because I was still alive. One reason I may have pulled through was that I had a very big heart—literally—due to all the competitive swimming and water polo I'd done throughout my life.

When I got back to France a few weeks later, though, I got really sick because the toxin had traveled to my stomach and pancreas. I was staying at my best friend Yann's parents' house and they called a doctor. The doctor said the toxins were going to be with me for many months, years even. And the problem was that if I got stung again by another one I could have a heart attack. (Needless to say, from that point on I've been careful of scorpions.)

So I'd gone to Ethiopia to cover a war for almost a month and nearly died, yet in that whole time I didn't witness a single firefight. Nevertheless, the Oromo soldiers left a deep impression on me. They had an integrity that was almost impossible to find in our atomized societies. They were living to fight for an ideal—an ideal in which their identity was inseparable from that arid earth we walked across all day long, a landscape bathed in moonlight or shimmering under the Milky Way at night. Everything—family, tribe, nation, land—was part of a single soul dependent on God. And they were fighting to keep that soul alive and integral.

What I did witness was a primordial way of living that you simply couldn't duplicate in any modern city. We walked, talked (or at least the other soldiers did), ate, and tried to survive amid the vastness of a landscape that was pure fiction to people who had grown up in cities such as Paris and New York, like I had. It was something out of *National Geographic*. You wanted food? You killed a goat or a camel, or hunted some other animal; you gathered what plants and roots you'd been taught could sustain you. It was so far removed from any office-job apartment living that—by nearly dying—I felt like I was giving birth to a new me. That's what kept me going.

AS I LAY in the dark with a keffiyeh wrapped around my eyes, I knew I needed to adopt the same attitude as when I had learned that the scorpion sting could stop my heart. I just wouldn't let that happen. It would be an act of sheer will. *I won't let them kill me*, I kept telling myself. *I'll make them understand. One way or another, I'll get them to let me out of here.*

In the room that would become mine, they placed a loose mattress on the ground parallel to the couch. It must have been a room for kids because there was a bunk bed and stickers of Care Bears, Mickey Mouse, and other cartoon characters on the wood. I kept leaning my head back to peek under the blindfold, trying to see where I was, what was going on around me. I was hearing a lot of voices in Arabic. Sometimes they were loud, and that would scare me. It was easy to become very paranoid and think that everything was about me. So if they were screaming I began to worry that they'd take out their aggression on me. And if they were laughing I assumed they were going to be gentle—unless, of course, they were laughing at me.

All day long it was a constant struggle with my hopes and expectations. Back and forth, up and down. Anything—a cross look or a skewed smirk—could set me off on a secret emotional tailspin. But it almost never had anything to do with me.

ON THE SECOND or third night of my captivity I had a nightmare. I woke up screaming and panting. I couldn't breathe because I was panicking. One of the guards came over to me, put his hand on my shoulder, and asked if I was okay. He was an ex-police officer who had deserted from Assad's forces. I called him Flic to myself ("cop" in French). He was probably in his forties or fifties, constantly chain-smoking cigarettes—a bit crazy, but he took a liking to me.

Flic eased me out of my nightmare. But as I awoke, my entire being felt compressed by the captivity. I was sleeping on the floor, surrounded by furniture. Three young soldiers were sleeping in the same room. The worst aspect was that I was no longer free to do as I wished. My life was not just out of my hands, but in the hands of someone, I don't know who, using me as goods to make money—or worse, to make a point.

A few nights later, while dozing off, I felt hands reaching for my feet. It was Abu Talal, cuffing my ankles. Now I was even less free than before. It meant my situation was getting worse. I couldn't walk or move my feet because the metal was going right through my tendons and it hurt like hell. I felt like I was on a slow spiral downward.

I convinced Mej to loosen them up. He was the first one I started talking to, because I'd immediately sensed that he was the key to making my situation easier. His cheeks puffed out a bit around his eyes, so you couldn't really tell what color they were, but the roundness gave his mouth a very affable expression that seemed to extend to his whole being.

Whenever I had to go to the bathroom, I always tried to ask Mej because he was the one who would offer me kindness.

In those first few days a routine developed. Every morning I would get up early, right after dawn, and wait for Mej to wake up. I'd lie there chomping at the bit to see his eyes open so I could ask him about my situation and hear more information.

But Mej was young and liked to sleep in. He'd wake up about an hour or two after I did and then doze off again. Once he was up for good he'd throw on his long three-quarter shorts, skulk into the bathroom with his mullet trailing behind him, and wash up.

As soon as he got out I'd try to strike up a conversation.

"Is everything okay?"

"It's okay, Jon," he would say. "Very good, no problem, you go home."

That little bit of reassurance gave me hope. Even though I knew it was fake hope, it didn't matter. It was enough to keep my will going. To make sure my heart wouldn't stop.

The routine turned into a ritual for me: getting him to give me information. There was an armchair between the bunk bed and the open doorway covered by a curtain, and he would sit there and look at me. I'd ask him, "Is everything okay?" And he'd reassure me. Then he'd feed me tomatoes and fries.

We'd teach each other words in Arabic and English, simple words that revolved around communal living: bathroom, food, hungry, sleep. Gradually we built up to more intimate words: happy, afraid, bombs, war.

The words out of his mouth—"It's okay"—were like the Gospel to me, and I forced myself to believe them.

BABY DONKEY WAS STILL a kid, barely sixteen and "intellectually deficient," to say the least. It didn't take much intellect to figure out that someone like that with access to a Kalashnikov amounted to danger.

He was often used to spy on me. He'd stand behind the curtain and peer out to see what I was doing in the room.

I did all kinds of things I wasn't supposed to do. For example, above the bunk bed there was a very bright fluorescent strip light that always annoyed me. It was right in my face and I couldn't sleep. If no one was in the room, I would jump on the bed quickly and rotate the tube just enough so it would stop working. Then I would sit right back down and pretend nothing had happened. Somebody would walk in afterward and ask where the light was. Then they would fix it. That little act of defiance also became a ritual. And even though another culprit would have been unlikely, they never figured out that I was the one doing it.

There was also something repulsive about Baby Donkey. I didn't know how he had gotten his nickname, but I knew the other men had given it to him. In many languages, like French, calling someone a donkey is the equivalent of calling him a dunce, so I assumed it was an affectionate tease on the part of the older soldiers. In what became a running joke in the room, the men would ask me, "Who is Baby Donkey?" Invariably I'd point to the kid, and all the men would get a good chuckle out of it. Obviously it didn't ingratiate me with him, but he remained rather harmless to me.

Psycho, on the other hand, scared me. He was barely eighteen and looked like a kid who needed to prove something. In the context of a war with little discipline, that factor, combined with his nervous, suspicious nature, spelled trouble for me. He had that look on his face of someone who is constantly having an argument with himself, battling inner demons that seem to spring up from nowhere.

The officers were more aloof. They could be frightening or kind, depending on their mood. The alpha male of the house was Abu Talal. The commander of the entire unit was a man called Essad. Mej always referred to Essad as "Number One Man, the chief." Mej said he was a good man. I didn't see much of him because I was usually blindfolded, although I assumed he was there, in and out. Whether or not Number One Man was a good thing, I'd have to find out.

AFTER THE FIRST FIVE DAYS all the young men left the house to fight. The government forces, backed by Hezbollah, were pushing in from various directions. I was left alone with Flic, and the area surrounding our house suddenly started getting shelled. Then helicopters arrived to bomb us. They launched rockets and the windows shook. Flic came into the room, took off my blindfold, and led me as the shells hit all around us. You could hear a hissing noise just before the explosion. When the bombing got too close, Flic and I would hit the ground and cover up. One time I saw a pickup truck pull up next to the house with a machine gun bolted into the bed. It started shooting at the helicopters. Then just as quickly it went away.

After the first few times we survived the shelling, Flic began taking me in his arms and giving me a big hug and kiss, the way effusive Arab men do. His beard smelled like burnt tobacco.

Then there would be a lull and we'd smoke cigarettes together. I was never a real smoker, but whenever I was in a conflict zone I'd start bumming the occasional cigarette. In captivity, I'd smoke every chance I got and I'd regularly steal cigarettes from the men—especially

Baby Donkey. They were harsh, local brands that reminded me of the dark Gauloises in Paris. But occasionally some of the men would score Gauloises blondes, which everyone liked.

THERE'S SOMETHING TRULY FEARSOME about an artillery barrage. All you can do is hunker down and hope you don't take a direct hit. The terror generated by loud explosions and shaking earth are enough to unhinge anyone—hence shell shock is not just a metaphor. And the heroism that springs from an artillery battle usually involves a willingness to risk getting blown to pieces in order to drag out someone unluckier than you who got hit with shrapnel. No stealthy Rambo-style prowess through the jungle involved, just a crapshoot in the midst of a hailstorm.

I'd first experienced getting shelled by artillery in the 2008 Russo-Georgian War. I was on the Georgian side and the shells were coming from Russian troops firing out of South Ossetia.

I waited it out in an abandoned house, then linked up with a group of independent Russian journalists in Gori, Stalin's birthplace. I hopped on a Russian tank and went deeper into the Kartlia Valley with them. A lot of the villages were bombed out. Many tanks were destroyed. The Russians were convinced I was a spy because I'd left my documentation behind in Gori, where all I had was an American passport. Being an American is not a good thing when you're riding a Russian tank through a country that wants to be part of NATO. Fortunately the Russian journalists were able to convince the soldiers that I was actually French. I told them I'd lost all my documents in a direct hit. They felt bad about it and gave me permission to shoot photos around the valley for about three days.

The shelling, both in Georgia and Syria, was terrifying. But in both places, during the lulls, I couldn't help think about what troops in the trenches during World War I had to endure, especially on the western front. It was beyond my imagination, even though so many of my childhood fantasies were fed by stories of ace pilots and French heroes during the First World War. I kept having to remind myself that what I was experiencing was just a training exercise compared to what the soldiers in the Battles of the Somme and Verdun went through.

AS THE DAYS PASSED I spent less time with the blindfold on and my feet were cuffed only at night. So much of my time was spent just sitting, watching, trying not to think too much, and keeping my spirits from plummeting.

I thought of my father. He was no doubt worried by now, and as his concern grew, he would have called my mother. I was supposed to have been back in Paris. I'd even set up a date with a woman through Facebook. She must have assumed I'd stood her up. But I couldn't dwell on these things.

Usually the officers, like Ali and Abu Talal, woke up at around ten or eleven. I would have been awake and anxious since five or six, just waiting to gauge their moods.

Meanwhile my parallel universe consisted of a gentle young man with a mullet who kept telling me everything would be okay, an adolescent imbecile, an aspiring psychopath eager to vent his rage on me, and a bunch of bearded men for whom I was just merchandise to be traded in the name of a cause that had nothing to do with me.

But that was also to my advantage. As merchandise, they needed to keep me healthy.

The most immediate danger, however, was the bombing all around us. Every day our position looked more vulnerable. Hezbollah had sent in reinforcements from Lebanon in support of Assad's army and were pressing against the rebels. The men holding me fell under the umbrella of the Free Syrian Army, a relatively moderate group of rebels compared to the organizations fighting throughout the rest of the country. A good number of the officers had deserted from Assad's army. They'd been secular before the war. Many of them probably used to drink and smoke hashish. Then, when the shooting started, they grew beards and became devout. Not only did they want to get rid of Assad, but many were no doubt sympathetic to a new state grounded in the teachings of Islam. War has a way of bringing tepid believers closer to God. Since virtually everyone in Muslim culture believes in God (the only Muslim atheists I've ever met have been educated in the West), it's only a matter of how zealously they uphold Islamic principles.

Being surrounded by believers made me wonder about my own relationship to God. I had certainly been brought up in a secular world: France until I was fourteen, and thereafter in New York. My mother was nominally Catholic but not religious, even though she sent me to a private school run by Jesuits while we lived together in Paris. My parents divorced when I was four, and at the age of fourteen I went to live with my father, who had moved to New York, where he worked at one of the premier international headhunting firms. My father's father was a secular Jew (Alperovich was the name before he francofied it), and he had emigrated from Minsk (then part of the Russian Empire) to France as a child just before World War I broke out; my father's mother was French, and a devout Catholic. Ultimately my relationship to religion was more or less an intellectual and cultural one. I never spat on it or even disregarded it completely the way most of my peers did; I became interested in it from a historical and political perspective. I didn't doubt that there was some metaphysical force out there, but it was never something I truly felt I had access to. Prayer, the way it was taught in the Jesuit school, always struck me as somewhat contrived. I tended to rely on my intellect and intuition. I felt I didn't need the benefit of so many stories the way others did.

Now, though, I needed to tap into whatever wellspring of strength could get me through this ordeal.

FIRST INTERROGATION

MEJ SEEMED TO RESPECT ME. He kept telling me that the authorities in Yabroud wanted to kill me because they thought I was a spy. But I was under the protection of Essad and his troops, who were about a thousand strong. "Jon is very safe," he'd say. "Number One Man friend to Jon."

Seven days into my captivity I was sitting in the room blindfolded and handcuffed when Mej came up to me and said, "Hey, Number One Man here. This good for you. You go home."

All of a sudden I was full of hope. He uncuffed me, grabbed my arm, and walked me from the bedroom to the TV room. I was still blindfolded and had no idea that there were about twenty or twenty-five people in that room until they finally took the keffiyeh off my head. All the men except for two were in uniforms. Most of the older ones had beards. It was the first time I saw that room. I looked into the corner and there was all my gear in a pile. Everyone was calm. I thought, *This is it, I'm finally going to be released. It's all just a misunderstanding.*

I looked at Mej and he was smiling at me. There was a translator on my left: no beard, wearing jeans and a leather jacket. He introduced himself in French and had a smile on his face—not an ambiguous grin with sinister implications, or one meant to disguise fear or some other emotion. He was genuinely friendly.

"Your name is Jonathan."

"Yes," I said.

"You're French."

"Yes, I'm French."

I often get asked how a Frenchman got the name Jonathan. My father's name is Jean-Louis. I was concerned they might think mine was a Jewish name and I'd get penalized for it. Actually, my mother named me after Jonathan Harker, the main character in Bram Stoker's *Dracula,* the hero who is taken prisoner by the vampire, then escapes, and later returns to hunt him down.

"Jonathan," he repeated. But he didn't seem to notice any incongru-
ence in the name.

I asked him how he knew French. He said he taught it in a school.

A puffy-faced bear of a man was sitting to my right, smiling. I
noticed that he was wearing my belt.

Two men sat on the ground because there weren't enough seats in
the room. One had a beard and wore a uniform. The other was clean-
shaven, blond, and dressed in civilian clothes. At first they just stared at
me. Clearly, they didn't have my best interests in mind.

After a few questions from the translator the two men on the
ground started asking questions in Arabic, back and forth, with my
translator relaying them to me in French.

"Where are you from?"

"France."

"What are you doing in Syria?"

"I'm a photojournalist. I'm covering the Syrian revolution against
the Assad government."

"Who do you work for?"

"I work for Polaris Images."

It was all matter-of-fact. Bureaucratic.

"Where are you from?" they repeated.

"France. Paris."

"Are you Jewish?"

"No, I'm French."

"Why did you come to Syria?"

"I'm a photojournalist. I've been to Syria before. Two times since
the revolution began. I'm here to cover your side. I want the world to
know about your struggle against Assad."

There was a man sitting beside the burly bear to my right, and he
was looking at me sympathetically. I sensed that he'd been in the house
before, but there was no way I could be sure because I'd been blindfolded.

"Are you a spy?"

"No, I'm not. I'm a photographer."

"Are you CIA?"

"No. You can look me up on Google and see I'm a photographer." Unfortunately there was no Wi-Fi in the house.

The translator was very mild-mannered. Even the original questions in Arabic from the men sitting on the ground came out mildly. It all felt like a formality. Something that would settle the issue for good, and then I could be on my way home. Everyone seemed to understand. There was no ill will apart from the odd stare.

"Do you work for the CIA? Or the FBI?"

They kept harping on the American spy angle, but I'd made a decision to insist on the French card. "I'm French. I live in Paris." I knew the fate of American hostages was usually worse than those of most Europeans because, in general, European governments (the French in particular) were willing to go to greater lengths to accommodate hostage takers, even if it meant paying an exorbitant ransom. The Americans refused to pay ransoms, and their citizens tended to get used for propaganda purposes. In places like the Middle East, which was a hotbed of anti-Americanism, it didn't matter who the United States was supporting with covert aid. Killing Americans amounted to credibility on the Arab street.

"You say you're here to help our side. What side is that?" the translator asked, spinning variations of the same questions over and over.

"The side fighting against Assad, the dictator."

I was under the impression they were all Free Syrian Army; at least that was who I was told I was going with on the day I got kidnapped. But I couldn't be sure. And the two men asking questions so seriously from the floor could have been anyone, although I assumed they were part of the rebel administration from Yabroud.

"And you want to help?"

"I want to bring your story to the world. I'm a photojournalist."

"Do you work for the CIA?"

And back they went, to the same questioning. They asked me so many times that I started hearing a creak of doubt in my own voice. *Maybe I am CIA? Maybe they know something I don't?*

Then after an hour the burly bear-faced man left and the translator walked out with him. The door was still open and I saw them talking for a while. I expected them to come back in and for the whole ordeal to be over. Then suddenly all those new people walked out and drove away. The blindfold came back on. I was led back to the other room and cuffed to the bed.

I felt totally deflated. My world was dark again. Mej didn't say anything. I could have used his reassurance, but I knew he didn't count for shit in this situation. I needed to deal with the darkness on my own.

———————

I MADE SURE to always stay aware of the date and count the number of days; losing track of time would cut me off from the world outside of captivity. The house was fairly spartan, but there were arabesque designs on the curtains, cushions and wooden molding. I'd count the repeating designs over and over. On one stretch of wood there were eighty repetitions of a geometric pattern, and I took it as a sign that I'd be there eighty days. Maybe it was wishful thinking. But it gave me a time frame to elaborate a strategy for getting my captors to liberate me, to somehow penetrate their psyches so they could see me as person, a human being who needed to be free—or at least a human whom they needed to set free. It didn't matter. Whatever worked. After the interrogation they left the cuffs off my feet for most of the day, and even on some nights.

Mej and I continued our exchanges. He revealed to me that the bear-faced man was Essad. "Number One Man still helps you, Jon." He was the one wearing my belt and I wasn't sure whether to be pissed at him or take it as a good sign.

Repeatedly the outside world would break into my handcuffed and blindfolded bubble in the form of Dashar's bombs. That in itself put us on a level playing field, since the helicopter pilot or artilleryman couldn't tell the difference between captive and captor.

But one morning, while everyone was sleeping, I lifted my blindfold and walked around. I peered into the TV room and saw my gear in the corner. My cameras, my computer. Not much stuff, but it felt like a limb I'd lost along the way. In many respects, those cameras were extensions of my eyes. At the moment, though, I had more pressing issues at hand—like simply staying alive. For once my stuff didn't matter.

Still, I tried to imagine what I'd do if I could hook up to the Internet that instant. Contact family? What would I say? *Help me, I'm screwed. Don't let these bastards cut my head off.* The mere sight of Facebook's blue layout might launch me into a tailspin. All those people taking photos of what they were eating and farting their thoughts to the world at large. I could post a picture of my tomato and rice dinner, night after night, along with the occasional goat meat. I'd comment on how the portions were getting smaller because they were running out of food. The pressure from Bashar's troops was building and everyone seemed more and more preoccupied with holding their positions. The kids would spend the night on the lines and whole days would go by with just me and Flic. My secret hope was that Flic's kindness or inattention might offer the key to my escape.

I started to develop scars on my wrists because of the handcuffs. I kept complaining, so they made them much looser, to the point where I could basically remove them if I wanted to. After about a week, though, Abu Talal realized what I was doing, that the cuffs were too loose. He didn't say much, but he looked at me like, *You sneaky punk*, then had the cuffs tightened again.

INITIALLY I WAS RELEGATED to the children's room. But one of the first times the officers allowed me to hang out with them in the other room was when Abu Talal grabbed me and showed me a little bottle full of liquid. He was losing his hair and the contents of the bottle must have been a product that helps slow baldness. There was something written on the label in Russian.

"Is this good?" he asked.

I said no. He paused a beat, assessed my attitude, then nailed me with a punch to the solar plexus. It knocked me on the ground and I couldn't breathe for about ten seconds.

Then he picked me up off the ground, laughing, and said he was only joking. I looked at him like, *Sure, joking just like when you were kicking me in the head and stomping on me that first day.* Maybe it was my imagination, but I thought I detected a little regret in his smirk while I was trying to catch my breath.

Either way, that little exchange between us meant something. He had revealed one of his insecurities to me—his thinning hair. That was a lot in a macho culture.

SECOND INTERROGATION

SEVEN DAYS AFTER my interrogation with the French translator, the two men from Yabroud and their entourage came again to interrogate me. This time it was different. There were fewer people. Mej was there. Essad wasn't there, and I didn't know what to make of it, but it couldn't have been good. They had another translator, one who spoke English, a soldier. His English was good, but not as good as the French translator's French. He wore khaki desert camouflage, which seemed to be the unit's standard uniform.

I was sitting with the entry door to my right side. No one seemed to be in a very good mood. I attributed it to an uptick in the bombing campaign. Occasionally I could make out the word *Hezbollah* in their conversations, and I asked Mej if they'd encountered any Hezbollah, which would have been bad news for the rebels. He never gave a clear answer, but I could tell from his facial expression that they probably had.

Just as we were settling in around the table, a guy came in with two kitchen knives and sat right across from me. I felt my esophagus tense up and tried to brace myself by showing no emotion. He started sharpening one knife against the other, the metallic clang cutting through all my thoughts. Then he came up behind me, pulled my head back, and set the blade against my neck, withholding just enough pressure to keep from drawing blood. My diaphragm seized up in terror; I stopped breathing. He could feel my fear, milked it for a few seconds, then let go and swaggered back to his seat with a satisfied grin.

They started the interrogation. This time there were hardly any questions.

"Okay, we know you're CIA," the translator said. "We checked you out. We know you're working for the American intelligence service."

"It's not true. I'm a photographer; you can easily find out."

"You're lying. Why did you come here?"

"I'm a photojournalist. I came to Syria to cover the war. This is my third time. I wanted to follow rebel troops to get their story out to the world."

"You're lying. You're CIA, you came to see who we are. Your government wants to know who we are, who is fighting, what kind of weapons we have."

"I'm French. I've never met anyone in the CIA."

They kept rehashing the same line of interrogation, sometimes with slight variations.

"Just admit it. You're FBI."

"I'm not FBI. I'm not CIA. I'm a French photographer who wound up in the wrong place at the wrong time. I'm on your side in this," I told them, trying not to sound like I was pleading, or desperate. "I want to help your cause."

"That's what the Americans always say. But we get no help. Only spies. You're a spy."

They repeated it so much that the seed of doubt started growing as I got tired. I kept trying to remember if I'd written any address in my French passport. If I had, it would have been my New York address. I tried to remember what was written about me on my online profile. Maybe they'd found out that I was based in New York. I could cover that lie by saying it was my father's address. He's still in New York. I was concerned that I might break down, but surprisingly I kept believing my own lie: that I actually lived in Paris (even though I hadn't lived there since I was fourteen).

However, along with my growing conviction in my own half-truth, an insidious doubt kept growing way beneath the surface of my words. I started to wonder if perhaps I wasn't actually an unwitting informer for the CIA. Maybe one of my contacts in Lebanon or a colleague I'd met on a previous assignment had given me away, and this was a matter of guilt by association. And if they kept up the interrogations, if they kept putting knives to my throat I would eventually break down and tell them I lived in New York. Not only that, but it might become so harrowing I'd start admitting to anything, that I was not only in the CIA, but I was also Napoleon's right-hand man, that I was a reconnaissance scout for a Crusader force bent on retaking the Holy Land and all of the Levant.

I needed to focus on the facts. Keep it simple: *I'm a nobody. I'm a misplaced pawn. I'm a small enough fish that you won't get much out of me, but I'm valuable enough to use as bait.* I tried to lock myself into an unflappable mode, always aware of the knives at the opposite end of the table.

"What about your parents? If you're a famous photographer, why aren't you on television? Why is nobody talking about you?"

The reasoning was logical. But I had no way of knowing why. I had no clue as to who knew what outside my bombed-out little bubble.

"I don't know. I'm not that famous. I don't know how these things work. Maybe I'm not that important. I'm just a photographer."

They kept at it for almost two hours. On the one hand, I was exhausted; on the other, it was a sign that things were moving. In which direction I didn't know, but it could have meant an opening. I tried not to get my hopes up like the last time. Instead, I did my best to analyze the situation and spot any signs of progress.

The fact that they were worried about me being CIA could go either way for me. They might trade me off to the Syrian government in exchange for some concession somewhere along the convoluted line. Or they might hand me over to a more fanatic group, one that has an ax to grind with the United States as an enemy of Islam. The bottom line was that I was better off staying French, a more low-key player in the context, one that was known to pay out ransoms.

When the men finally got up to leave, I felt like I was about to pass out. As he was walking out of the house the knife guy smiled and patted my shoulder, as if to say, *Nothing personal.* I shot him a massive fuck-you with my eyes while trying to keep my face relatively expressionless.

BEFORE THEY PUT THE BLINDFOLD back on I caught a glimpse of my boots by the entry. Every time I looked at them I thought I'd definitely be set free. Strange how something these men deemed as unclean as any shit could become another man's symbol of freedom.

Back in the dark, I felt the pressure of the knife on my neck suddenly come back to me. During the interrogation, in that airless fraction of a second when I had the blade up against my skin, I got sucked back into one of the most traumatic episodes of my childhood. Now, alone with the tension lifting, I could delve into the unpleasant memory.

Throughout elementary school I had a best friend, David. I was a skinny, gangly kid, a late bloomer, and David was bigger, more at ease in his own skin. He was popular with all the other kids, and their parents would hold him up as an example. If an adventure ever presented itself to us, he was the one to insist on taking the invitation, whereas I was always hesitant. And I loved David because every time I deferred to his sense of adventure, I grew, I learned more about myself, and I was that much closer to becoming a man. Little things: jumping over a ditch, walking down a street where a gang of other kids were taunting us, defying their disrespect. He always confronted such situations head-on.

But David, I'd gradually come to realize, was unable to control the violence that seemed to run in his blood, under the surface, a violence that gave him a glow that drew me to him like the fated moth to a flame. He didn't suffer fools easily, and I was often foolish. One time, when we were about eight or nine, I was at his house and I saw a packet of gum on his night table. When he went out to talk to his mother I casually took a piece of gum and started chewing. Then, when he came back into the room, he said, "Where did you get that gum?"

He asked in such a menacing way that I just lied. "I had it."

"No, you didn't. You took mine."

Suddenly his voice turned scary. The logical thing to do was say, *Yeah, I took some gum. Big deal.*

Something sinister welled up in his face and he pulled a hunting knife from out of his desk drawer. He gave my shoulder a quick poke, and suddenly I was bleeding.

"Tell me the truth!" he said, grinding his teeth with a feral look in his eyes.

"Okay, I took your gum."

I was holding my shoulder, terrified by the sight of blood. I wanted to scream, call his mother, who was in the house at the time. But this was his world. We had to play by his rules.

In any case, he'd made his point and put the knife away. Then he went into the bathroom and came out with bandages and disinfectant and cleaned me up like a little nurse. I probably needed a stitch or two, but I didn't want to betray him.

Later, when my mother saw me without my shirt and asked me about the cut, I looked at her like I didn't know how it happened. She looked at me suspiciously.

"Did you do that to yourself?" she asked.

I said, "No. Why would I do that to myself?" And then let it sit as a mystery. Because I was loyal. I didn't want to betray my best friend. And I felt more like a man for having sucked up that fear and dealt with it.

So at the interrogation, with the knife up to my throat, I distinctly remembered the tone of David's voice. Only this interrogation was much easier to deal with because I had no emotional attachment to my interrogator. I was able to become impassive, despite the initial fear that overtook me.

Over the subsequent days I played the two episodes back in my mind, almost conflating them, and it shed some light for me on why I'd always been so attracted to violent conflict. It was more than just a way to test my limits and confront my fear. The fear that sprang from random violence was connected deep down to a sense of loyalty and devotion.

I REALIZED THAT MY CAPTORS must have gone through my gear with childlike curiosity. Already I'd noticed Essad wearing my belt.

A few times they brought my computer to me and told me to type in the password. They went through various files. As I guided them through the contents of what was essentially a memory bank for me, I could see I was becoming more human in their eyes. I remember my mother telling me, before a previous trip to Syria, that if I ever got the chance I should show Muslim fighters my pictures with the Ogaden rebels on the Ethiopia-Somalia border. In 2009 I went to the Somali region of Ethiopia for three weeks to photograph the rebels of the Ogaden National Liberation Front, who were all devout Muslims. One of the first chances I got, I showed my captors those pictures, and that scored me a few points with them.

But one time while they were going through my medicine kit and checking out what brand of toothpaste I used, the mood suddenly changed. The laughter shifted to harsh sounds of indignation.

Abu Talal lifted my blindfold and put a foil packet up to my nose. "What's this? What the fuck is this?" That much I could figure out in Arabic.

It was a stray condom that had probably been sitting in my medicine kit for months. He'd ripped it open just a little.

I caught a backhanded slap to the face. My cuffed hands were too slow together to raise them high enough to protect me. Ali came around, too.

How could I explain to them that I'd never had any intention of going to Syria on a sex holiday? The condom was just an oversight. One of these you-never-know type things. And even though I didn't understand any Arabic, it was clear as day what they were thinking and saying: *You come here to fuck our women? Take pictures of our dead and then fuck our women?*

I tried to explain to them that it was a just-in-case precaution, but it was hopeless. I'd have needed a translator. These people probably didn't have the kind of casual sex with women (at least women who weren't prostitutes) that we Western men were used to. I knew it was best to just shut up, take my beating like a man, and hope to earn some respect from it.

I reproached myself for not having packed with more attention. I hadn't expected to fall hostage to Arab men jealous of their women's honor, though.

Turned out the beating wasn't as bad as I'd anticipated: just a few smacks and a perfunctory punch in the gut. I accepted it as a matter of course. No point pleading or whining. I gave them a look that said: *Do whatever you want. I wasn't interested in fucking your women. If you need to smack me around to feel good about your honor, then go ahead. There's nothing I can do about it.*

That attitude seemed to register with them on an animal level. After the last few halfhearted slaps, they lost interest and left me to my darkness.

I WONDERED WHAT Abu Talal's woman might look like. Or even if he had a woman. Was she as chubby as he was? He looked like he'd crush a skinny girl if he got on top of her.

The others must have had mothers, sisters, aunts, but I hadn't seen anything feminine since the barbecue with Alfarook's family. The young men were very affectionate with each other. By American standards it would seem gay, but in the East, and even in parts of Europe, men touch and kiss each other much more readily as a sign of friendship. If the boys had sex with each other or just jerked each other off, then it tended to be a functional homosexuality—there were no women available, so they needed to make do with what was there. Inevitably some of them come to realize that's what they prefer.

In the back of my mind, though, I kept thinking *I* was what was there. If they wanted, they could make do with me. I knew if I broke down, I could wind up one of their bitches. So far, though, there was nobody who seemed interested in me. And they were all fairly busy with the fighting. But in my bleaker moments all kinds of worst-case scenarios floated to the surface.

They had families. We all had families. Now we were stuck under the same roof, at times with the same fear of falling under the same mortar or rocket fired from an airplane. If I could get the sense of family going . . . Already Mej had become my lifeline. He reassured me every morning. He'd tell me who was a good man, who was a bad man. He spoke some words of a language I understood. I needed to become their brother, but I was like a helpless embryo cuffed by my umbilical cord. That image helped. Especially when I imagined myself floating in all that amniotic fluid, as if in some huge ocean where my troubles seemed insignificant in the greater scheme of things and I realized that my freedom—everyone's freedom—was merely an illusion; because real freedom entails the ability to remain fully human even in that embryonic state of captivity we've all been subject to. In particular, this illusion tends to afflict those who believe they are absolutely free, like I used to before I got captured.

These men had to become my brothers. But that was something else I needed to learn. I never grew up with brothers. My father had a daughter, Lauren, with his second wife, but I'm ten years older than my sister. In a sense, my father was somewhat of a brother, in that I'd always confided in him. I tried not to think of him, but there was no getting around how much I missed him. He used to tell me stories, read to me: Jack London, *Moby-Dick*, the Knights of the Round Table. All the notions of freedom, honor and chivalry he helped instill in me were now coming in handy. I sensed somehow that the language of honor and courage was something these pseudo-brothers holding me captive understood—despite the linguistic gulf.

My mother, for her part, imbued me with a stoicism that helped me deal with the daily sense of deprivation. She'd had a very harsh childhood, which she never talked about, and escaped by traveling the world. Her capacity for solitude and ability to adapt to foreign cultures had rubbed off on me.

But now my parents were each on opposite sides of a continent that was an ocean away from me. I couldn't afford to worry about them worrying. I needed to cultivate this new family—even though I hated them and would kill them if I could.

EVERY MORNING I'D SAY "*hamam*," bathroom—usually to Mej, who was watching me. He would always say he didn't have the key. Later they cuffed me to the bedpost and I could only sleep on one side. I would motion to them to uncuff me. And they would make the gesture that means wait. Sometimes Mej would agree and sneak into the other room and get the key, then he'd open the cuffs and I would go to the toilet. They would wait for me outside and I would go out. Then we'd come back quickly and he'd cuff me to the bedpost again.

Throughout the day they would give me water. I had a gold-colored glass sitting on my right side, from which I would drink. But of course the water would make me want to piss, and they wouldn't let me go to the toilet unless I pleaded with them and looked like I was about to explode. So I would just piss into the glass. The window was usually open, so I'd toss the piss out the window, but often I'd miss and some would spill onto the sill and the outside wall. The acrid smell of dried urine would waft through the room. I didn't care. I was leaving my mark like a dog. If for some reason I disappeared from the face of the earth and wound up buried in an impossible-to-find Levantine hole, at least I had left a mark for some other dog; at least I had created some discomfort for the fucks who took away my liberty.

I piss, therefore I exist.

It was a minuscule consolation, possibly even more fodder for despair, but any little act of defiance gave me strength, made me feel a little more alive, a little less pliant. And that somehow might translate into respect on their part.

PSYCHO WAS ALWAYS an immediate concern. One minute he was a squirrelly teenager, the next a rabid assassin. And with no life experience to speak of under his belt, he needed to make a name for himself.

One day I was only cuffed with my hands in front of me, and not to the bedpost. So I stood up. It was early morning and everyone was sleeping. Sometimes the younger guys would sleep in the TV room with Abu Talal and Ali, and I'd be on my own. I liked that.

I was already thinking about how I could escape. I stood up, opened the curtain, and looked into the kitchen to get a sense of the layout. The bathroom was on the left. I tried to figure out the doors leading outside, and how my captors blocked them with metal bars, which I heard every night. They were probably closing it for safety reasons, not necessarily to keep me in. But it made a lot of noise. In planning my escape I kept imagining different scenarios, different exit routes. I drew the curtain a bit and ventured into the kitchen. There was a drape and another drape and then the TV room. I looked in and saw that they were sleeping— everyone except Psycho, who clearly saw me.

I went back and pretended nothing had happened. But he came right in with his AK-47, loaded it with a magazine, and pointed it at my head. He kept screaming at me, cursing incomprehensibly. Mej woke up and asked what was going on. I looked down and saw the cigarette I'd just finished smoking on the floor. I could feel the cold barrel of the gun on my forehead. Psycho kept cursing at me in Arabic. Then Mej nudged Psycho's weapon away from me and said, "No, no." Ali came in all gruff because of the rude awakening and grabbed the gun from Psycho.

I didn't do anything or show any emotion. Something in me was already numb. I felt like I could say, *Do it now, I don't care anymore.* At one point I even had a smile on my face. I was just sizing Psycho up, thinking, *You have a gun now. But if you didn't, in this situation, just you against me, I'd kill you without a second thought.*

Later Mej pleaded with me not to do that again. But Ali and the other guys never said anything. I'd been sneaking around, pretending I needed to go to the bathroom, but I didn't really have to go to the bathroom. I'd been exploring my options, planning to bolt. Something in me sensed they knew that's exactly what I was doing and they could only respect me for it.

The next day Psycho was gone. I never saw him again. I asked Mej, and he said, "No good man. He went back to Yabroud, to his family." It dawned on me that they thought I was too valuable to have a loose cannon like that around. I was precious merchandise.

AFTER A WHILE BOREDOM started to become demoralizing in and of itself. Just sitting there in the dark, doing nothing. The men smoked a lot of cigarettes and watched TV. Whenever I heard them light up I'd try to bum a cigarette.

I was getting a bit more comfortable and decided I needed to be friends with them. Otherwise I'd just be aggravating the torture.

One evening Abu Talal walked by. My blindfold was lifted because they'd just fed me. I motioned for him to come over. He did, and with a few gestures I asked if I could watch TV. He said okay and uncuffed me. From then on I started watching TV at night, mostly Egyptian movies, often with the famous comedian Adel Imam. The men in the room were always laughing, and I would just sit there and smoke cigarettes. Obviously I didn't understand a thing, but the laughter helped—any laughter that wasn't directed at me had a healing effect. We were all able to share something, and as a result they were getting used to me, like a new piece of furniture. At times it almost felt like I was free, just hanging out with these rebels.

But then they would put the cuffs back on me before going to sleep. Or whenever a car pulled up to the house they would hurry me back to my room, cuff me again, and lower my blindfold. Then some officers would come in and take a look around, and the men would act like everything was in order.

I NOTICED THEY HAD MADE dumbbells out of tin cans filled with cement. While I was sitting there blindfolded, Ali would come into the room and work out in front of me as if I weren't there. But one time he saw me looking at him from under the blindfold, my head tilted back, and

I made him understand that he wasn't doing the exercise properly. He was trying to do curls with his elbows out, and that made for a jerky motion that would eventually cause back problems. I stood up and put pressure on his elbow so it was closer to his body; that way he could isolate the bicep.

He suddenly became interested, so for about a half an hour I showed him how to lift weights, basic exercises.

They had a series of makeshift dumbbells and one barbell made out of a metal pole with two huge aluminum cans on the end. Both the cans had USAID written on them.

When the other rebels found out that I knew what I was doing technically, many of them came in to train and I'd lead them in a workout session. They came into the house to do push-ups, sit-ups and squats together. I'd spend an hour every day teaching everyone how to lift weights and showed them how to do dead lifts and curls. We even set up a makeshift bench for bench presses.

It was good for them because it built a routine. Ali was especially into it. So was Flic, even though he smoked cigarettes between reps. I knew lifting weights would build the soldiers' morale, because so much of a man's morale is tied to his physical strength. But I also made myself needed, and that built up my morale as well.

THIRD INTERROGATION

SEVERAL DAYS AFTER the interrogation with knives, the same men came back again. Abu Talal and the others were out. They had a document with many pages in Arabic and told me it was a transcript of my testimony. They wanted me to sign every single page of it. I didn't even bother to bring up the objection that I could have been signing my own death warrant for all I knew. It would have been as pointless as saying, *Talk to my lawyer.*

They looked at the papers and picked up where they'd left off, still aggressive—minus the kitchen knives, though. "You're lying, we know it." The fear was steadily building inside me. It set off a metallic taste in my mouth. I had a queasy feeling that I wasn't going to get out of this one. "You're an American. We know you're working for the Americans. We're going to kill you. We're going to execute you. You're a spy and we kill spies."

I stuck to my story and tried not to think about the ridiculous logic of what they were saying. Why would they want to kill an American if they were hoping to get aid from the Americans? There were already rumors at the time that the CIA was vetting rebels for a covert training program in Jordan. They must have already had operatives on the ground. I assumed none of them had ever shown up in these parts and the rebels were getting disillusioned. During the beginning of the war there was talk that the Americans would funnel tons of arms to the rebels and create a no-fly zone. All I saw was Russian-made equipment (probably captured from Syrian army stocks) trying to shoot down helicopters that were bombing the rebels mercilessly. So resentment against the Americans was understandable.

Still, I intuitively felt that the interrogators were grasping at straws, trying to trip me up in my story. They were hoping I was more important than I was, but it was becoming clear to them that I was just a paltry young freelance photographer who'd gotten a little too hungry for the right shot.

After about an hour, as the interrogation was winding down, Abu Talal showed up with Ali and the other kids. They gave me the papers to sign, which I did, and then suddenly everyone was very nice to me, like, *Hey it's okay. It's all over.*

The sudden switch caught me off balance. Abu Talal was my buddy now. He told me to grab my computer and open it up with the password. I assumed he wanted me to show them pictures of me with the Ogaden rebels in Ethiopia. But as soon as I opened it he knew exactly which folder he wanted me to double-click—my personal photos.

"What is this?" he said.

My heart sank. I suddenly realized that they'd gone through my computer at some point and found the folder with all the pictures of my past girlfriends. One of them had been a very successful model for a well-known lingerie company—as well as somewhat of an exhibition-ist. While we were going out, before one of us had to go on a lengthy trip for work, she'd sneak little videos onto my computer to tease me while we were apart.

Abu Talal went straight for her. The two interrogators were sitting next to me. A few minutes earlier they were telling me they were going to execute me for being a spy, and now they were all pals of mine antic-ipating a hormonal rush. I clicked the video and my girlfriend appeared sauntering around in her lingerie. She uttered a few seductive words that the men clearly couldn't give a rat's ass about, and then slowly started showing her magnificent body, bit by bit.

They called in other guys from the unit waiting outside. Two more showed up and sat next to me to watch my ex-girlfriend spread her long, sensuous legs and finger herself for me. For me exclusively.

This video used to drive me crazy. She knew all the teases and reveals that could press my buttons. Now I was just feeling depressed because I had to share it with this band of troglodytes drooling over my shoulder.

This was the life that I'd left behind, the life they'd taken away from me. And they were all just laughing. My intimacy had become a mockery to them. I tried to feign indifference, but I felt mortally wounded deep inside, in a place I hadn't even realized existed.

———————

IT SEEMS THAT even when I felt good about something I was doing, even when my morale was high—all things considered—something would happen to put me back in my place. In ordinary life, the life that had been taken away from me, such instances tended to involve little shots of humility to set you straight and put things in perspective. Working in conflict zones makes you acutely aware of what a spoiled lot we Westerners who grow up relatively wealthy with a sense of entitlement are: you come face-to-face with people who have lost everything—home, loved ones, hope—because of a random artillery shell. Fate literally comes crushing down on them. But there's a fine line between humility and humiliation. In the context of my captivity, humility usually had to come as a by-product of humiliation.

In my case I was very happy to finally be allowed to help the soldiers with some sort of physical fitness routine. I'd gained some respect in their eyes. I was making them feel better about themselves. We were building a sense of fraternity.

Then Abu Talal got involved. He liked to walk into a room and start roughhousing with the younger guys—wrestle them, slap-box a little. Sometimes he seemed to just want physical contact. Other times he looked like he needed to prove a point.

I happened to be in the room one day and he said, "Come here." I went over to him and he gave me a shove. As soon as there was a little distance, he waved me back toward him. As I approached he put his hand behind my neck in a wrestling lock and put his weight on me. You have to find a way to fight back that isn't so aggressive as to be disrespectful, but not too passive, either—enough force to let him know you still have some dignity to defend. Abu Talal was tall, at least my height, but much heavier. I knew with utter certainty that if we had been alone on neutral ground, unarmed, with all my built-up rage, I would have not only killed him, but probably disfigured his body for good measure, maybe ripped off his balls and shoved them into his fat mouth. But I also knew that showing my anger would be like committing suicide. So I wrestled, and resisted just enough.

He felt me resisting, pushing him back, and then basically started whaling on me with looping haymakers. I covered up and closed the distance. We got into a clinch and he started to strangle me from the front. Somehow I manage to trip him and we wound up on the ground, with him on top. Suddenly I felt two of my ribs snap. One after the other—pop, pop. While I was on the ground he got up and started kicking me as I lay there unable to move or breathe. Then another guy came in and held Abu Talal back, but it was too late. My ribs were broken.

FOR THE NEXT FEW DAYS every movement that involved my abdominal muscles—that is, just about every single movement, including the indispensable one of breathing—was accompanied by a pain that practically made me convulse. I tried to will it away, but my will was just a shadow of what it once had been.

Exacerbating matters was the fact that my difficulty in breathing and the consequent lack of air summoned up another memory of my childhood friend David. With the arrival of puberty he became more erratic. And the more erratically he behaved, the more I was drawn to him. We became inseparable. I'd sleep over at his family's house in Normandy and we'd play war for hours in the woods with the local boys, or sneak wine and cigarettes from his parents. One time I was in his room, we were playing Risk or some other board game and he exploded. I don't even remember why. By that point some itch that was imperceptible from the outside would get into him and he'd go ballistic. This time I wound up on the floor, on my belly. His hands were wrapped around my neck and I couldn't breathe. I was helpless, but I remember seeing a small stuffed Mickey Mouse lying at the foot of his little brother's bed. When I clutched Mickey, David let go. I'd almost passed out from him squeezing the sides of my neck.

After he released me, the blood rushed back to my brain. He didn't say anything, and I didn't say anything to anyone. But that was when I decided I wanted to go live with my father in New York. I needed to get David out of my life.

As with the knife incident, I played the choking episode over again in my mind, conflating it with my current predicament as a hostage. David had been my lifeline to the outside world, and he was tainted by violence. Inevitably I'd come to see the whole outside world as tainted by violence. I began to understand how the conflicts I've always been drawn to were connected at the deepest levels of my psyche to a sense of loyalty and devotion—imperatives which are manifested to the extreme by soldiers willing to take orders and sacrifice their lives for an ideal. Over time, violent conflict had become the magnetic north for my compass. At university I wrote my thesis on the Viking invasions of Carolingian France in the ninth century. Violent conflict gradually became a framework of worship for me. As such, war was a sacred rite that reenacted the human drama. But of course this kind of reverence for violence bordered on idolatry, at best. In the worst cases, when entire societies fell under the same ferocious spell, the historical ramifications have been devastating.

As I lay on my mattress, in pain every time I inhaled, I was in no position to work these ideas out. All I felt was that the mere thought of breaking away from the violence that had informed me was like being confronted by the prospect of losing my identity.

IN RETALIATION FOR THE BROKEN RIBS, I tried to lash out in a way that only I would notice. Ever since they put me in that house I kept unscrewing the neon strip light above the bed when the others weren't looking. I must have done it about twenty times. Then finally I got the chance, despite the pain in my midsection, to reach up and smash the light's contact altogether so it wouldn't work again. For a fraction of a second I felt triumphant.

But that didn't last long.

Soon after, I really needed to go to the bathroom, but my wrists and ankles were cuffed—during the day this time—and I was blindfolded. My ribs were throbbing with pain. There was only me, Mej and Baby Donkey in the house. The others were out fighting. I told Mej, but he said he didn't have the key. I couldn't walk, so I went on my knees. But I couldn't really move my feet because the cuffs on my ankles were so tight and the chain was very short.

The two of them looked at me like, *Where are you going?* And I glowered back at them, *Fuck you, I'm going to the bathroom. I'm really in pain.* So I started crawling and they just watched me. I could tell Mej felt bad. But Baby Donkey was laughing at me. I wanted to grind his face into a pile of shit. And then I realized I was peeing all over myself. I wanted them to feel bad about it, so I just stayed there, sitting in my own piss.

They felt sorry for me and dragged me back. Mej asked if I was okay. Baby Donkey just laughed that imbecilic laugh of his.

WHEN NOBODY WAS LOOKING I curled up into a ball as best I could and tried to become numb. It was dark enough to imagine myself elsewhere, as a boy, my father reading some adventure story to me.

I tried to breathe in a way that minimized the pain. Of course, it wasn't so much the physical pain in my ribs, which was bad enough, as it was the psychic pain of captivity. Along with freedom you lose all the other entryways to joy that you never realized were contingent on that freedom: the smell of the surf just as the morning fog is lifting; the sound of a campfire crackling under a desert sky whose stars multiply with every step you take away from the firelight; the womblike sound of your head underwater when you're swimming on your back for miles parallel to the shore with the horizon in the distance; your father's impish laugh when you recount a funny anecdote from your adventures; the thick, sweet taste of that condensed milk you drank as a kid; your mother's coq au vin; how she tells you you're crazy when you're about to travel, but says it with admiration; the rumble in your gut as you cross into a country you've never seen before, one in the process of a historic upheaval; the look in your lover's eyes when she sees you for the first time after a long absence, the first feel of her freshly wet lips, the taste and squeeze of her. I lost all these things as soon as I lost my freedom. And they kept wheezing away with every labored breath in the silence.

Then Flic walked into the room and turned on the light. He shook me up, told me to grab my clothes. I asked where we were going and his normally jovial face looked grave, as if to say, *Just shut up* . . . Then he dragged me outside into Abu Talal's car. What little gear I had at that house—my computer and all the memory stored in it—I'd never see again.

THE LIGHT HOUSE

THE CAR TOOK OFF IN THE DARK. I thought they were driving me to where I'd be executed. They no longer needed me. I'd become a liability. But the level of tension on their part seemed a bit too relaxed. I started to think they might be taking me to where I'd be free. My hopes rose and fell with the car over the potholed road.

In the end the ride was brief, only about a mile or so. We parked on the side of the road and got out at the gates to a villa. Once inside I was led down a slight slope. As soon as we stepped into the house, old man Flic, who had shaken me out of bed, was in a much friendlier mood. He led me into a large TV room. There was a young man sitting on a couch: good-looking, stubbly beard outlining his aquiline features, dark intelligent eyes, and lashes that practically cut into his brow. He was medium height and thin, relaxing with his hands behind his neck, wearing jeans and a T-shirt.

"*Alors, ça va?*" he asked, just to show that he knew a little French.

He said his name was Fares. I registered his features, his natural way of looking into things, and trusted him immediately. Instinct told me he might become the key to my well-being in this new situation.

I asked Flic where the bathroom was. He pointed and said, "Just go." He didn't even walk me. Still cuffed, I went to the bathroom and then washed myself. The old policeman eventually came by to see if I was okay. My ribs were killing me and I winced with every breath. I saw him in the mirror and could tell he felt bad about it.

I went back and talked to Fares for a few hours. Flic was also there and he didn't say anything. He just sat smoking. I asked about the progress of the war, where the enemy was. And among the questions I'd casually drop one like, "Why do you think they brought me here?" Fares kept his responses vague enough to give the impression he knew little, but I got the sense that what little he did know involved me being part of some deal. And by the way his eyes looked downward I also got a sense that he wasn't entirely optimistic.

He noticed I was in pain and asked what had happened. I explained to him that Abu Talal had challenged me to a wrestling match. Fares didn't seem at all surprised.

Flic offered me cigarettes as he watched TV. One after another, like he wanted company smoking. Fares didn't smoke and I couldn't keep up with Flic. I was on the verge of passing out from exhaustion. I'd been in that other house for three weeks, blindfolded. Here it was just me, Fares and Flic—no one else. So I was very hopeful as I crumpled into the couch with my hands still cuffed.

I WOKE UP the next morning and saw everyone from the Dark House surrounding me. Mentally, my universe collapsed. Whatever hope had wormed its way into me while smoking cigarettes with Flic dissipated in the daylight. I almost wanted to be blindfolded again so I wouldn't have to look at their crusty mugs.

Almost. Because as soon as I looked outside the window and saw the sun, I knew I could regain some of my psychic strength, and one way or another that would lead me to a way out of there.

In the daylight I got a better look at the location. We were in a fairly large compound, about a hundred yards by eighty. There was the house in which we stayed and an adjacent swimming pool, which was empty. The compound was surrounded by a cement wall along the road, and the wall turned into a fence as it wrapped around the back of the house. Behind the house was an orchard of apricot trees, and the land sloped downward to the west, where you could see the Qalamoun Mountains on the border with Lebanon about a dozen miles away.

They put me in the room next to the TV room and chained me up to the bars on the window, a long chain so I could sleep better. But every time I moved you could hear it. Sometimes when I needed to piss I'd rattle the chains out of frustration and make a lot of noise so they would come to me.

One of the windows in my room looked east onto the road. On the other side there were twin villas, apparently built by two brothers to house their families. One of them hadn't been occupied for a while because it had taken a direct tank hit.

Farther up the road was a four-story building with an empty swimming pool. I later learned that the building was being used as a headquarters by the rebels holding me. From my window I could also see the main entrance to our house.

There were plenty of new faces in this new location. One was Noor, the man in charge of the house. He was in his early thirties, balding, with a thick black beard and big crazy eyes. He'd created a little garden of potatoes and salads in the yard and spent a lot of his time tending to it.

Then there was Rabiyah, a skinny kid in his twenties who usually did the cooking. We ate a lot of potatoes, tomatoes, and eggplants fried in a rather disgusting cooking oil—which I assumed was vegetal rather than industrial, though I couldn't be sure. In the kitchen there was a

propane canister for the single-burner stove where the meals were prepared. They were very fattening, and I could feel myself gaining weight
each day, which I needed because the three weeks blindfolded had
stressed me to the point where my appetite had started to wane.

Another guy living in the house was Mahmoud, a short, stocky
man who actually looked like a Westerner. There were so many Mah-
mouds that I referred to him in my mind as Pech, because his weapon
of choice was a Russian-made PKP "Pecheneg" machine gun. He was
very friendly with me and explained how his wife was in a refugee camp
in Lebanon with their children, but he had to fight. When I first asked
Pech about his weapon, he lay on his back to show me how he liked to
shoot at passing MiG jets.

In those first days at the new house there were weapons and
ammunition in every room, all over, including the Pecheneg and RPG
launchers. At one point, just a few days after I'd arrived, I was in my
room, and the Pecheneg was there, fully loaded with the belt cartridge
and ready to go. I knew I could just pick it up and mow everyone down
in a few seconds. There was also Mej's RPG, which was harder to use
and less effective for my purposes, but ready nonetheless.

I quickly assessed where everyone in the house was. There were
only four or five people. But there were people in the houses across the
street. I hadn't been to the headquarters yet, so I didn't know how many
people were there. There was a car in the gate, but I wasn't sure where
the keys were. I could see a dirt road heading west, and I assumed it
would eventually lead to the Lebanese border.

I could have grabbed the loaded Pecheneg and pulled a Rambo—
taken out the two men in the next room, snatched an AK-47 and a 9 mm
pistol, shot through my cuffs, and made a run for the Lebanese border. It
would have been spectacular, worthy of a Hollywood action-hero movie.
But it was pure fantasy.

I'd never fought in a war or shot at people. But I'd already seen
enough combat situations to know that such acts of heroism are rarely
choreographed. Rather, they tend to spring up from a chaotic mael-

strom—the proverbial fog of war. I hadn't thought out my escape, at least not in any realistic way. And as soon as I started to think about how to mow everyone down—with no previous training—I knew it wouldn't happen. Such skills come from training and repetition aimed at developing muscular memory. Professional soldiers are drilled to confront danger and cut it off. Repetition combined with indoctrination make that attitude second nature. On top of all that, with my ribs still broken the heavy breathing involved in any run would have been painful to the point of paralysis.

Over the years, by dint of sheer curiosity, I may have developed a second nature to walk into danger, but I didn't have the muscle memory when it came to handling weapons. I'd need to develop a plan, an escape route, work it out in my mind, and imagine it over and over.

Shortly after I began imagining my escape, they moved the weapons out of my room. It was as if they could see me studying their potential.

I LIKED TALKING TO FARES. With me he'd build up his French and English vocabulary, and I'd learn some Arabic. The men would greet each other with "Shlaunak."

Fares wasn't a fighter. He just volunteered to help those who did fight. He talked about his student days before the war in Damascus, where he studied French and engineering. He and Mej got along well, so that little alliance helped keep Baby Donkey at bay, who always risked becoming a nuisance. My world was confined to that room, and I wanted to ensure that the vibes in there were as sympathetic to me as possible. My ribs still ached and I needed to focus on them healing. But that wasn't always easy since this new house saw a lot of traffic and men would walk in and out looking at me very suspiciously.

As I sat on my mattress, chained to the window, I noticed that the red paint above my feet had flaked off in places, creating little patches by exposing the previous layer of white. Out of boredom I started scraping some of the looser bits off. There was one little patch that had the shape of Syria. I imagined I was looking at a map and following a time-lapse progression of territory being conquered by the rebel forces. In my own fantasy universe I visualized a victory for these men holding me captive. Slowly the areas to the east of Homs and Hama would get flaked off and fall into rebel hands. Then, from the northern part of the country, near Aleppo, the rebels would push southward, and even encroach on the Alawite stronghold of Latakia and the coast. I chipped away sections with my fingernails till all that was left was a little rump state run by Bashar al-Assad.

But I knew that was wishful thinking. What seems clear-cut and simple when you analyze a political situation from behind a desk starts flaking apart as soon as you hit the ground and get mixed up in the mud and rubble of so many conflicting aspirations.

I remembered the first time I'd been to the Syrian combat zone, in the summer of 2012. I was with a Greek journalist, Giorgos Moutafis, and we crossed over the northern border from Turkey. After spending a week and a half in northern Syria we ended up staying two days in the worst part of an enclave, holed up with a dozen or so rebels trying to contain whatever government troops there were. The fighting was very intense, getting closer and closer. I no longer felt comfortable because I didn't trust the rebels' tactical sense. They kept saying how everything was okay. But I didn't buy it. Giorgos and I discussed bailing out. Then we were attacked in a raid by government troops and all the rebels just rushed out of the house, basically leaving us to fend for ourselves. We had to make a decision quickly and it was hard to understand what was going on since very few people spoke English. When the fighters came back they said they'd pushed Bashar's troops back. But now there were twelve tanks five hundred yards away and we had no idea how these rebels would react to another assault, so we decided to leave.

I found out later that, about twelve hours after we'd left, our entire position had been destroyed.

We wound up walking to the Turkish border with a wave of refugees. It was a real scoop for us because up to that time there were very few pictures of refugees fleeing. Most of the images had come from the camps across the border. There were many children and at one point I had to carry one of them because they slowed everyone down. Then they had to put us on a truck to speed everything up. We walked through the mountains with them to the Turkish border, but eventually we had to split up because the refugees at the border could just go to the Turkish army and get channeled through, whereas journalists had to be smuggled back into Turkey illegally so as not to get deported and possibly blacklisted.

At that point in the war, after it first broke out, people were predicting the quick overthrow of Bashar and the rise of a new Sunni-dominated government, probably linked to the Muslim Brotherhood, which was supported by Turkey and had just come to power in Egypt. Even Western countries were considering arming the rebels. Over time, the United States and the West would choose not to support the rebels too enthusiastically, partly because they just assumed the rebels would overwhelm the Bashar regime with sheer numbers and partly because of concerns that they were becoming increasingly Islamist. That resulted in foreign policy paralysis.

From my point of view, I could see how ragtag these fighters were. All I had to do was take a look at Baby Donkey's dim-witted expression. Our positions were getting hit by heavy artillery, helicopters, even jets. The Alawites backing Bashar may have been outnumbered, but they knew they would probably be massacred if they lost, so you could be sure they would fight to the death. Moreover, the area we were in was already having to deal with Hezbollah, the well-organized and battle-hardened Shia troops from Lebanon who supported Bashar militarily and were financed by Iran, the country that had created Hezbollah back in the 1980s.

Many of the rebels had already become disillusioned. Fares kept asking me when France and America would set up a no-fly zone, like they had done in Libya. I tried not to be too pessimistic, but I'd been to Libya less than two years earlier, right before Muammar Gaddafi was killed. From the ground it looked highly unlikely that those rebels could bring order to a country like Libya—full of tribal rivalries—without some colonial power stepping in. And none of the NATO powers that bombed Gaddafi's forces were even remotely inclined to occupy that tar baby. So based on the Libya experience it was clear that Barack Obama, who was gun-shy to begin with, would look for any excuse to stay out of Syria. I didn't want to put it so bluntly to Fares, but I knew they were on their own. And from the continual shelling getting closer and closer, it felt like it would be a long, drawn-out war.

AFTER TEN DAYS, they stopped tying me up during the day and would only cuff me at night. Most of the soldiers were just kids and the war was wearing on them. They wanted a sense of normality. Having a tall foreigner chained up in the house must have struck them all as a bit awkward. If he's a prisoner or hostage, then you bring him to an isolated room and interrogate him, after which you lock him up. It wouldn't have been unusual because I'd occasionally see them taking prisoners to the house across the road, or to a room below mine in the one where we were staying. I could even hear the interrogations: crying, pleading, beating, and then, when the dogs started barking, the full-on screaming. In short, torture.

But I'd been with Mej and Abu Talal and even Baby Donkey long enough to have garnered at least a modicum of sympathy out of them, and it probably disturbed them to see me sulk and brood in the room. If I were a fresh hostage—and therefore less human—they could beat me with little remorse. But I was gradually seeping into the fabric of their existence. I represented the world beyond the war, and they were reluctant to antagonize that world. So they let me roam somewhat free through the compound, at least during the day.

I'd lie by the empty pool and take my shirt off to get some sun, letting my leg dangle off the edge. We were already past mid-May and the weather was getting hotter. You could see apricots ripening on the branches throughout the orchard. The sun on my face and the faint smell of slightly burnt skin felt miraculous. It picked up my mood like a drug. Like everything was going to be all right. In a strange way these were my brothers-in-arms. We were in this together, on the same side, and whether they realized it or not our well-being was intimately connected. Or at least that's what I told myself.

Those first few hours of sun made me giddy, like when I was six years old on the beach in Normandy and had just discovered the sea at Madame Poudardin's vacation colony for the first time and listened to the waves while walking below the cliffs. I felt so good there by the pool because I could actually see something beyond my mind conjuring all sorts of unseemly fates and unlikely escapes.

Then the novelty wore off. It was like a drug, and I soon needed more. After a few days, lying by the pool and sucking in the sun just didn't cut it anymore.

Now that I could see the lay of the land, my escape fantasies whittled down to more realistic scenarios. I noticed there were two big white dogs (I was never sure if they were the ones I would hear during the interrogations). If I ever hoped to run away from there I'd have to make sure the dogs became my friends and didn't bark at me. Occasionally I'd give them bits of food or offer to feed them. I'd pet them, scratch their necks, and get them used to my presence.

At times I'd test my captors to gauge how far they'd let me go. Behind the house there was a cherry tree that gave me cover. I figured I'd put a chair down and sit beneath it to see what their reactions were. Sometimes they wouldn't say anything; other times they would grab me and throw me back in the house. Or they would call to me and point at the building down the road, as if to say it's not cool to sit there because people could see from the top floor and they were always watching. I tested them to see how far I could go with my freedom.

Soon I started just walking for hours. I'd get myself so tired that I'd pass out at night. It would take me about five minutes to walk the perimeter. Then it occurred to me that I hadn't heard any of my own music in weeks. All I had was the dross coming off the TV—pop and

Arabic songs. My computer had hundreds of tracks with an emphasis on hard rock, especially bands like Uriah Heep, Deep Purple and Black Sabbath. So, as I started walking, the Scorpions song "Still Loving You" welled up spontaneously from my lungs: "Time, it needs time to win back your love again . . ."

I was in between serious relationships when I left for Syria, so there was no woman I was particularly pining for, which oddly enough made the lyrics even more poignant because it became an anthem to my lost freedom.

As I repeated my Scorpions mantra, I eventually overstepped my bounds. I'd started out by the brick barbecue oven where they often cooked and walked down the side of the house, continuing along the fence. Usually I'd turn back at one point, but this time I kept going, to get a little farther from sight. Suddenly Mej and another guy, who were sitting in the orchard, started calling me and waving. I came back and they were very angry. They grabbed me, brought me to the TV room, and chained me up as punishment.

I ALWAYS TRIED to make the best of my punishment. Here at the new house I could at least look out the window and imagine. Otherwise I could continue scraping the red paint.

There was a patch that vaguely resembled the shape of Germany after the Treaty of Versailles in 1919, with East Prussia as an exclave of Germany. I started chipping away at the gains the Third Reich made during World War II. First I chipped off Austria, which was annexed by Germany in the Anschluss of 1938. Then I lifted a sliver of the Sudeten-land in Czechoslovakia, which was easier. After that I scratched off the Danzig Corridor and started dividing Poland by gradually flicking off significant paint chips. It was a bold move at the time—signing a secret pact with Stalin—and now, with our historical perspective and access to so many archives, we know that Hitler's plan was to colonize all the Soviet lands up to the Ural Mountains.

Then came the invasion of France. As I chipped away at the French border my uncle Theo came to mind. Theo was probably my first encounter with a real war hero. I met him several times when I was a kid and my father would take us to the South of France. My childhood was filled with stories of his exploits and he became a cornerstone of my own personal mythology.

Born in 1910 in Berdychiv, a small town with a large Jewish population in what was then the Russian Empire (now central Ukraine), Theophile Lieberman arrived in France when he was only three months old. Theo's father worked as a showman. When the war broke out in 1914 he enlisted. He fought in the Dardanelles, and then at Verdun in 1916. He came back from the front in February 1919.

Theo stopped going to school at the age of fourteen. The children had to work in show business to help earn money. In the 1930s Theo decided to leave his father to set up his own troupe, which was rather successful.

As soon as World War II broke out in September 1939 he volunteered in order to obtain French nationality. He was enrolled in an anti-tank unit, then transferred to the all-black Eighth Senegalese Colonial Regiment. He was a sergeant with a four-gun battery of antitank guns and fought at Sedan in May 1940. His unit was hit hard by German infantry and tank attacks. Because of the Eighth Regiment's heroic resistance, the Germans sent in Stuka dive-bombers to finish them off. It worked. Theo and a few other survivors—most of them wounded, including himself—dragged themselves into a ditch near a small bridge. After an agonizing time in that ditch a German column passed nearby. A Wehrmacht soldier unloaded his machine gun on the wounded black troops. Fortunately for Theo the Germans ran out of ammo. But he still got hit in the groin. He spent three days eating worms from his wounds, after which he was picked up by another Wehrmacht column with a doctor. They sent him by rail to Germany to be treated. A German surgeon saved his life but had to amputate a leg. I was also convinced that he'd lost the function of his genitals, though I can't recall anyone telling me this explicitly. Nevertheless, the assumption itself left an impression. Theo recovered for nearly two years in a hospital bed before being repatriated to Nice. Before his departure, the German officers present at the hospital honored him with a full military ceremony, even though he was a known Jew.

Theo spent the rest of the war hiding guns and grenades under his wheelchair for local partisans, while being pushed around by a priest, who would later become the bishop of Nice.

After the war he received the Grand Officier de la Légion d'Honneur (created by Napoleon), which is the closest thing the French have to the Medal of Honor. Theo had lost everything, so the city of Nice gave him an apartment and a store very close by. He became the seller of high-end Bally shoes. He married his sweetheart Fanny, my father's aunt, and they stayed together for forty years until he died in 1992.

I always have to laugh at the irony of buying shoes from a one-legged shoe salesman. Unfortunately I was too young to have adult conversations with Theo before he died. I would have asked him what it was like to be so close to death, to be treated by men who could send you to a near-certain death for being a Jew. I also wondered what it was like to live without being able to use your penis, though I doubt I would have had the nerve to ask him outright. War hero or no war hero, it's hard to imagine anything being worth that price. In my "what if" moments I often ask myself whether I'd prefer keeping my genitals and living with dishonor, or accept dishonor and retain my ability to fuck.

That kind of question over the years has been completely conditioned by Theo, who continued his life with honor and continued making love to Fanny—though perhaps not strictly speaking. Ultimately I believe dishonor is the real punishment of war. I mean real dishonor, the kind where you are forever known as a coward or a scumbag. Most people to whom I say such things think I'm either crazy or fanatic or just posing—which is why I rarely say such things. But the memory of Theo—that perfect example of honor at the price of pleasure—keeps everything in perspective for me.

Some shelling in the distance roused me from my paint-flake reverie. I was fully immersed in the world of my forebears. There was movement all around me. One of the fighters unlocked my chain and we all proceeded to the basement, which would be safer in the event of a direct hit.

As we waited out the shelling I looked at the young men around me, working out their own heroic aspirations—all of them to some extent driven by a chain of events their own forebears had set into motion. I wondered how many of these men would finish the war in a similar state to Uncle Theo. How many of us would make it through alive?

I PAUSED MY PAINT-SCRATCHING project at Operation Barbarossa, when on June 22, 1941, more than three million German troops invaded the Soviet Union. I've never seen anything even near that scale; no one in my generation has. And I doubt something like that could be repeated in my lifetime. In fact, there are few people alive who have witnessed Operation Barbarossa from the combatants' point of view.

The only massive invasion to have occurred in my adult life was when the United States and Britain invaded Iraq in 2003 with more than 150,000 troops. But I had only recently started my career and was focused on Africa at that time. To get close to the invasion forces you needed to be embedded, which meant already having credentials and connections. I was at a stage when wandering through jungle, savanna, or desert with a ragtag group of forgotten freedom fighters suited me better than competing with CNN embeds in an Abrams tank racing across Mesopotamia.

In any case, the Germans invaded with a number of troops that was an order of magnitude greater than any invasion in recent memory—in all of history, for that matter.

Ukraine was to be deurbanized and serve as the Reich's granary, while the Slavic populations would provide slave labor. Ironically, the colonization model Hitler had in mind was based on America's notion of Manifest

Destiny: in the United States, Europeans subjugated or simply liquidated the indigenous population and imported African slaves for hard labor as they expanded westward into what was deemed uncivilized emptiness. In Hitler's plan he would subjugate the Slavs *and* use them for labor.

But nobody could take such an audacious plan seriously in 1939—at the time of the Polish partition—notwithstanding the fact that it could be found black on white in *Mein Kampf.*

History buffs often like to play "what if" in their minds, and Operation Barbarossa always offers some of the most disturbing what-ifs in recent history.

Initially the invasion was to take place on May 15, as soon as the ground, still muddy from winter snows, hardened enough to ensure the mobility of the German panzers, which were crucial to Blitzkrieg tactics. But the invasion was delayed for a number of reasons. Hitler's Balkan campaign in April was one; others included delays in distributing motor transport, problems with fuel distribution, and the difficulty in establishing forward airfields for the Luftwaffe.

The bottom line was that the Wehrmacht was at the outskirts of Moscow in late October when the first snows fell. After that, the Soviets had winter on their side. Eventually the Germans, who were not prepared to fight in cold weather, had to hold their positions desperately and initiate a series of tactical retreats when the Soviets funneled in reserves from Siberia.

What then would have happened if Operation Barbarossa had begun just a few weeks earlier? Europe and the rest of the world would no doubt be entirely different. Or would they? Here it depends on whether you believe in a historical destiny that compels peoples and nations toward certain ineluctable actions, or whether you believe history is just a random concatenation of causes and effects that we call destiny to appease some deep-seated teleological need.

As I scraped away at Belarus and Ukraine I wondered whether it was my destiny to be captured by Syrian rebels, or if I was just an unlucky schmuck.

THERE WERE ABOUT a half dozen young guys who came in and out of the house and they were all very friendly with me. They weren't really soldiers, more just helping the rebels in whatever capacity they could. They would always greet me with, "Hey, Johnny." So it was a pleasure to spend time with them, a tinge of normality.

One of them was an officer's son, a young kid about twelve or thirteen who would show up at the house once in a while. Sometimes he wore kids' clothing; other times he sported a desert camouflage outfit. Whenever he saw me he would light up and say, "Hey, Jon."

One morning I was next to the covered area near the pool. Rabiyah was there with the officer's kid. We were just standing around, talking. Then suddenly we heard the ominous whistling sound of a mortar, and it was coming straight for us. Rabiyah and the kid ran for the house, but it looked too far away for me, so I jumped into the pool and instinctively ran toward the deep end, which was opposite the direction from where the shells were being fired. I hunkered down into the corner and bits of metal and earth started raining all around: on the road and throughout the orchard. The house didn't get hit, and the other two made it back there safely. All told it lasted only about thirty seconds—just a few shells. But I stayed in that corner for a while, kind of dazed.

I wondered if I could ever get used to being shelled. It always made me think of World War I in the trenches, the literally shell-shocked soldiers. Could a human being ever get used to something like that without going insane? I found it hard to imagine.

UP TO THEN the heaviest shelling I'd experienced was from the giving end, in 2010 when I was in Afghanistan embedded with the French Foreign Legion, with whom I'd already embedded six years earlier in Côte d'Ivoire.

I arrived in Bagram Airfield near Kabul with another photographer and there they arranged armored vehicles to get us to the base at the

front lines. After a few uneventful days on patrols, one of the captains
came up to me and said a major operation was going to start the following day: five hundred men, mortar teams, armored vehicles. "There's
going to be firefighting," he said. "We're going to kill some Talibans."

They'd set up a sort of diorama in a huge sandy area, re-creating
the landscape with flags and soldiers, so people could really get a visual
understanding of the terrain. The commanding officer pointed to specific buildings and hills with a stick. There were some Afghan auxiliary
units looking at it, too. They gave me full access.

The following day, after everything had been prepped, we went into
a typical Afghan village full of mud houses. On the left there was a large,
not very deep wadi in which they were cultivating crops. Beyond that
was a mountain range, not very high but with steep hills. We took up
positions behind a low dirt wall. There was fighting about two miles
away. Machine guns. Suddenly the platoon leader, a Frenchman (the
platoon leaders are always French in the Foreign Legion), said, "Guys,
we have to go. There's a counterattack." There was an ambush and we
had to help them out.

At the time my arm was basically paralyzed because I'd torn all my
shoulder muscles in a water polo game the week before. I lied to them,
because if they had known they would have sent me back to Paris. So
I tied it up and spent three weeks in Afghanistan with my arm loose. It
was very painful, and the armored vehicles were high because of all the
gear. With only one arm I didn't have the strength to hoist myself up, so
the guy behind me gave me a push.

You could tell the soldiers were nervous. As we drew closer we
heard the boom-boom of 20 mm rounds landing and RPGs being fired.
We got into a village on the outskirts of the town and unloaded. There
was fighting. I ran with the men at the point of the attack. We got cover
from an armored vehicle shooting 20 mm rounds, just blasting things.
Moving closer and closer, we soon entered the actual town. They were
running from street to street, a column of guys. At one point we stopped
because one of the men had stepped on an unexploded ordnance. I got

a picture of it. It didn't blow up. Then I looked to my left and there was a closed door where civilians had just taken cover inside a house. It was raining and I saw a small puppy all wet, looking at me and shivering, terrified from the fighting. I wanted to take him in my arms, but obviously I couldn't.

We continued and then made a right into the street. Suddenly one of our soldiers got shot, though not badly because he was wearing a flak jacket. He pointed and said, "They're right here." We went down the street and there was more and more shooting going on. Then we took a left into a square. All the guys took positions. I found cover along a wall. Then one of the soldiers went into a very narrow street and boom! . . . He got shot, then dropped. I got a picture. His friend came in to help him, and he got shot, too, in the head. He died almost instantly. I didn't get pictures of that because they grabbed my camera. All the guys were firing everywhere. Then we went from one area to another and started cleaning things up. Eventually it wound down and stopped completely.

We stayed put in another street for a while, then suddenly the Taliban ambushed us again, with RPGs, so suddenly there were forty to sixty guys all shooting at the same time. It was what they call a fireball—a mad minute when everybody shoots at the same time. I couldn't even take pictures because I was doubled over. And then it stopped.

I saw two crazy American mercenaries I'd befriended. They were on their way to check the house where they thought the two Taliban who had just ambushed us were. One of them looked at me and said, "Hey, man, we're gonna fuck these guys up."

Then the men captured a Taliban and the Romanian lieutenant beat him up viciously because they'd just killed one of the lieutenant's men. I took some pictures but I felt very ambivalent about it.

After cleaning up the town we left. We slept on the ground, and the following day we were ambushed again. They hit us with RPGs. There were always two F-15s on call to help the French, and the Americans wanted to solve the problem with a five-hundred-pound bomb. The French dissuaded them: "No, don't do that, you're going to hit civilians."

The officer was laughing. "These fucking Americans, what's wrong with them?" he said. "They just want to blast the whole thing." Instead they compromised with a show of force: basically the plane flies fifty yards off the ground to scare the enemy. It usually does the job.

Then they moved us to the wadi area, where we took up positions. We heard on the radio, "They're going to attack you guys, so be ready." Thirty to forty men were spotted from a satellite. They were coming on our left side to flank us and attack. The foreigners were very excited about it, because it was a wooded area, and it was a little bit elevated. Then you had the wadi, and after that the mountains. They lined up all their heavy machine guns along a huge tree trunk that had fallen down. They were up on a slope, so they would have simply mowed the Taliban down. We waited about an hour or two, but nothing was happening so I went to where that trunk was. One guy from Russia gave me a cigarette and said, "You want some action? Wait a little bit."

The lieutenant came and said, "These assholes in the artillery unit want to take care of it." Everyone started complaining about their fun getting taken away from them. I could see on the side of these hills, about a half a mile away there was a platoon with armored fighting vehicles that carried 120 mm cannons. They were French, very good.

Suddenly we heard *boom, boom, boom*. And then they started launching 120 mm mortar rounds. That was terrifying. They hit a mile away and everything was shaking. Afghan dirt is very fine, so it explodes into a mist. The men coming up on the flank were finished. The sound was so loud. Thirty Taliban were killed. The legionnaire who died was a lance corporal from Slovakia.

It might be one of the most tired commonplaces of war, but it's true nonetheless: the rush you feel in the middle of a firefight, when something within you knows you can die or be maimed from one moment to the next, is unlike anything else. Never have I felt so alive, so fucking happy to be alive. I'm sure that's what keeps so many soldiers coming back to the front lines—not to mention us photographers and reporters, who don't even get to fire a weapon. There's something about the thrill of surviving a brush with death that begs repetition.

I didn't climb out of that empty pool until I was reasonably sure there were no more shells on their way. But when I did, I felt renewed.

THE DAY AFTER I took shelter in the pool I looked around at the pale blue paint chipping off the sides. So many of my first experiences in how to overcome fear took place in swimming pools. I learned how to swim late, at the age of nine. My father had taken me to l'Oustau de Baumanière in the South of France, where there was a swimming pool. It was an old-school swimming lesson, put the kid into the deep end and let him figure it out for himself. I swallowed a little water and almost panicked, but then managed to dog paddle to the edge. It didn't take long before I developed a taste for it, and in no time you couldn't get me out of the water.

I eventually took such a liking to the water that I started to swim competitively. In 1997, between my junior and senior years of high school, I'd just broken up with my first love and was very sad. To take my mind off my loss I convinced my parents to send me to a three-week Jack Nelson swimming camp in Fort Lauderdale, Florida, where they train Olympians.

It was hell. They'd wake us up at four in the morning and we'd have to run an hour and a half on the beach. Then six hours of swimming, then weight training, then classes. After the first day of training I said to myself there was no way I could go through with it. It was too hard. I went to one of the pay phones at the camp and called my mother, who was still living in France at the time. I was eighteen years old and whining with a face full of tears.

My mother, who had always refused to cosset me in any way, was unequivocal. "You wanted to be there. You're there." And she hung up on me. She refused to talk to me the entire trip. I never tried to call her, because I knew she'd say something to the effect of "Don't be a wimp."

I wanted her approval, for her to say, "Okay, you can go home now." I knew I could have gotten some money, hopped in a cab, and been on a plane back to New York very easily. But no. I had to face my fear. That's what she was saying in her very undiplomatic way.

So I sucked it up and went through the three weeks, winning all the races in my specialty, the 100-meter backstroke. I was so good that the coach took me out of the group and trained me by myself. I even qualified for the Junior Olympics. By the end of the three weeks I was like a machine.

Back in New York, at my regular training pool, it felt like I was cutting through water like never before. The coach during my senior year in high school was Cesar, from Venezuela, who led a team at the 92nd St. YMCA. He separated me from the team and said he was going to train me individually. I spent that year swimming more than twelve hours a week. I was so tired at school that I often slept in class. He would pick me up in his shitty little car at five in the morning and drive me forty-five minutes to another pool just to train me. Then he would kick my ass for two hours, drive me back, and drop me off, after which I'd put my uniform on and go to school.

Thanks to my mother I became a competitive swimmer. She was an adventure-seeking woman who flaunted an air of fearlessness that she hoped would rub off on me. As a single mother she felt she needed to toughen me up, perhaps to compensate for the lack of a male figure. She pushed from the beginning. I remember when I was nine and a friend of hers with a motorcycle came to visit. He offered to take me for a ride, but I was scared and refused to get on. She insisted, despite my crying, and forced me to hop on and go for a spin. Years later I'm one of the few nutjobs I know who move around New York City on motorcycles.

As I walked around the empty pool I noticed there was shrapnel everywhere. If I had stood there instead of jumping in, I would have been killed or badly injured. I picked up a few metal shards—some pieces were almost as big as my hand—and gave them to Abu Talal.

He examined them with his blue eyes, very impressed, as if I'd brought home a trout from a nearby river.

OVER TIME FARES AND I got closer. He was smart, and he was the only one I could have a real conversation with. I kept trying to get more information from him, but he'd told me all he knew. The upshot was that no one really understood what I was doing there. There was no useful information they could squeeze out of me. I assumed there was a price for my release, but no one was willing to pay it. For all I knew I may have been forgotten. My family back home may have just thought I was missing in action.

On the opposite side of the main entrance there was a big balcony that overlooked the entire valley. Fares and I would sit there with charcoal left over from burning fires and on the cement he'd draw a map of where we were.

"That's Lebanon—five kilometers," he said, pointing to the Qalamoun Mountains to the west.

"Is someone trying to get me out of here?"

"Don't worry, Jon. You'll go home."

I didn't want to press him on how he knew. He said it with conviction enough to have me believe it was more than just wishful thinking, as if he'd overheard something.

Fares gave me hope. In the meantime I'd become a fixture in the house. Early on, while I was still tied up, Noor walked by and looked at me with disapproval, then shot Abu Talal a look like, *Why is this guy tied up? This is stupid.*

Shortly after that, they stopped cuffing me and I became a "free-range hostage."

A few times they took me to the headquarters. Headquarters was the four-story building just across the road from where I was being held. Up close I saw it had tinted bay windows.

One time I went there with Essad's brother, who was very nice to me. He paid us visits on occasion and during one of them came up to me and said, "Hey, come over with me," or something like that. So I crossed the street with him. Essad was "Number One Man," so going over with his brother, who fought alongside him, raised my status with the others. He brought me in and offered me some Marlboro cigarettes. We smoked in a large empty living room with just couches. After a few smokes he told me I had to go because his brother and the other officers were on their way back.

The second time I was at the headquarters was when we'd come under heavy artillery strikes. I'd been sitting in the living room of our house with Mej and we got hit pretty hard, mostly around the yard. At one point the grass started burning. But we didn't take a direct hit. We were lucky.

When it stopped, Mej told me to run out of the house with him. The headquarters had much better protection. As we ran out of the gate and into the street, the shells started landing again. In the front part of the building there was a protected area. At the gate two rebels fell off their motorcycle. I could see them trying to lift up the bike as I ran, with shells landing all around. One shell landed a bit too close so they left the bike there and ran into the house, where the others were waiting.

Once in the house we went down to the protected area full of boxes and waited an hour or two for the shelling to stop. One of the soldiers lit a cigarette and I bummed one off him. Just as I took a drag, one of the officers started yelling at us: "You can't smoke here!" I looked around and noticed that this was where they kept a lot of their ammunition and explosives for making IEDs.

Sometimes they had big gatherings with all the leaders, and they'd put a large carpet on the ground. They would invite me, too, except for once or twice because they were talking about military plans. They served hummus and other Levantine fare. I stole a jar of cheese. I don't know why I stole it. I probably could have just asked for some cheese and they would have given it to me. It may have been an unconscious attempt to remind myself that I wasn't, in fact, a guest—which was an easy illusion since my conditions had improved at the second house. But I was still a hostage, and I needed such little acts of defiance to keep my morale up.

For example, I really enjoyed fucking with Baby Donkey's mind. He was such a simpleton, but with an innate violent streak—the kind of boy who in the wrong hands can become a dangerous man. I stole cigarettes from him every chance I got.

One day he captured a fairly big turtle and put it in the empty swimming pool. The boys always captured animals. Once they caught what I thought was a beaver. (I found out later that there aren't any beavers in Syria, and it was most likely a hyrax or hedgehog or some other rodent-type mammal. But in my mind, with no Google to fall back on, it was a beaver.) They shot it and tried to cook it. It was disgusting, so they left the cooked carcass next to the house for weeks. Another time they captured a big snake and wound up killing it. I'm not sure if they tried to eat that.

So Baby Donkey and I sat around the pool watching the turtle try to get out. When he went back in the house, I jumped into the pool, grabbed the turtle, and walked really fast to the orchards on the other side of the house. I put it right by the fence, where it started digging immediately with its long claws until there was enough space to sneak underneath. Then I went back to the pool and lounged in the sun as if I'd been sleeping. When Baby Donkey came back he asked where the turtle was. The puzzled look in his eyes—as if one eyeball didn't quite know what the other was up to—convinced me he was a legitimate idiot and not just on the stupid side. I adjusted myself in the chair and looked at him as if I didn't know what he was talking about. He gave up and walked away.

While sitting at the pool one day it occurred to me that since we'd moved to the second house, I hadn't been beaten. Obviously my status had changed, but I wasn't sure whether that was to my advantage. Of course, as soon as I started to count my blessings, something happened to undermine my hope. I was just sitting outside in one of the garden chairs, smoking with a bunch of the other guys, who usually ignored me, when Abu Talal drove up to the house. He stepped out of the car in a visibly shitty mood, grabbed me, threw me out of the chair brusquely and sat in it. I skulked back to the house. I thought the beatings might start again, but later Fares told me something bad had happened to Abu Talal's family.

SOME AFTERNOONS were very relaxed, especially when everyone else was out fighting. One time Rabiyah, Mej and I were just sitting in the TV room disagreeing about what to watch. I grabbed the remote control and put the news on, hoping to glean some information even though I couldn't understand the Arabic broadcasters. As soon as he heard something he didn't like, Rabiyah would just grab the remote from my hand and switch the channel to dancing women or some retro Syrian variety show that looked like it was stuck in the seventies. There was a round stage with pouty Arab girls sauntering around, not seeming very happy with their work.

"They're *hajiah*," Mej said. "Prostitutes." Every time we watched these show girls someone had to say they were all prostitutes.

Sometimes I'd take back the remote and we'd go back and forth, like Ping-Pong, anything to bide the time. It was an easy way of communicating, given the language barrier.

Mej watched the girls and sighed. Then he looked at me and shook his head. "Jon is beautiful man," he said. "Me no." Indeed, there was something disproportionate about his stocky build. Apart from the fact that his hair was in a mullet, and a bad one at that, his limbs looked too short, or maybe too long. It was hard to tell, but the sum effect was just lopsided.

He'd already told me that he liked a local girl named Nermin. When we were alone he would pull out his cheap little flip phone and show me a picture of her. Not exactly a beauty, in fact she looked as lopsided as Mej did, but there was a wholesome quality to her. A girl who was made to nurture. He didn't want the other guys to know because he was afraid they might try to steal her, or make fun of him.

He gestured to me. "You make picture."

I shrugged my shoulders. Why not.

He went into his room and brought in the RPG launcher he liked to fire. I lowered myself to get on the same level, but when he saw the shot he said, "No, that's not good."

"How the fuck would you know what a good picture is?" I said. "I do this for a living."

Still he insisted I take the picture from higher up. I tried to explain how that would make his legs look short and he'd appear even more out of proportion, but it didn't manage to get through.

After the RPG he went out and got the Pecheneg machine gun, then did his tough-guy pose with that. Once we had a couple of shots he was satisfied with, he sent them to Nermin.

Not long after he sent the photos I saw Mej moping. As soon as we got alone I asked about Nermin. His face went sad and I could see him trying to hold back tears, but they streamed down anyway.

"She doesn't want me," he said.

I didn't want to make him feel too awkward, so I said, "Don't worry. It happens to everyone. I have the same problem."

That seemed to give him a glint of consolation. He looked like he was hungry for me to elaborate, but the language barrier precluded it. In any case, there was no point delving into heartbreak, not given the circumstances.

RABIYAH, I WOULD QUICKLY LEARN, was obsessed with sex. A wiry, high-strung young man with pitch-black hair, who probably had to jerk himself off and shoot his wad on a regular basis just to keep from short-circuiting, he was always talking about pussy and tits and wanted to know how to say those words in French and English.

Once, while watching the prostitute showgirls on TV, Rabiyah looked at me and Mej and said something in Arabic as he grabbed a pillow and started riding it like a jackhammer, pogoing in and out. Then he turned to me with a thumb up and said, "Good, okay?"

I looked back at him appalled, shaking my head, "No good, not okay." Mej was watching the whole scene, embarrassed, but still curious about what my reaction would be. Rabiyah handed me the pillow to show them how it's done.

So suddenly I was holding a pillow and kissing it with gentle caresses. Basically I tried to explain foreplay to him. I showed him how to move his hands, and was trying to make him understand that you had to work your way in gently and not just impale her like you would a randy nanny goat.

They were all watching me intently, studying every gesture. I tried to show them how to be smoother with the hips, so they could understand it wasn't simply about pounding your prey into submission. I started slow, building up rhythm, back and forth. And they studied me, nodding, saying okay, giving me the thumbs-up.

But it was very embarrassing for me, so I stopped after a while and handed the pillow back to Rabiyah. He took it enthusiastically and started going through the motions, more slowly this time, looking toward me for approval. I gave him a thumbs-up and left it at that.

Later, when more dancers came on the TV, Rabiyah mimed my lesson again, thrusting his hips back and forth deliberately, face glazing over with the expression of a rabbit in a lettuce patch. I couldn't help but laugh.

He swallowed my snicker like a healthy dose of derision and timidly asked me to show him again. I was more than a decade older than him, and I obviously had more experience with women than he did—which wasn't difficult, considering he almost certainly had never had sex with a girl in his life. He mimed the gestures, but it was as if he were saying, *You have experience, you can imagine how I feel. Help me get through this unbearably awkward phase—old enough to perforate a man and bore a hole through half his body with a lethal projectile and expected to do no less ... but forbidden from entering a woman.*

Even though I was embarrassed, I humored him, mimicking kisses and caresses. It felt sort of like playing air guitar, only more ridiculous. But I got over that quick enough, because I knew how awkward it can be to walk around with a full-grown, well-functioning male body and not know how to use it properly. I sensed that he knew something from porno videos, but he also understood that porn was the emotional equivalent of action-hero war movies. Having experienced real war, he already knew the Hollywood variety was just two-dimensional. *His* war wasn't just those moments of noise and blood and heightened aware-ness; it was all that *plus* the endless boredom, fear, bitching and con-vincing yourself—more chaos and luck than clear-cut heroism. And because Hollywood also aspired toward realism, it was even more a travesty than some mythographic heroism. Likewise with porn. They try to keep it real enough so that the effect is always somewhat of a travesty compared to either idealized romance or the real emotions and sensations of making love.

Deep down I think Rabiyah wanted to know how to bring a woman to ecstasy. When at last he showed me his hips moving more slowly, more sensually, I realized he sort of got it. It's less about rhythm and friction than it is the easy giving up of one's entire being.

It certainly looked ridiculous from the outside as we both stood there in the middle of the room, air-fucking some imaginary lover, but it took us away, albeit briefly, from the awareness that we might not survive the coming days—and that's already an accomplishment.

As soon as we heard footsteps in the house, we stopped. It was our secret. Mej, Rabiyah and I: all three of us dreamt of making love. So did many of the others, I was sure, but these two were willing to open up, each in his own way, and share that vulnerable space inside them.

Something within me sank after that episode. It was the core in me that wanted to make love but didn't want to be reminded of the fact that this luxury, this gift had been taken away from me. I thought about what making love might mean to virgin warriors like Rabiyah or Mej, and what it meant to me, a privileged young man growing up in the frenetic capital of the world.

I LOST MY VIRGINITY as a matter of course. It was almost a nonevent. Lovemaking was never that idealized. It was more like getting laid. Eventually I'd fall in love with other women, but there was always some obstacle, some snag or circumstantial impediment. One of my most recent girlfriends, Tara, was older than me and already had a son. She wanted to have a child with me and was approaching the age when it would be too late, but I was too absorbed with my career, gone for too long and too concerned with navigating conflict zones to focus on a family. She was mature enough to recognize as much without giving me grief. The relationship disintegrated organically with the help of distance when I was away in either Africa or Asia. In the end we wound up remaining dear friends.

Other women were much younger than I was. There was all the passion and intensity you could imagine from hooking up with a beautiful woman, but the urge that drew me to watch historic events unfold close-up was made up of a very similar passion and intensity. Ultimately the openness to events seemed irreconcilable with the commitment and giving involved in a stable emotional relationship. The two modes of passion often crossed wires and the relationship came undone as a result of the centrifugal force.

The natural solution might have been to find a woman who did the same work. The love affair between André Friedmann and Gerta Pohorylle comes to mind. They worked together during the Spanish Civil War under the name Robert Capa. Friedmann was also a mentor for Pohorylle, who became the first female photojournalist to cover the front lines. When the identity of Robert Capa became known, Friedmann continued using the name and Pohorylle took the pseudonym Gerda Taro. Sadly, the affair was short-lived because she died while reporting on that war. Capa continued shooting conflicts and he, too, died in action: stepping on a land mine in 1954 while covering the First Indochina War in Vietnam.

I'd certainly met quite a few women in the Gerda Taro vein. But that would have been a nonstarter. Apart from the constant concern for your loved one plunging headlong into harm's way, the last thing I wanted was to come home to a nurturing situation in which I wound up talking shop—politics, insurrections, and the attendant human tragedy: dawn light filtered through ordnance dust and the sheen of blood on a sidewalk. Not to mention the competition involved. Conflict reporters can be fiercely competitive and, as a result, highly opportunistic. Sometimes you can't afford to help colleagues too much—especially if they want to be cowboys or are just plain stupid. So what about me? Was I stupid or just unlucky? I kept wondering—more so in my darker moments. And in this line of work you wouldn't want to associate with too many unlucky people, lest the bad luck rub off on you. Mixing all these contingencies up with making love and nurturing, then giving yourself up entirely, seemed like a recipe for disaster and precluded any romantic affair with a colleague, no matter how beautiful.

That said, there's no doubt that now, frustrated, often scared, but mostly bored in a house I knew I might die in, whiling away the time by chipping paint off the wall and teaching kids how to kiss, caress and fuck the woman of their dreams, I would have loved to have a female companion who understood all the risks I'd taken and, moreover, all the ones I'd avoided.

NOOR WAS ALSO A SEX FIEND. But unlike Rabiyah, who had a romantic streak and was secretly preparing for the arrival of some princess conflated from an MTV video and the *Arabian Nights,* Noor was a veritable pig. He would come up to me with his thick neck and bon-vivant smile peering through his beard under the receding hairline and spew the

English word *ass* from his mouth. He was a self-avowed ass-man. Pussy and tits, too, but he was definitely in the big-butt school of women. "Nice ass," Fares and I taught him to say.

I'd echo his sentiments in Arabic. "*Kess*," I'd say, which meant pussy or ass. I was never quite sure.

Noor's was a fiendishness based more on a reality-tempered aesthetic than Rabiyah's. Noor was married, with children, so I assumed he had experience. I had no idea what his wife looked like, but tastes in the Arab world tended toward chubby women.

If we were watching some variety show with dancers, or Jennifer Lopez on MTV, Noor would let out his Neanderthal grunt: "*Keeessssss,* I want *keeessss*. Cuunnnt."

From time to time he'd spit it out like machine gun fire. "C-c-c-c-cunt!" It was as if he were acutely aware of the similar thrills involved in coming into a woman (or man, for that matter, or, who knows, even a goat) and shooting a gun—and he was acknowledging as much in the face of the young virgin boys' starry-eyed dreams of conjugal bliss.

Noor probably had a wife who was tired of his sexual appetite, even if she may at one time have enjoyed it. I could picture him coming home from work, scarfing his dinner down, belching loudly, smoking four or five cigarettes, then grabbing his chubby wife and lifting up her abaya. One, two, three . . . twenty pumps at the most and he was done. Then he'd roll over and leave her there . . . not so much "unsatisfied," as you'd imagine a Western woman, but resigned. *That's the way it is. That's how men are.* And then she'd tend to the children and household chores.

At times sitting around in the second house I felt like I'd gone back in time. Soldiers' lives—if you disregard the technology involved—have always been extremely primal. Maybe that's what drew me to conflict photography: the opportunity to spend time with soldiers without being forced to take orders. Sort of like a spectator at an orgy. I wondered how many photographers before me had traded in their cameras for Kalashnikovs.

RABIYAH MADE ME SHOW him how to dance a few times—always at night. Once it was just me and him watching TV. Some of the guys were in the other room. He put on the Lebanese channel that played music videos from the West and started busting a move. When I laughed at how he danced, gyrating his hips like a spastic Elvis, he ordered me to the dance floor to show him how it was done.

There were a lot of Jennifer Lopez and Pitbull videos for some reason. The boys were in love with Jennifer Lopez. I taught them how to say "J-Lo," and Noor, of course, turned the name into an obscenity: "J-Lo'kess," like some half-wit brute waking up with the name of his Irish whore, Jail O'Kiss, on his lips. I taught him to say "booty" but it didn't have the same impact.

So Rabiyah and I were both standing in front of the TV, with no one watching. We danced together and he imitated me. He didn't have the natural groove of Africans, and I wasn't exactly Fred Astaire, but I'd been to enough clubs in New York and Paris to feel totally comfortable dancing.

I actually got into it. J-Lo was moving on the screen and I was swaying my hips in sync with her. A couple of the other boys came in from the next room and joined us, each pretending there was a girl twerking away uncontrollably in front of him.

Then suddenly, from under the music, I could hear the familiar whining and pleading. Directly across the road from the TV room, in the villa, there was a room where the troops used to carry out their interrogations. Until about a week earlier they'd been doing it in the lower floor of the house, right underneath us. A couple of times I saw men being dragged out of our house in the evening and taken up the road to the headquarters.

So while J-Lo was shaking her booty and lip-syncing whatever the song was about—the magnetic power of her own booty, I presume—the voices across the road begged and pleaded. Since I couldn't hear the sound of anything being struck, I assumed some even more sinister torture was being applied, like cattle prods, or cigarette burns, or some

sort of testicle twist. Then I heard the dogs barking and those unmis-
takable screams.

I danced to drown out the sound. Even the boys were disturbed by
the torture. Noor tried to gloat: "Assad something-or-other," he said. I
gathered they'd caught some of Assad's men, or people they thought
were spying for the government. When he said, "Christian man," a chill
cut through me.

And all the while, J-Lo was on the verge of something resembling
a twerk on TV and I was boogieing down with Rabiyah and the boys.
As I moved to the music I wasn't sure how much longer I could last
before I started whining and screaming like the guys across the road.
Something in me would have preferred to join these people in their
fight rather than wind up pleading under their torture.

THE TV AND BOREDOM brought us closer and closer. One night we
were sitting around: me, Mej, Noor, Baby Donkey and Abu Talal. They
were zapping the channels between Arab variety and talk shows. Abu
Talal had the remote and landed at the beginning of *The Green Lantern*
dubbed into Arabic. Everyone wanted to watch it. But when the star of
the film, Ryan Reynolds, came on the screen, they all did a double take
toward me. For several years now, I'd been getting stopped in clubs and
on the street by people asking me if I was Ryan Reynolds. I didn't think
we looked alike, but I could see how other people did. We had similar
height and build, and both of us had short hair and elongated facial
features.

Abu Talal, though, was convinced I was on TV. He started blabber-
ing something at me while pointing to the screen. All the others kept
studying my face, going back and forth to the movie.

At first I laughed and took it as a compliment, the way I would if
I were on a New York street. But when my denials weren't swallowed
right away, it occurred to me that if they suspected I was a Hollywood
star, then my ransom price would go sky-high and I'd never get out of

there. So I had to deny it vehemently and present my case: "No, no, look at my nose. That's not his nose. Look at these eyebrows. Not the same."

They all got a kick out of my little panic flare-up and eventually bought my denial. Then we all settled back down to watch the film.

I'd seen it before, so the Arabic didn't bother me. I remember thinking that the emotions they tried to draw out of the film were overly sentimental: a young pilot coming to terms with his own fears in order to save the universe. But as is often the case with Hollywood films, they're done so well that you can't avoid getting absorbed. Now, as a captive, all that superhero business made me a little queasy. I wasn't sure why. I didn't need to come to terms with my own fear. I needed to eliminate it. And I wasn't interested in saving the universe. I was determined to save my ass. Everything was so black-and-white in the film. In real life, though, apart from surviving, everything is one big muddy gray zone: good and evil, courage and cowardice. The only thing that's relatively clean and simple is the division between life and death.

SEVERAL NIGHTS LATER I was dozing off in my bed. I could hear the TV on in the background. I was in that half-dream state where I wasn't sure whether a nightmare was coming or not, but I instinctively tried to stuff whatever was happening and get as close to comatose as possible.

I felt a presence come into the room, but it could have been the dream. Then I felt Abu Talal nudge his butt against my legs and I woke up completely. He was sitting at the foot of the bed in his ratty boxer shorts. My reaction was pure instinct. I raised my voice loud enough to be heard in the TV room. "No, no, no. Get out. Don't even think of it."

Abu Talal tried to shush me, but not violently. As if he had something important to tell me. But with the language barrier there was nothing to say. He put his hand on my lap and I recoiled. "Don't even think of it," I said even louder.

He must have been embarrassed, because he didn't pursue it. And a few days later he was joking about the incident in front of me to one of the other officers, imitating the panicky way I said "no."

I'd been waiting for something like that to happen for a while. I was surprised he hadn't tried earlier. Occasionally I'd see Abu Talal with a handsome young visitor, another soldier still too young to shave, and they'd horse around, very touchy-feely, even tickling each other. It's hard to say if they were romantically involved. It could have gone either way. Arab men can be very affectionate with each other without there being a sexual vibe.

I was somewhat used to it from growing up in France, where it's common for men to greet each other with a kiss on each cheek. Boys would hang out with their arms around their buddies. Older men would walk down the street arm in arm. In America you just couldn't do that without it being equivocal. A bro-hug and pat on the back was cool, but kisses were for faggots. Any other kind of touching was borderline.

But I think it would have been safe to assume that Abu Talal was interested in more than just a bro-hug or a kiss on the cheek. In fact, when I brushed him off and embarrassed him, instead of getting all alpha-male on me and trying to turn me into his bitch, he just waddled out of the room disappointedly. I started to suspect that he might, in his own awkward way, be falling in love with me. I realized it was a double-edged sword, but one I could play to my advantage.

ONE OF THE BEST developments since I'd been captured was simply the weather. In the first house I was always cold. It was May already, but there was no heating. Cold tends to compound fear, and vice versa; both make you shiver.

Now in the new house, with the blindfold off and a little more mobility, I could feel the sun. The light led my thoughts along a more rational track. For example, I could assess my possibilities for escape much more clearly.

Back at the first house I was fairly irrational: I'd convinced myself

that the reason I was still there and not free was that there were helicopters above us. I started to obsess about clouds, lifting the blindfold
to check how overcast it was. Because under cloud cover, they could
take me to safety, to freedom—though I wasn't exactly sure who "they"
might be. All I knew was that the menacing sound of helicopters and
its potential to rain fire from the sky was what kept us inside that little
jail. It kept me inside a mind warped by fear.

I started to make halfhearted vows. *If I ever get out of here I'll change
my line of work, I'll be a better person.* Something within me knew they
were halfhearted, but that's how my mind was working. I was grasping
at anything, knowing full well that I was grasping, but hoping nonetheless to effect a change in my situation.

But now it was early summer and the backyard was full of apricots
ready to fall off the trees. I'd walk around and eat the ones that looked
ripe, even help the men pick them off the branches. A few times Abu
Talal drove me to the fields a few miles away where I would help the
local peasant men gather the fruit into big bushels.

To me it seemed as if the trees needed to be picked and the aim of
their natural profusion was to draw me out of captivity. Those sweet,
succulent apricots tasted just a little like freedom, because otherwise I
might be stuck inside a room watching bad Arabic TV—or much worse.

At the height of the apricot season, Noor and his brother took me
with them for a drive about an hour into the mountains, where entire
slopes were full of orchards and the apricot trees were exploding with
their little orange grenades.

As I was picking the fruit and putting it into the bushel, I could
see two peasant girls in the distance. It was the first time I'd seen any
females (apart from on TV) since I'd been taken. They were shy, but
they didn't bother covering their faces, and I was struck by the girls'
dark eyes and sultry gaze. I had a weakness for dark women—New
York was full of Latinas and black women who seemed to still have that
charge of femininity that many of the Waspy white women have lost in
their drive for equality or career or whatever. The girls kept looking at

me, obviously a foreigner, and I felt exposed, as if a sniper could hit me at any moment. I ran my thumb over the slight fuzz covering an apricot and tried to imagine what stroking their faces might be like. After all this time surrounded by beards, I missed being near feminine energy. At one point I imagined they could read my thoughts, and I didn't want Noor or his brother to think I was ogling one of "their" women. Then Noor gave me a friendly nudge saying, *They're looking at you.*

That little nudge broke the spell for me. There, in the mountains, near the border with Lebanon, in the proximity of the peasant girls, I caught a glimpse of what freedom in its deepest sense might mean. Not that I was in possession of it—or ever had been. Not by a long shot. But I could get a taste of it somewhere in the sweetness of the apricots I kept stuffing into my mouth.

Then, as if to confirm (or maybe to poison) my epiphany, Noor offered to let me shoot his AK-47 into the mountain. I took him up on it, and that little ballistically induced rush only amplified my taste of freedom. And that kept me going.

I STARTED SEEING ESSAD more and more often. In total I met him about ten times. He was Number One Man, and whenever he came the men liked to have him join them in prayer.

Depending on the military situation, the men prayed five times a day. These were the so-called moderate rebels. They weren't ISIS, which had just begun to form out of al-Qaeda in Iraq while I was captive. They weren't Jabhat al-Nusra, which was allied with al-Qaeda. Still, they were devout. Many of the men were almost secular before the war (in the Muslim context that would probably mean they believed in God but didn't follow all the precepts and proscriptions of Islam, such as praying five times daily or not drinking alcohol).

They knew I was Christian, but in the first house they made it clear: "You're not here because you're Christian." It had nothing to do with faith. Yabroud had twenty-five thousand people, of which anywhere from a quarter to a third were Christians. There may even have been Christians among the fighters, but I never met any. The only person who was Christian for sure was the one getting tortured along with two other Muslims—at least according to Fares.

They always prayed very late at night—often in the room where I slept. They would go in separately. More often than not I was asleep and they were quite discreet about it. Old man Flic had a very soothing voice when he prayed, which lulled me to sleep if I wasn't already passed out. But Abu Talal's voice had the opposite effect; I'd feel like ripping his tongue out of his mouth.

In the first house I never prayed. I was in a constant state of agitation. In the second house, though, I developed the habit of going to the balcony that overlooked Lebanon. I would pull up a white plastic garden chair in the late afternoon and just sit, staring into the distance. There was a peak on the mountain and the sun would hit the peak just before dusk. As soon as the sun touched it, I would start praying—always the same prayer, the only one I knew by heart: "Our Father" in French. I'd repeat it over and over until the sun disappeared.

Several times I prayed with the men on the balcony, facing Mecca—which was almost due south, so the mountains that symbolized freedom for me were to my right and slightly behind me. I joined them and just imitated whatever gestures they made. When it was over they would give me a smile.

One of the times when Essad and his lieutenants were there, an artillery round hit the eastern side of house. We all ran to the sheltered area under the balcony because it was safer; the strikes were coming from the east, and the slope in the yard behind the house offered extra protection. There were at least fifteen of us waiting it out, and I was sitting among them. One guy looked at me and said, "Johnny, are you scared?" So I said "*Bein Allah.*" God help us. They all started laughing and even threw me a few cigarettes in approval. They were very pleased that I remembered these things. *Bein Allah* was a pious way of saying it. I kept hearing it, so at some point I'd asked what it meant.

After that incident they asked me a few times if I wanted to convert. They taught me the Basmala in Arabic, which opens every sura of the Quran: *bismillahi rahmani rahim.* (In the name of God, the Most Gracious, the Most Merciful.) But the last thing I wanted was to convert to Islam. Not only would I appear to be opportunistically ingratiating myself to them, but I also saw Islam as a threat to my own culture. In any case, I had my own faith (weak though it may have been) and I didn't want to betray it. I believe they respected me more for that.

PRAYER USUALLY HAD a soothing effect on me. But not always. On occasion, the calm it induced would unexpectedly lead to waves of hatred welling up from my belly. I wanted to kill all of them. But especially Abu Talal—for his grating voice, his troglodyte eyes and Neanderthal brow, for snoring in front of the TV, for making swinish sounds when he ate, for having taken away my precious freedom with a smile on his face.

I imagined myself walking the streets of New York, very specific spots, like Thirty-fourth Street, right around Broadway: I bump into Abu Talal by pure chance. He smiles and tries to greet me as if we're friends who haven't seen each other in ages. But as soon as he comes toward me with his arms open for a hug, I throw him to the ground and start beating on him. I kick him in his ribs and then rain fists and elbows across his face until it's full of gashes. People start crowding around and I'm turning his fat face into a pulp. Police come but they can't hold me back. Everyone is amazed by the fury in me and they can't help but understand that such fury must be justified somehow. Everyone asks themselves: What did that fat Arab do to incite such rage? And everyone knows he's getting what he deserves.

IN THE BEGINNING of June the fighting flared up. Fares and I often wound up alone in the house, so one of those times he invited me out for an excursion. He put me on his little motorcycle and rode up into the mountains, toward Lebanon. It was very near where I was captured. He said he had cousins there.

On the sides of the little road the gentle slopes were cultivated with orchards surrounding modest houses. At one point we stopped and he greeted two men—kiss, kiss—who were watching their children run around. They prepared a meal for us. I assumed Fares hadn't seen these relatives in a while.

I almost felt like I was free. Fares and I simply relaxed, eating casually, lounging out in the afternoon sun. Then we walked behind the house and went to an area on the side of a hill. Fares told me that before the war he and his friends used to hang out there and drink Coca-Cola. We climbed up the hill, which got quite steep, over an outcropping of rocks until we hit a plateau that seemed to lunge toward Lebanon.

From that height you could see the village where I was being held. I studied the layout and eventually made out the very house. I tried to mentally photograph the image and lock it into my memory. This was just one of the hundred times every single day that I wished I'd had my camera. Everywhere I moved among these men—no matter whether they were sympathetic, like Fares, or assholes, like Abu Talal or Baby Donkey—I had become privy to their most revealing gestures and expressions. If I'd had my camera I could have recorded all the nuances they were sharing. And it's a rare privilege when soldiers caught up in fighting open themselves up to that extent with a noncombatant.

A pleasant gust of wind kicked up as the sun began to drop, setting free the dandelion puffs that were strewn across the plateau. The sun skirted the grass and cast a yellowish light filtered through the swarm of fluff. It was like a salve for my eyes. I had to accept that I couldn't capture it with anything but my memory. Sort of like accepting my own captivity.

Nevertheless, the image of our village from above was seared into my mind as though it contained photographic film, and my subconscious was already elaborating an escape route.

I followed Fares along the edge of a meadow and felt the last rays of light soothing my face. He pointed to a rock. There were rectangles carved out of it and I immediately recognized that these were ancient Roman tombs carved into the rocks. They had been emptied, so they were just holes now. But they were in good condition. Perfectly carved. Obviously the top had been removed. When I was an aspiring archeologist I'd taken part in some digs in Spain, so I'd already seen similar artifacts. I examined the tomb and imagined myself inside. I wouldn't have fit. The average height of an ancient Roman was five feet five inches.

We walked down the hill with the wind kicking up. The last light silhouetted Fares in front of me as it sifted through the dandelion snow to caress my face.

It was already dusk when we got back. Everyone had returned to the house. As soon as we got off the motorcycle, Abu Talal scowled at us and said, "Where the fuck have you been?" Fares just told him he'd taken me along with him on an errand. It didn't seem to matter as long as Essad didn't know.

Just before it went completely dark I retrieved the bird's-eye view of our village and looked out toward the hills to calculate where we'd been. I closed my eyes and saw the rays of light streaming through the dandelion fluff, as if refracted by a shattered lens, each floating seed one of us.

ESCAPE

MEJ AND I WERE WATCHING TV like an old couple: hardly aware of the other's presence, though just aware enough to know it wouldn't be the same without someone to share it with. The Egyptian actor Adel Imam was in an old black-and-white movie trying to weasel his way out of a comical misunderstanding—that much I could understand.

A very Western-looking man came into the house: clean-shaven, polo shirt, jeans, armed with a couple of cell phones, exuding the air of someone who is always conspicuously busy. He sat down on the couch beside me and kept looking at me, almost staring. Then in English he asked, "What are you doing here?"

I looked down at my own body, then back at him as I shook my head.

"I've been kidnapped."

"What do you mean, 'I've been kidnapped'?"

"Just what I said. I've been a hostage for two months. I'm just here because this is where they're holding me—against my will."

"Oh, I see," he said, digesting the information as he turned back and forth from the TV, watching the movie like he'd seen it before. Mej was somewhat put off by us speaking a language he didn't understand and went outside.

"I'm Fares's cousin," the man said. "Are you a journalist?"

"Yes. A photographer."

"A photographer. I see."

The way he said "photographer" made me suspect the questions were just a formality, that he'd already heard about me and was trying to make the planned visit seem spontaneous. But there was no way to be sure. Every day I had to struggle with flights of paranoia concocting all sorts of conspiracies.

"So what do *you* do?" I asked.

"I import and export cars . . . between Syria and Lebanon." *Probably a smuggler,* I thought.

We made a little attempt at small talk, but it wasn't going anywhere. He'd come for a purpose and I was anxious for him to spit it out.

After a few more awkward exchanges he finally said it: "We have to get you out of here."

I agreed, trying to rein in my enthusiasm. "Yes, you have to get me out of here. As soon as possible."

So he took his newest-model iPhone out and started filming me.

"Just say who you are."

"I'm Jonathan Alpeyrie, a French photographer kidnapped by Free Syrian Army troops in Syria. I'm being held captive in a village between Yabroud and Damascus, near the Lebanese border. I've been held hostage since April twenty-ninth, 2013."

"Okay, that's good. I'm going to go back to Lebanon tonight and I'll bring this to your embassy."

Then he stood up and left.

Fares came in right afterward and I told him his cousin had just been here, but he knew that. Fares had asked him to come in the first place.

"He's going to help you."

I was still wary and didn't want to get my hopes up, only to be let down.

"Why would he help me?" I said.

"Because this is not good for the Syrian people. It's not good that we're doing this to Westerners. We need your help. Why are they doing this if we need your help?"

SUDDENLY MY HOPE LEVEL shot up. It was almost unbearable, because it conflicted with the fact that I couldn't really do what I wanted. I imagined myself free, wandering through other people's lives invisibly, the way I'd trained myself, armed only with my camera.

Then two days after my visit from the car smuggler, I was back to doing my regular laps around the swimming pool. Fares had just returned from a visit to his family's country house; with him was a small man wearing glasses and a baseball cap. I greeted Fares near the main door of the house. The man in the baseball cap looked at me very intensely, like he wanted to tell me something as soon as Rabiyah and Mej were beyond earshot. I understood he wanted to communicate, so I winked at him and he sort of winked back, confirming my hunch.

Apart from Rabiyah and Mej walking around, it was just Fares, myself and the new man there. It was afternoon, right about the time the temperature started to cool down. Noor and the other men were away fighting. We went inside and Fares told me that the man was his uncle. He sat on the couch in the living room and kept looking at me, a little jittery. It was clear he wanted to tell me something, but Mej and Rabiyah were continually coming in and out of the house. He kept reaching into his pocket, like he had something to give me, but Rabiyah and Mej were always too close.

Finally I decided to go into the kitchen. I caught the uncle's attention and cocked my head a bit for him to follow me. He sat down at the table and I took a seat right next to him. He then reached into his pocket and was about to pull out a piece of paper, but Fares walked in. I assumed

Fares knew about whatever he had to tell or show me, but suddenly I wasn't even sure of that. Then Rabiyah and Mej came in and joined us, talking and laughing so he couldn't give me what was in his pocket.

After a while he went outside, back to his car, and returned with a hookah pipe. That way we could gain some time with a leisurely smoke. The uncle filled the bowl with tobacco and lit an ember to place it on top, hoping everyone else would find something more useful or pressing to do. But Mej and Rabiyah wouldn't leave. There was a new face at home and they wanted to enjoy a little break in the routine. So they kept coming in and out.

Then at one point, when the younger men casually stepped out for a second, I finally found myself alone with the uncle. He pulled a folded piece of paper out of his pocket, placed it in my palm, and closed my fist with both his hands. I put the paper into my pocket. The uncle stood up, went through all the salaam-motions of excusing himself because he had to leave suddenly, then grabbed the hookah and was off in his car.

Within a few seconds I was in the bathroom slowly unfolding the paper. I felt like a genie would suddenly manifest itself from out of the creases. But I was also paranoid. Every crackle of paper sounded like thunder that could incriminate me. If anyone found me with a piece of paper in my hand, it would mean that I was doing something wrong.

I opened it up and saw there was writing in English. The printed letters had a very deliberate posture, as if they were written by someone not totally comfortable with the Latin alphabet: "I come for you at midnight. 48 hours after you have this note stay outside house and this man will come in white car to go with you to Lebanon."

I kept reading the note over and over in the bathroom, trying to understand. Why did he say exactly forty-eight hours and also midnight? I thought one of them might be idiomatic, similar to how we say "eight days" to mean a week in France, or "fifteen days" to mean a fortnight. *What if I get the wrong date? What does he mean by forty-eight hours?*

I folded the paper and hid it in the rolled-up cuff of my pants. As soon as I got out of the bathroom I was waylaid by anxiety, constantly checking if anybody was looking at me strangely. The only people in the house were Mej, Rabiyah and Fares. In all likelihood, nobody noticed anything weird, but my mind was racing and I could hear every blink around me.

THE OTHER MEN CAME back later that evening. For the next two days I was hiding a lot and taking the paper out to read it again. I was constantly worried about them searching me. Twice since we'd come to the second house they had told me to empty my pockets and given me a gentle pat down.

During these days the area around the house was being shelled. Assad's forces were increasing pressure and toward the end of May a major battle had been raging around Al-Qusayr, about forty miles north of us. Hezbollah was now backing Assad openly, and the rebels holding me were sandwiched between Assad's troops to the east and Hezbollah to the west in Lebanon. A government offensive in the Qalamoun Mountains was imminent.

The very evening after uncle had left, Abu Talal walked in and told everyone to pack up. We were moving back to the first house, where I'd been blindfolded and handcuffed for three weeks. I started to panic a little and asked Fares why we had to leave. They felt that the second house was too much of a target, so they were moving some of us back to the first one.

I loathed that house and tried to tell them politely that I didn't want to go there, but Abu Talal wouldn't even take my dissent into consideration. I was little more than a heavy bag they had to lug around. I started complaining more vocally. "No, I don't want to go. I want to stay here." But Abu Talal was already pushing me into his car. I looked at Fares, but he said he had to go back to his own house, with his family, so he couldn't stay with me. There simply weren't enough men. Abu Talal wasn't going to stay just because of me. The others were already at the first house and I would have been on my own, which was a nonstarter.

So they forced me into the car and drove me back to that dreaded Dark House. It was the middle of the night. Not only was I beginning to relive that darkness and fear, but my whole plan for escape was crumbling between my fingers.

By the time we got back to the first house I was already in a foul mood—brooding, irascible, practically throwing a hissy fit. I couldn't find my socks. I bitched about the belt they'd stolen from me. I felt like spitting in the back of the car. I had to piss.

Then once we were inside the house I caught a waft of something rancid and it triggered an avalanche of memories: the mock executions, the beatings. I took a deep breath. My ribs still hurt. I complained so much that Abu Talal couldn't stand me anymore. I was like a nagging wife tormenting her husband—easier to satisfy than to cross and be subjected to death by a thousand cuts. He got on the phone with Fares and ordered him to go back to the villa and wait for us. Abu Talal drove me back. So it was just the three of us at that house, and the odd shell landing very close to our position. Every time we heard an explosion Abu Talal glowered at me. *You see? It's because you're a whiney little bitch that we might get blown up.* But I'd rather have been anywhere than that first house. I'd won my little battle—maybe not in the noblest manner, but I got my way.

Eventually, when the shelling subsided, Abu Talal drove back to the other house to mind Baby Donkey and Mej. Fares and I fell asleep in the TV room. And whenever I could, I'd sneak the note out from my cuff and imagine the escape panning out.

BECAUSE OF THAT SUDDEN attempt to move me, I became convinced that they knew someone was planning to pick me up and usher me to freedom. Paranoia became my default mode. My confused mind shifted into overdrive and I even mistook the day the car was supposed to come. I calculated twenty-four hours instead of forty-eight, and realized that I was losing my sense of time.

In order to wait for midnight I needed to know what time it was. But the only working clock in the house was on top of the door in the TV room. That was the only way I could tell the time, and after a certain hour, if there were others in there, it would seem suspicious for me to be constantly checking the clock. I'd noticed that Rabiyah wore a nice watch, which he'd hide at night. And I knew the hiding spot because I'd seen him stash it there. The house had a couch that you could lift up, and there was a storage area built into it, which was divided into compartments.

They were all in the living room chatting, so I went to the corner of the sofa and lifted the cushion where he hid the watch. In one swift move I grabbed it, put it in my pocket, and walked outside. I hid it under a rock, then took it out in the evening so I could check the time without having to walk into the TV room.

That evening I stayed up past midnight, well into the morning, but the guy didn't show up. After waking up, I realized I'd miscalculated. Only twenty-four hours had passed, not forty-eight. I felt like along with my grip on time I was also losing my mind. I wasn't even certain the note was real, so I kept touching my cuff to make sure it was there.

The following day it was just me and Abu Talal in the house. I was waiting for midnight, wondering if this was going to work, if this man would ever show up. I was tired, but I couldn't let myself fall asleep. I had to stay up until midnight. So I went into the TV room. Abu Talal was watching TV on his own. I sat down and smoked cigarettes with him. I kept watching the clock. Then I decided to go to bed—not too late, not too early, because I wanted Abu Talal to fall asleep. By eleven I said good night and I was in the bedroom, just waiting. One hour went by. From my bedroom I could see the big porch and the street and anyone walking in. I was constantly looking up from my bed, then checking Rabiyah's watch in my pocket. Midnight—no one. Twelve thirty—no one. Twelve forty-five, forty-seven, fifty—still no one.

Finally, a little after one, the uncle suddenly showed up. I was ready to go. I slipped out of the bedroom very discreetly, hoping Abu Talal would be sleeping. I opened the door where the man was standing and I was ready to scurry out to the car. But he stopped me and said no. "Not tonight. It's too dangerous."

As he was telling me the bad news, Abu Talal walked up to the door a little groggy and looked at us like, *What the fuck is going on?* I feigned ignorance, shrugging my shoulders, *I don't know, some guy was knocking on the door and I just sort of opened it.* The two men started speaking in Arabic and I caught Fares's name. Basically he was saying that he was looking for Fares. Abu Talal, still grumpy from getting woken up, said something to the effect of *I don't know where Fares is so get the fuck out of here* and shoved him out the door.

I slipped back into my room like nothing happened, but I was expecting trouble. Abu Talal walked in and I was already numbing myself in preparation for a long-overdue beating, but instead he just scolded me. "No, no, no!" He made it clear that I was not to open the door or talk to anyone. That was all. He didn't even seem to suspect that visit was about me.

OVER THE NEXT FEW DAYS nothing happened. I kept waiting for the uncle. But the prospect of escape took control of me and I began hatching a new plan in my mind. I'd stolen some paper and a pencil, and set out to draw a map of exactly where we were. Enough with the fantasy maps made out of scraping paint chips off the wall. Now I was going to confront reality head-on. But the only way I could draw this map accurately was if I had a 360-degree view from the top of the villa. Since we had arrived at the second house I'd noticed that every couple of days they would bring a water cistern pulled by a tractor and link it up with big hoses, then somebody would have to climb to the third floor of the villa, which was still under construction. Up there they would transfer the water into a big plastic cylinder.

Usually Mej was responsible for filling up the water tank, so I offered to do it for him. He told me to go right ahead, happy to have one less chore to do. The plastic cylinder took about twenty minutes to fill up. So as I was transferring the water I looked all around the house, surveying the fence and trees and slopes, and did my best to memorize the whole thing: road here, walking path there, this is where I'll hide, this is where they'll come and pick me up, and so on.

After I filled the water I ran back down and drew two maps on the paper I'd stolen, both maps exactly the same. I drew exactly where we were. I also drew a stick figure of myself . . . the house here . . . the road there . . . the promised land of Lebanon to the west. Then I drew their car with uncle beside it, wearing his baseball cap, indicating exactly where he was supposed to wait for me. I drew little lines to show my path. Then in the upper right of the page I drew a clock face, saying two, with a crescent moon on top, so they'd know it was nighttime. I wrote two in the morning because midnight was too early.

After I finished the two maps, I kept one on me, again folding it up and tucking it into the cuff of my pants. (I'd eaten the previous note that uncle had given me bit by bit, so as to not leave any evidence.) I hid the second map under a rock beside the house.

The plan to escape set my mind on fire. I came up with a new idea. I'd stolen some pieces of charcoal and started drawing an encrypted map on the marble balcony looking out toward Lebanon. So just in case the uncle came and I didn't have any paper on me, I could bring him up to the balcony so he could see the drawing.

All that creative energy, combined with the heat, the regular shelling, and an already heightened state of paranoia, was causing me to lose my grip on what was real. I had no way of being objective. I didn't understand the language beyond a few basic words and I had to extrapolate volumes from the little information I got from Fares or Mej. Planning my escape was the only way to keep any focus apart from the brief moments of prayer on the balcony at sunset. But even that prayer was directed at Lebanon, which I could literally see.

I started walking around the pool like a madman, memorizing over and over how I was going to do this, repeating the plan to myself like a mantra. *This path is a hundred and fifty meters. If I'm walking five klicks per hour it will take me about two minutes.* Then the plan would ramify as soon as I inserted contingencies. *If I take this route it's going to take me less time but they can see me more. If I go through the orchard it's longer, but I can hide. But then I have to go through the fence . . .*

I walked around that pool for hours memorizing every minute of my plan to escape. From time to time there would be shelling in the distance and I'd have to remember to go into the house so as not to seem too crazy and raise suspicion, even though I knew a direct hit on the house might be the very thing that allowed me to escape.

Inside the house, for more than a week, I physically prepared myself for how I was going to escape. I repeated the exit routes dozens, maybe hundreds of times, trying to look casual as I calculated the number of seconds it took to get from my bed to the door. I would walk against the wall to avoid passing in front of the curtain through which they could see movement. I'd walk to the main door, open it, and exit through the little alley to the main porch. One problem was that the door creaked. And they would lock it at night. I solved the problem by taking some olive oil from the kitchen and dripping it onto the hinges. The creaking stopped immediately.

The alternative to the main door was going through the kitchen and then the back door. I calculated how many seconds it took. They used a tall propane canister to keep the door shut, so I trained myself over and over to move it without actually lifting it off the ground. I would tilt it toward me and roll it once or twice in the sand, then go around it, open the door, walk out, and close the door behind me. Once outside, either I went one way, back toward the orchard, or the other way, alongside the house, then through the alley and onto the porch, after which I'd get out onto the road and either hop in a car or simply run. So I trained up to the porch. But of course I wasn't allowed outside of the porch and onto the road. To complicate matters, I had to be able to do all this in the middle of the night, when it was dark and there was always the chance of dogs barking at me.

For days I kept repeating the routine, over and over. But no one seemed to notice. They thought I was going crazy, always walking around the pool, absorbed in my own thoughts. But my behavior was innocuous enough to keep me somewhat invisible.

MEANWHILE, I KEPT WAITING for either uncle or the smuggler to show up again. Then, in the middle of my mad pool laps, the smuggler finally showed up in a beautiful SUV. He milled about the house a bit. When he got a chance to exchange a few words with me, he said, "It didn't work. But it's okay, we're going to make another plan. We have to organize. In a couple of days we'll come get you again."

By this time I didn't trust him as much. I asked Fares about him, and Fares said, "This man is dirty. Be careful with him." I started to suspect he might have helped set up my kidnapping in the first place.

The following day the smuggler came back. But Noor and Abu Faras—the commander of the small unit I hooked up with the day I was kidnapped, the man who in all likelihood organized my kidnapping—had already told me to come with them in their SUV into the mountains. Abu Faras had been appearing more and more during the days I was planning my escape. It only heightened my paranoia. So when I got into the car and sat back, I was convinced that they knew what I was planning. They knew I had maps drawn out, and the smuggler had to be in on it.

The drive into the mountains took about an hour. Abu Faras sat shotgun and kept looking into the mirror at me. I felt like he could see right through me, that they were just toying with me. It was all about psychological torture now. They were going to let me go through with the plan and hook up with uncle and the smuggler until they could catch me red-handed.

Once we were well into the mountains, they parked the SUV and led me into a huge cave. That was it, I thought. They were going to execute me right there and dump me in the cave. But Abu Faras didn't seem to have any bad intentions in his eyes. In fact, he was inordinately friendly.

Inside the cave I saw two older men who had been digging and were now just resting beside their shovels. Next to them were piles of ceramics and greenish bits of metal. I recognized them immediately as Roman artifacts.

Abu Faras pointed to odd bits and asked me what they were. Fares must have told them that I had a background in history and archeology and knew about these things. I assumed they were looking to sell the objects for the war effort, so I gave them the thumbs-up to let them know that these objects were valuable. Especially a few coins I'd noticed, on which you could barely make out what looked like the head of an emperor. They went back to at least Byzantine times, if not pre-Christian.

From the cave we went to the village where Fares was from, which wasn't far away. I recognized the landscape. As we drove along the dirt road, up and down hills, I saw a white car coming toward us. It was the uncle. Noor and Abu Faras stopped to say hello. Uncle exchanged a few words with them. Then, when he got a chance, he made a discreet gesture to me with his fingers together, which means "wait." Everything was about waiting and it was slowly driving me insane.

When we got to our destination, I saw a small house still under construction with a big tent pitched beside it. The car smuggler was there. I looked at him and he greeted me like a long-lost friend. He invited us all to sit and have tea. It seemed like he was trying to talk as much as possible to the others to buy time. While I was in the tent, he came up to me and said, "Let me show you something." Abu Faras and Noor looked at us very puzzled. We walked away about fifty yards and he pretended to show me the foundations of the house. "We tried to do it the first time," he said, "but it didn't work out. We'll try again."

I quickly told him that I had a plan, I'd drawn a map, I could give it to the uncle. But just as I was about to elaborate, Noor and Abu Faras showed up, a bit suspicious because we were speaking English. I couldn't prolong the talk. It was very frustrating.

Once we were all back in the tent, the smuggler skillfully managed to lead everybody out. So it was just me and the uncle. He was standing right in front of me and he said, "*Bad bokra.*" *Bokra* means tomorrow and *bad* is after. Just to make sure, I added another day, "*Bad bad bokra?*" He said no, and corrected me: "*Bad bokra*"—the day after tomorrow, in forty-eight hours.

WHEN I GOT BACK to the house I waited, still rehearsing my escape every chance I got, just in case the smuggler didn't show up in forty-eight hours. I waited for him, but this time without too much optimism.

The forty-eight hours passed and no one had shown up. But a couple of days later the smuggler returned. He came up to me and said, "It's okay, I'm going to get you out today. I'll talk to Essad and get you out." I asked him if he'd been to the French embassy? He said yes, he had, but it was complicated. It sounded like a lie. But I was still willing to grasp at lies.

He left the house and walked across the road to the headquarters building. On top of the building there was a balcony, and I could see from my window that he really was talking to Essad, so at least he wasn't lying about that. After his conversation with Number One Man, the smuggler came back to the house and said, "Don't worry. I'll get you out." But he didn't take me with him in the car.

I thought of giving him my map, but by now, exhausted from all the paranoia and false alarms, and crippled by so many letdowns, I felt like it would be futile. Something deep down told me I'd never see this man again. And I was right.

A couple of days later the uncle came back. He was sitting on the porch with Fares, and if I'd ever had any doubts about whether Fares was in on the escape plans, they were dispelled. Fares insisted that his family would try to get me out. At that point I wasn't going to hold my breath.

RAMADAN STARTED ON JULY 9. I'd already been captive for nearly two and a half months. For the start of the fasting month they had a big get-together at the headquarters and I was invited. We all ate together: soldiers, officers, volunteers.

I was mentally exhausted: all my escape preparations, the worry that came with it, the disappointments, the lies, and all the underlying fear that at any moment someone could change his mind and have me killed or turned over to a crueler group.

Eating the hummus and cheese and lamb with the others was the closest thing I had to any sense of community—and that was tenuous at best. But for their part they seemed to accept the presence of this foreigner, this infidel (although Christians were very common in that part of Syria). At times I suspected they'd gotten so used to me that they were reluctant to let me go, like some sort of mascot. Their lives would have lost that tinge of cosmopolitanism had they not been able to say "Hey, Jon . . ." a few times a day.

Letting me take part in their pre-Ramadan festivities and prayers meant I was in their good graces. After their holy month started, though, I don't remember any of the men fasting during the day, as Islam required. I assumed men fighting a war were exempt because they needed to keep up their strength. And I know from history that Ramadan has never been a serious impediment to war among Muslims.

BY NOW THE WEATHER was hot. The headquarters building had a pool attached to it. And unlike the pool at the house, this one was now full. The cistern truck that had spent all morning there must have been filling it up.

Noor brought me over there once and I noticed some of the men were diving in to cool off. I asked Noor if I could go for a swim, panto-miming a breaststroke. He shrugged his shoulders as if to say, *Why not.* I stripped to my boxer shorts and dove in.

At first I did a whole length of the pool underwater, to block out the world around me. In the water I was in another reality, free—no one could touch me. Then I did a few lengths of freestyle and eventually backstroke. I fell into a good rhythm, looking up at the sky, my breath in sync with my strokes. I noticed the men watching me from the edge of the pool, but as long as I was in the water they didn't really exist. I swam for at least fifteen minutes. I could have easily gone for an hour but I didn't want to overstay my welcome. This was a privilege I was hoping to repeat.

When I got out of the water, Noor and the others said, "Very good, Jon. Good swimming." I'd told Mej that I used to compete in races and played on a water polo team, but this was the first time they saw me in action. He relayed to the others that I was an Olympic swimmer, or some such, and they all nodded in approval. Then one by one they showed me their respective freestyle techniques and asked me to give them pointers. As with most people who don't swim well, it was a matter of keeping the body perfectly horizontal and synchronizing the breath—both very hard to do if you've never been properly trained.

A few days later, in the late afternoon, Noor came into the TV room and said we had to go. Essad wanted me. We walked up the road to the headquarters and straight to the pool. Everyone was there, and Noor explained to me that Essad didn't know how to swim. He wanted me to teach him. At that point Number One Man stepped out of the house, a fat hairy lug wearing a ridiculous pair of red and orange Hawaiian-print bathing trunks that came down to his knees. All the others were practically doubled over in laughter until he scowled at them self-consciously.

He waded into the shallow end. I was already in the water. I urged him to show me what he knew, so he splashed around helplessly. He knew nothing. He would have easily drowned despite the fact that he was built like a buoy.

I had him lie on his back with my arms underneath so he could get comfortable floating. Once he was relaxed I had him turn over and do a few strokes while I was holding him. Then I stood him up and corrected his arm motions.

As uncoordinated and out of shape as he was, Essad was determined to wipe away the friendly derision of his men. I stood beside him and studied his strokes, then stood with him to show him what he was doing wrong. I tried to get him to relax, to keep his back parallel to the surface of the water and time his breathing with his strokes—all the while holding him in the water like a baby whale. And like a true warrior he was eventually game to try on his own. With me guiding him ever so slightly, he managed to put together a few steady strokes.

"Relax," I explained to him with pantomime. "That's the key to everything. Don't tense up everywhere. Only the muscles that need to be tensed." The others translated what didn't get through, but I could see Essad was picking it up rather quickly.

Our swimming session was interrupted when one of the men came to the pool to tell Essad something. Essad lifted himself out of the water like a walrus and told me to come back the following day for a second lesson. In the meantime I was instructed to get dressed.

Twenty minutes later a man who was obviously some sort of sheikh arrived, accompanied by a soldier. His fat face was framed by a gray beard that somewhat mitigated an idiotic smile on his face. His turban gave him an air of authority, but there was something about his mouth that telegraphed bad breath, even though I wasn't close enough to detect it. By the way everyone was deferring to him, I understood he had a lot of clout. The soldier accompanying the sheikh took an interest in me and even filmed me a bit with his iPhone. I couldn't tell if it was just out of curiosity or because he'd been specifically ordered to film the foreigner.

After that, the sheikh went to talk to Essad alone and I was escorted back to the house where I stayed.

The next day he was already in the pool warming up when I got there. We worked on his breathing, and he managed to swim back and forth the whole length of the pool on his own. Once he'd figured out that by relaxing he would simply float, you couldn't get him out of the water.

I was proud of him. And he was beaming with a sense of accom-plishment. I'd never taught anyone how to swim before and it gave me great pleasure to offer someone else the sense of freedom that swimming gave me. Of course, I couldn't help but hope that he would return the favor by setting me free.

IN THEORY, THE SWIMMING lessons should have solidified a certain bond between me and Essad. But I was growing more and more numb by the day. My capture had slow-baked me into a fragile shell that used to hold feelings. I was now just a friable effigy of the person who'd lost his freedom, skittish of flames like a scarecrow would be, grasping at the very straws I was made of to make I don't know what.

I latched on to anything that could change my position—though change it to what, I wasn't sure. I was gradually forgetting what freedom meant, or at least doubting that I'd ever known.

At about the time that my escape plans had become a perpetual tease, a man came knocking on the door early in the morning. I opened it for him. He had a bag filled with ancient Roman coins that he must have collected from the ruins and caves all around that part of Syria. He was giving them to the rebels so they could sell them in Lebanon and make money for the cause. I took the bag from him and he left. My immediate impulse was to take a fistful of those coins for myself—for when I was freed. So I took about half a dozen and put them in my pocket, then gave the bag with the rest of them to the men when they woke up. I took the coins and placed them under a rock where I'd been hiding shrapnel pieces gathered from around the house. I kept thinking, *When I get freed I'm going to take these with me.* But what for—as souvenirs, sources of cash? I tried not to ask myself too many questions at this point because I knew that I was already losing my bearings.

This may also have had to do with the fact that I was inevitably bonding with my captors. Somehow I sensed that real freedom could not be divorced from your social context. We're really only as free as we deem ourselves in relation to others. The paradox is that we are all dependent on others. In my better moments, during captivity, I started to fantasize about my previous life—the freedom it entailed—and realized how despite the illusion of freedom afforded by a seemingly inexhaustible array of movement and choice, I wasn't all that free. Or at least I didn't fully understand what freedom was, or could be. Here in the Light House, I was totally dependent on these fighters. This much was obvious. But over time, they had become increasingly dependent on me as well, on my eyes watching them. Because I represented the world outside their simple yet insane little corner of the civil war. And without that outside world, they would have no point of reference from which to justify their struggle.

Even my relationship with Abu Talal was becoming more fraternal. He noticed my hair and beard had grown very long, so he gave me a trim. Surprisingly, he didn't do such a bad job, and he was very proud of his work. But when I looked into the mirror, it was almost painful because it reminded me of who I was before I'd lost my freedom.

Not long after Ramadan had begun, a government MiG fighter dropped a bomb right next to our house. Abu Talal took me out and walked me to where the ordnance had exploded, about a hundred yards away. It was a huge crater, which must have come from a 150-pound bomb. He showed all the destruction as he would to a comrade-in-arms. But I felt almost nothing, just the vague echo of a desire to maim him beyond recognition. And all the while I must have given him that sinister grin that had crept across my face during those mad walks around the pool.

I came back to the house and took down the two T-shirts, socks and underwear I'd washed in a bucket and hung to dry on the balcony. I folded them on my mattress. Suddenly I unfolded the white T-shirt, held it up to the light, and stared bemusedly into its blankness. *This is all I have. This is all I am.*

I wasn't able to move, but my whole body felt like it was trembling. Tears started streaming out of my eyes at first. Then they gushed, with snot filling up my nose and me desperately trying to muffle the gasps in my throat and chest. I crumpled to my knees and buried my face in that shirt in the hope of stemming some incipient collapse. But my body could scarcely keep from shaking. I felt as if all I could really hope for was to catch my breath and prepare to die because there was nothing left of me.

April 2004, Aghdam, Nagorno Karabakh Republic, South Caucasus: NKR soldiers rush out of a trench on the front lines as Azeri troops are firing machine guns at their positions. The NKR is an enclave populated by Armenians who have declared independence from surrounding Azerbaijan.

April 2004, Aghdam, Nagorno Karabakh: NKR soldiers are helping each other leave a frontline trench.

September 20, 2004, South Ossetia, then part of Georgia: As we get closer to the Cossack positions, the guide puts on his mask so he cannot be recognized. He is carrying a Russian uniform and gun that he kept from his days in the Georgian army in the early '90s.

February 3, 2006, central northern Kenya, south of the Ethiopian border: Oromo Liberation Front (OLF) rebels are regrouping in northern Kenya for safety. The OLF is organized militarily as a conventional army, with platoons, battalions, and regiments.

October 15, 2006, Ogaden region, eastern Ethiopia: An Ogaden National Liberation Front (ONLF) freedom fighter shows wounds sustained six months earlier when a grenade blew up near his hands.

October 24, 2006, Ogaden region, eastern Ethiopia: A rebel has just hit the ground after shots were heard coming in this direction. The rebel is taking cover behind a small bush, enough to give him camouflage while he waits for a potential target.

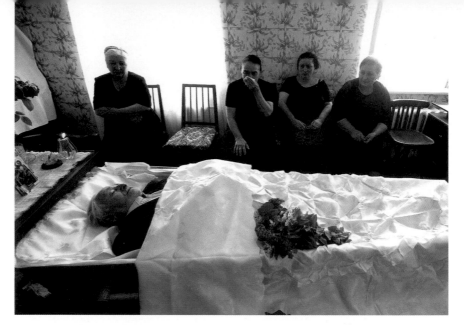

August 14, 2008, Gori, northern Georgia: A family is mourning the death of a relative who died during the bombings in Georgia. It is traditional to have a wake for a few days after someone's death.

February 23, 2009, Galashe, Ogaden region, eastern Ethiopia: An ONLF soldier is taking a rest inside the town's school during a sweep in the area for government soldiers. The school was destroyed by government forces in order to make sure no one returns to their homes.

June 6, 2010, Shelwatay, Tagab Valley, eastern Afghanistan: A local Afghan man is walking close to the command armored troop transport for the Third Company. At this point in the operation, the company's commanding officer is leading his men from inside it, gathering information, before the move northward.

June 7, 2010, Shelwatay, Tagab Valley, eastern Afghanistan: Soldiers from the Third Company, Fourth Platoon are counterattacking from the east side of the village in order to get closer to insurgent positions only a hundred yards away. Firing is getting intense, and coming closer.

October 20, 2011, Athens, Greece: Communists are charging down a street to attack anarchist groups in the center of Athens. One man dies after fighting erupts between protesters at an anti-austerity demonstration outside the Greek parliament.

March 17, 2012, near Al Janoudia, Syria: Rebels are resting after a gun battle with government forces. About eleven rebels, survivors of the fighting in Idlib and Al Janoudia, are holed up inside a small house. Most have deserted from the Syrian army to join the rebellion.

March 18, 2012, near Al Janoudia, Syria: Rebels are drinking tea and washing up early in the morning inside their makeshift defensive position.

March 18, 2012, Turkish border, Syria: With Bashar al-Assad's troops in the area, a truck full of Syrian families tries to escape into Turkey.

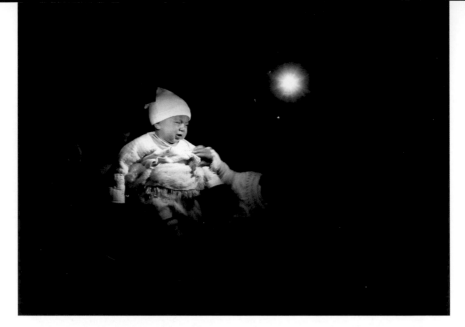

March 19, 2012, Turkish border, Syria: Syrian families are hurrying toward the Turkish border with the help of local fighters. Many children are present. The rebels still hold a mountainous area around a few villages such as Al Chatouria.

March 22, 2013, Mokattam Hills, Cairo, Egypt: Muslim Brotherhood members are charging by the hundreds up Mokattam Hills to attack opposition rioters. Clashes in the Egyptian capital erupted between supporters of the Muslim Brotherhood and protesters who oppose the leading party.

March 22, 2013, Mokattam Hills, Cairo, Egypt: Opposition rioters are clashing with Muslim Brotherhood members. The violence has injured at least forty people, and police have fired tear gas at protesters in order to protect the Muslim Brotherhood's headquarters nearby.

April 25, 2013, Yabroud, Syria: A Free Syrian Army (FSA) fighter is taking aim at government troops controlling the next town over, Al-Nabek. Rebels from FSA have been fighting to keep the town and its surroundings clear of government troops, who have been shelling on a daily basis, killing civilians as well as fighters.

April 25, 2013, Yabroud, Syria: An FSA fighter is on the lookout from inside a defensive position after government forces just shelled the area with tanks. This area is attacked often throughout the day and night.

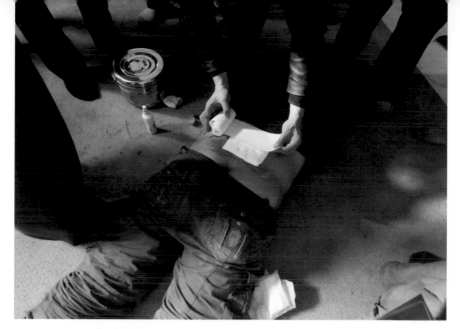

April 25, 2013, Yabroud, Syria: In a secret field hospital, an FSA fighter is being treated for wounds received in battle.

April 25, 2013, Yabroud, Syria: Two civilians were killed on this day because of government shelling. The local men pray together before the burial.

February 2013, Port au Prince, Haiti: A Haitian gang member shows his weapon inside the infamous Cité Soleil, impoverished, densely populated, and the most dangerous part of the Haitian capital.

August 18, 2014, twenty kilometers south of Donetsk, Donbas region, Ukraine: Separatists are burying four of their comrades who died in fighting against the Ukrainian army. The men were locals from a small village south of Donetsk near the front lines; their final resting place will be in that same village.

August 18, 2014, twenty kilometers south of Donetsk, Donbas region, Ukraine: Two women mourn at the burial of separatist fighters.

August 19, 2014, Maryanivka, Donbas region, Ukraine: A shopkeeper has been killed by a shell while walking on the street. Ukrainian forces are inching closer to the besieged city of Donetsk, where thousands of separatists have regrouped to secure one of their last remaining strongholds in the region.

August 24, 2014, Donetsk, Ukraine: A man who lost both of his legs during an artillery attack takes shelter in the hospital's cellar.

August 24, 2014, Donetsk, Ukraine: An early-morning artillery barrage landed on a hospital in central Donetsk. Although no one was killed in this assault, many wounded from previous attacks have taken refuge in the building's cellar.

February 3, 2015, Sloviansk, Donetsk Oblast (province), Ukraine: Two women pass by a damaged sign near Sloviansk. Each day many wounded soldiers, civilians, and refugees arrive in Artemivsk to escape the encirclement.

February 6, 2015, Debaltseve, Donetsk Oblast, Ukraine: A woman stands in front of a bombed-out house. Each day volunteers from all over Ukraine risk their lives to enter Debaltseve to provide food to the thousands of civilians still trapped inside, as artillery fire from both sides rains down in and around the besieged city.

February 11, 2015, Myronivsky, Donetsk Oblast, Ukraine: Civilians have taken shelter inside the Palace of Culture building as their town is hit by frequent shelling. About a thousand civilians are still trapped inside this small town on the front line where Ukrainian forces have set up artillery to shell separatist positions a mere three kilometers away.

May 2, 2015, Shyrokyne, Donetsk Oblast, Ukraine: Troops from the Donbas Battalion of Ukraine's National Guard return from a patrol along the cease-fire line agreed upon under the Minsk II Protocol.

May 2, 2015, Shyrokyne, Donetsk Oblast, Ukraine: A soldier from the Donbas Battalion of Ukraine's National Guard fires an RPG-7 at separatists while his position is being shelled by mortars.

THE ROAD TO DAMASCUS

THE UNCLE CAME BACK from time to time, and I always hoped he would give me a sign that everything had been organized, or pass me a note again saying, *Tonight we go*. But instead it was just that same hand gesture: *Wait*. In other words, be patient, don't get your hopes up. In other words, some things might take getting used to—war, captivity, death. In other words, *Bein Allah*.

My routine of praying on the balcony at sunset—repeating the same "Our Father" until the sun touched the mountain marking Lebanon and freedom beyond—had started to bleed into other parts of the day. I was there around noon, sitting in the plastic chair, and wasn't so much praying as merely emptying myself of as many thoughts and worries as I could.

Suddenly I saw Noor and Rabiyah running toward the house with big smiles on their faces. "Home, Jon! You're going home!" They grabbed me, then pulled me out of the chair and into my room.

"Hurry up, take your things."

So I grabbed whatever clothing I had and threw it into a plastic bag.

I didn't know where I was going, or even whether I should be worried. Every situation, even the happiest, felt like it contained a hidden trap. So as soon as I was alone for a second, I stepped out of the house and lifted the rock under which I'd hidden the Roman coins I'd taken a few weeks earlier. You never know. But for some inexplicable reason, I also took the pieces of souvenir shrapnel, which made no sense. I guess I just needed to minimize the gravity of the situation, make it feel like I was going home after a long vacation. I'd kept telling myself that when I was freed I would take these things with me, so I was not only preserving artifacts of captivity but also fulfilling something approaching a vow.

Outside there were two SUVs with a group of soldiers around them, waiting for me. I knew all of them. They were Essad's men. But Essad wasn't there.

They put me into the second SUV and we drove off, hitting one checkpoint after another, all manned by rebels, until we reached Yabroud. I remembered the area because that was the same road I'd taken on the day I was captured. I recognized many of the buildings, one specifically, a beautiful villa set in a neighborhood where wealthy people lived. Alfarook had pointed it out to me as I rode with him on his motorcycle: "My uncle built it." That ride seemed so long ago, part of someone else's life.

When we got inside the city, the driver pulled over. They all got out of the car and told me to stay in. I waited for almost an hour, alone in the car with no one watching—at least no one I could see. They'd all gone into a house where I assumed they were negotiating my price and other details. Then they came out, took me from the car, and brought me into that same house. Inside I recognized two top officers whom I'd always seen with Essad. They'd been to the house many times during my captivity and were always polite with me. They had me sit in the living room, where to my surprise I saw the sheikh who had come to film me along with a soldier less than a week earlier. I wasn't sure what to make of him. From the looks of the others, he was the most important man in the room. All the men were speaking in Arabic, and it sounded

like they were weighing various options. Everyone's reaction seemed
to be contingent on the sheikh's expression of approval or disapproval.
The air was thick with tension and all of a sudden I understood that the
sheikh was bargaining over my price. They'd brought me there to sell
me to a group of Islamists. Jabhat al-Nusra, maybe. Or worse.

A pang of panic cut into me. Though I couldn't actually smell it, I
imagined the foul miasma of the sheikh's breath gathering in a cloud
above him as it issued from between his jowls.

They kept talking, more and more casually now, as if they'd settled
a few prickly details. Occasionally one of them would turn my way and
nod. Then, as their discussion sounded like it was heading for a conclusion, I caught the word *Dimasha* several times, so I asked, "Why
Damascus?"

They addressed my question as if I were an insolent child and had
no say in the matter—which I clearly didn't.

"You're going to Damascus," one of Essad's men said.

Damascus meant I was being sold to the government. This, to
me, was as bad as the Islamists—possibly worse. Immediately I had
to stanch the gush of images revolving around Bashar's torture rooms.
Among the rebels, getting captured by the government was the worst of
fates, much worse than having to deal with al-Qaeda-affiliated Jabhat
al-Nusra, who were effectively the rebels' allies in this conflict, even
though they'd been known to fight each other in certain areas.

The men all stood up and shook hands. I stood up with them. Their
faces changed. Everyone suddenly had a grim expression. They said
goodbye to me stiffly—like *Good luck, man, and Godspeed.*

Essad's men left, and as soon as they did, two others came in. They
were dressed in black military uniforms typical of the Shabiha, the
Alawite militia loyal to Bashar and his regime. Shabiha means "ghost"
or "shadow." They had a fearsome reputation among all Syrians and had
already been accused of numerous atrocities since the war had started.

I sat back down when I felt the blood course out of my legs.

The two Shabiha looked at me with intense smiles—too intense.

Neither of them had a beard, which only confirmed they were Shabiha, as government troops tended to be clean-shaven. One of them wore Ray-Ban Aviator sunglasses. They both spoke English well.

The guy with the sunglasses waved me toward him. "Okay, now we go quickly."

The sheikh stayed behind and shook my hand goodbye.

They led me outside to a small white car and put me in the back, then we drove off, four of us: one driver and the two Shabihas I'd already met. The guy with the Ray-Bans rode shotgun and kept an eye on me in the mirror.

We headed east toward the road connecting Damascus to Homs; it passes a couple of miles east of Yabroud. It's a major highway, Syria's north–south axis, and it was controlled by government troops. About halfway to the main highway we pulled off where two white SUVs were waiting on the side of the road. We parked our car behind them and about six or seven men came out, dressed in black, carrying machine guns and kitted in military gear. These were government troops, for sure, and my panic welled up into a full-on rush.

Shortly after the Syrian protests had begun, in the wake of Hosni Mubarak's ouster in Egypt, Bashar al-Assad decided to use a heavy hand in dealing with the protesters. An array of stories about his torture chambers made their way around the press. It had never been any secret what kind of methods Middle East dictators and their secret services used to crush dissent, but with Syria in the spotlight every survivor's account became fodder for news. I remember detailed descriptions of beatings, electric shocks, and humiliation practiced by professional torturers—all of them dressed in Shabiha black, at least in my imagination.

The men in black told me to get out of the car and follow them to the second SUV. As I walked, one of them bumped my shoulder and scowled at me. I was queasy at the prospect of now being government property.

Still, the guy with the Ray-Bans suddenly became very friendly and

said, "You're free now, you don't have to deal with these bastard terrorists anymore." He started talking about how the rebels were planting
bombs near schools in Damascus, the massacres perpetrated in Alawite
villages. "They posted video of one bastard eating the liver from one of
our dead brothers. It's sick. Fucking sick. And the world wants to help
these terrorists."

The driver lit up a cigarette and I asked him for one. I still had all
the Roman coins and shrapnel in my pocket, and I realized that if they
found artifacts on me that belonged to the Syrian state, it would give
them even more reason to question me and poke my testicles with a
cattle prod. So at one point, when we stopped the car and the men got
out to pee, I stashed the bag of coins and shrapnel under the mat at my
feet.

They handed me a black military outfit, with a matching black cap,
so I could blend in. They also gave me a fake ID. "Whatever you do,
don't talk at the checkpoints."

I understood we were no longer in rebel-held territory. Everything
near the main highway was under government control, and all the men
suddenly seemed more relaxed.

The SUV ahead of us opened the road at each heavily guarded
checkpoint that cropped up every few miles, so when the soldiers
looked into the vehicle they weren't too curious.

As we drove, Mr. Ray-Ban could tell I was nervous. He kept saying, "It's okay." But I couldn't help imagining the torture rooms. Enough
people had escaped or been released from Bashar's prisons to recount
their ordeals. One technique that was common to nearly all of them
was having your body immobilized inside an empty tire while they beat
the soles of your bare feet with a wire cable. Other accounts involved
raping the prisoner's mother or sister in front of his eyes in order to
extract information. I knew this kind of torture was routine in most
Middle East countries (no doubt why after 9/11 the United States sup-
posedly outsourced some of their interrogations to Egypt and Jordan),
but Bashar's government had an especially sadistic reputation. So as I

tried to better hide the bag of Roman coins under the mat with my foot, I was preparing the latter for contact with the wire cable.

AS WE APPROACHED DAMASCUS, Ray-Ban started speaking on his iPhone. Shortly after he hung up he handed it to me so I could read a text message that had been sent.

"Now you're free. I'm the man who negotiated your release and paid the ransom for you . . . You're a very lucky man. Originally I was looking for two other French journalists and then stumbled upon you. Shortly we will meet. I'm very much looking forward to it."

I texted him back: "Thank you."

What more could I write? I had no idea who this person was, or even if anything written was true. All he basically said was, "I'm the guy who saved your life." He didn't even sign his name.

After a couple of exchanges I gave the phone back to Ray-Ban. In the distance I could see the anonymous buildings on the outskirts of Damascus rising up in the stark afternoon light, and everything seemed to crystallize into that distilled sense of exhilaration and anxiety that had been driving my life since I started taking pictures.

BY LATE AFTERNOON we got to Yafour, a suburb in the hills west of the downtown area, where some of the richest Syrians live. As we drove past a mall, Ray-Ban turned around and asked, "Do you need some clothes?"

"Well, I don't have anything."

"Okay. No problem."

We pulled into a parking lot and he went into a department store. About ten minutes later he came out with a huge roller suitcase filled with stuff. (Up till then I'd always hated those suitcases and never traveled with anything I couldn't carry over my shoulder. But all that changed when I realized that it was full of stuff for me, who'd been wearing the same ratty jeans and two T-shirts for all these weeks.) He heaved the suitcase into the back of the SUV and we drove to a safe house.

All the men, who had been so tense and stiff before, were now relaxed and friendly with me. There were about a half a dozen Shabiha types guarding the safe house—which was actually a beautiful villa. I walked in and the rooms were lavishly decorated with sculptures and art and a flat-screen TV. In one room there was a long dining table with a vast and varied spread of food freshly prepared: salads, hummus, baba ganouj, grilled chicken, meats floating in gravy. It was as if they'd been expecting the arrival of an important guest. We all sat and ate. I'd always been a light eater, but because I hadn't had anything similar in three months I dove in and stuffed myself.

Afterward we smoked some cigarettes and Ray-Ban showed me into one of the bedrooms. "This is where you'll be living for a while. I hope you're comfortable. You'll be in hiding, so you can't go out."

After nightfall three men came in. One man was in his late forties, short, fit and very deliberate in all his movements. He wore a baseball cap to hide his face somewhat, but his intense eyes still shone through with obvious intelligence. He was accompanied by a man who looked slightly older, with jowls, beady eyes and a receding hairline that made his head look like a peanut. The third man was a translator who relayed the information even though it was clear that both men spoke English very well.

The translator introduced them as Mohammed Aboud and Kamal Atrash, as if those names should have been familiar to me. (They weren't.)

"You're going to be here for ten days," the translator relayed. "Then you'll go to Beirut. Once there, you'll go the French embassy and tell them we helped you. But for now we still have to work something out. So you must stay here."

My stomach twisted a bit. So I wasn't really free. I was just in a much more comfortable situation. They told me not to go out. In any case, it was dangerous because you could hear sporadic shelling all around the city. Most of it, though, was the government shelling rebel territory, like the Ghouta neighborhood, and other parts of eastern Damascus.

AFTER THEY LEFT, I hung out in my room with Ray-Ban. He asked me about my work and what I'd seen so far in Syria. A bloody mess, I told him. He said it's always been a mess throughout history. Just not always as bloody. We became friends.

He left me alone to rest for a while and I checked out my bedroom, which was very impressive. I even had my own bathroom. I examined myself in the mirror. My beard was thick and I looked extremely gaunt. My ribs were visible from all the weight I'd lost, and I pressed the ones that had been broken; they were still sore. Suddenly a wave of emotion rose up in my throat. I felt as if I were seeing someone who had betrayed me long ago, someone I missed dearly. I touched the mirror like a man trying to break through and embrace the image, but as soon as I hit the solid glass the illusion dissipated. I shook my head and gathered my thoughts so I could assess my new situation.

I opened the massive roller suitcase and it was crammed with jeans, shorts, T-shirts, polo shirts, belts, toothpaste, toothbrushes, even deodorant. I took a shower, put on some jeans, and fixed myself up a bit.

Then my new friend came in and said, "We have to go. We're going to see your man, Aboud."

HE PUT ME IN the car and we drove about five minutes up the road. It was a clear warm night and both sides of the road were lined with opulent villas. The streets were full of men armed with machine guns and RPGs, all dressed in black.

We turned into a road that led to a manor. The gate opened up and we proceeded up a driveway lined with motorcycles and quads. The driver turned to me and said, "Aboud is a very wealthy man. He buys all kinds of stuff." It didn't escape me that I was now in that category of "stuff."

There were more armed men as we approached the house. He took me out of the car and we walked through an expansive garden full of palm trees towering beside a huge house and swimming pool. On one side of the garden there was a tent with a wooden table. Sitting at the table was a small man wearing a pink polo shirt and jeans. It was Aboud.

"Welcome to my home, Jonathan." He spoke impeccable English, so it took a few seconds to recognize him as the man in the baseball cap who'd come to my room only a few hours ago. It wasn't clear to me why he'd have brought a translator—but then again, less and less was clear to me the more I got entangled in this deal. Obviously I was in government-held territory. But I'd been handed over to these government troops by rebels ostensibly trying to kill them. It didn't make sense. Maybe Aboud's troops weren't as loyal to the government as they were to Aboud himself, I thought. Many oligarchs in this part of the world have their own personal battalions. I'd been in enough murky war situations to know that they rarely made sense the deeper you looked. And any notion of "us against them" is more often than not an oversimplification. In most armed conflicts throughout history—the current Syrian one is a prime example—common interests, which can be economic or military, serve as aggregating factors for forces. Usually these forces vie with each other in a dance of shifting alliances. It's more like eddies in a tide pool than a head-on collision. Right now I was swirling through a very complicated eddy, unsure of where I would wind up.

At first I wasn't even sure that the man in the polo shirt was the man who'd bought my freedom. Then he flat-out admitted it: "You know, Jonathan, I only wanted to pay two hundred thousand dollars. But Mr. Atrash, whom you met earlier today, said that I should pay more, because they originally wanted seven hundred fifty thousand. He said, 'You should pay more, it will be good for you. It will help your reputation.' That's how he explained it. So you see, Atrash saved your life. Because he convinced me to raise my offer."

I had the urge to ask him, *So what was I worth?* But I kept quiet.

"Eventually we settled on four hundred fifty thousand."

At that time I had no idea who these people were, but from the looks of his private Shabiha army protecting the villa, I assumed he was an important ally of the Bashar regime. As the conversation continued, he told me he was a parliamentarian. As for Atrash, Aboud himself said that the man was a Lebanese politician with close ties to Syria, a member of the Druze minority that has historically had to maneuver among countless factions with extreme caution—all of which merely confirmed my status as a pea in a very complex Levantine shell game.

"You see, I was actually looking for two other French journalists. Someone had told me Essad's group were holding a Frenchman, so I sent the sheikh and his men to verify the information. They came back with a video of you."

"So what do you intend to do with me?"

"Like I said, as soon as we work out a few things, we'll take you to Lebanon, where I'm counting on you to tell the French government that Mr. Aboud helped you and paid your ransom. You see, in this part of the world every action is in reality a transaction. I expect your government to return the favor and help me."

"Well, if you get me to Beirut, you have my word that I'll tell them exactly how much you're helping me."

"That's all I need from you, Jonathan. Here, take my phone and call your family. Tell them you're safe and you're going to be free soon."

I took the phone and thought, I can't call my father. He might break down and have a heart attack. Years earlier I was with him in the National Air and Space Museum in Washington, D.C., and he had a severe heart attack. I practically saved his life. I couldn't risk it. And even if I had been sure he could handle it, that call would have been too emotional for me. So I called Yann, my best friend in Paris.

"*Salut,* Yann. I'm in Damascus. I can't say much, but I'm going to be freed soon. You have to call my dad."

As soon as Yann heard my voice he started weeping with happiness.

"I felt it. This morning I felt you were going to call. When the phone rang I knew it was you."

I got off the phone quickly because I wasn't ready for so much emotion, especially since I wasn't entirely convinced that the ordeal was over.

ABOUD AND I CHATTED for a while. He told me that even though he was a parliamentarian, he'd been arrested by the government years back and jailed—but only briefly—so he understood my situation somewhat. He also suggested that when this whole ordeal was over, I could come back as his guest. He could even get me access to rebels in the Jobar area of Damascus if I wanted to do an exclusive reportage. I couldn't believe what I was hearing. Everything was so murky, and I just didn't have the strength to dig into his connections and find out who he was for or against, or even what he really wanted from me. I was in pure survival mode and didn't want to ruffle any feathers on my potential flight to freedom.

As we were talking, his son showed up out of nowhere. He was very Westernized, with short spiky hair and glasses, wearing an Iron Maiden T-shirt. There was something slightly goth to his look.

Aboud introduced him and said, "My son likes photography. Since you'll be here for ten days, most likely, would you teach him something?"

"Sure, I'll teach him. No problem," I said. And to myself I thought, *I'll teach him teleportation if that's what it takes to get me out of Syria.*

They took me to a small house on the grounds of Aboud's lavish manor, and as soon as I walked in I saw an array of camera equipment. D800 Nikons and other very expensive cameras, lenses and attachments. I got a sudden impulse to ask, "Can I have this stuff? Not all of it. Just some of it." At that time I had nothing. But what I felt wasn't envy; it was like seeing a lover from whom you've been separated for a long time. You just want to touch her, remember the magic you can make with her.

We set up a time for a lesson the following day, then went back to the tent to sit down. There were many servants hovering over us and they brought tea and little sweets. At one point in the early evening three men came in to negotiate a metal scrap deal with Aboud. He told me to stay and just keep quiet. The three of them were fairly young, in their thirties, and they must have assumed I was a very important person because they bowed to me deferentially. I had to restrain myself from saying, *Easy on the formality, boys, I'm just the hostage here.* So for a half an hour I sat there drinking my tea, not saying a word while they did the dance that captains of industry do.

As the evening progressed Aboud became increasingly nervous, and at around nine o'clock he said, "Let's go out for dinner." His wife came and we started walking to the driveway where all the cars were parked. We got into their Mercedes sedan, which looked so heavy that I assumed it was armored and bulletproof. Aboud drove, with his wife sitting in the passenger seat. There was no escort or bodyguard that I could see.

We drove to the luxury hotel that Aboud's friend owned and took a table in an open-air lounge where people sat drinking, smoking and playing cards around long tables. A server in the hotel came up to me and asked if I wanted a cigarette. I said sure and he came back with a whole carton of Marlboro reds. I tried to sit as nonchalantly as possible and some strangers started up conversations. No one really asked me why I was there, and I didn't reveal any information. Still, I noticed Aboud getting more and more fidgety every time someone exchanged a few words with me. We all ate dinner. But his wife left before dessert. Suddenly Aboud said, "Listen, I think I'm going to take you to Lebanon tonight."

My eyes opened wide and I tried to keep from fist-pumping the air. "Yes, please take me there tonight," I said, almost trying to convince him that Damascus was not a good place for me.

"I'm worried that people are going to talk. Even though I know many important people in the government, that didn't prevent me from being arrested in the past. You see, I have friends on all sides. And this can lead to misunderstandings."

WE LEFT THE HOTEL at around eleven. Aboud drove us back to his house, where he made some phone calls. Ray-Ban turned very serious and went about organizing everything. As he took care of the details, Aboud and I sat back down for about another hour or two. By now it was past midnight. I was anxious to leave, and a part of me was expecting someone to come in and say, *Sorry, but things have changed.*

Aboud saw I was nervous and explained: "We're preparing your exit now."

"How are you preparing it?" I asked.

"Well, I've sent a car ahead with men and a few thousand dollars, and we're going to pay off the Lebanese customs. Because, you know, the Lebanese love money," he explained with a grin. Then he looked at me and said, "What about you? I don't imagine you have any money on you."

"Zero."

Aboud casually pulled out a green wad of bills and said, "Just take it." I shoved it into my pocket with no questions, just a thank-you. It was about four thousand US dollars in cash.

After a couple of hours, once all the preparations had been made, we got into that same Mercedes sedan and I rode shotgun next to him. They threw my massive soft-shell roller suitcase into the trunk. Ahead of us they sent two cars, about a mile apart, to the border to pay everyone off and tell the Syrian army soldiers manning the checkpoints that a parliamentarian was on his way to Lebanon, so they shouldn't stop his car.

Once we were moving, we went through checkpoint after checkpoint, about a half a dozen of them, and nobody stopped us. All the soldiers simply waved Aboud onward, some actually saluting him. I thought there might have been another car farther behind us but couldn't see anything, and I had no way of knowing.

As we approached the border, I asked if I should hide, but Aboud said not to worry. At the Syrian side of the border they didn't even stop us. Then the road started winding, with switchbacks and steep hills on each side. He pulled over after one of the turns, opened the trunk, and told me to get in. I climbed in and he shut the hatch.

We drove for ten or fifteen minutes with me bouncing around in my little coffin. It was pitch-dark. Then we stopped and I heard people speaking Arabic. I knew we were on the Lebanese side of the border. They talked for a few minutes and then let us go.

Aboud drove another five or ten minutes, then pulled over. When he opened the trunk the first bluish light of dawn washed my eyes and I realized I was in Lebanon. I recognized how the little shops were laid out, just slightly different from Syria, but a world away. We were parked in front of a bakery that was just opening, and a waft of baking bread caressed my frayed nerves.

Two of Aboud's men were waiting in another car. Both wore suits and one of them had a pistol handy. They'd no doubt been sent ahead and had probably been waiting for a while.

Aboud led me to them and said, "Listen, I'm going to go back to Syria now. Remember what I told you. You have to tell the government I helped you."

Then he gave me a hug and just drove away, back toward Syria.

THE TWO MEN TOLD ME in Arabic to get in the car, and I sat in the back. As we drove over the mountains, I could see the sun coming up behind us. Soon Beirut came into view in front of us, then the Mediterranean Sea.

We drove through the city and I felt *almost* free. But that almost was like a fishbone stuck in my throat. At one point I considered just opening the door and running. Then we got to the harbor and the marina, with its posh high-rises. We parked right in front of the Marina Towers, which I remembered as a landmark from previous trips to Beirut. The men helped me with the huge suitcase. We got into the elevator and went all the way up to the top floor. As we entered the vast penthouse furnished with modern décor, I was greeted by two African maids. The men in suits led me to the balcony, where we each smoked a cigarette. The Mediterranean shimmered softly in the distance and some of the yachts moored in the harbor were getting ready to set sail. What a contrast to the shrapneled house I'd woken up in the day before.

The maids brought us breakfast. They were from West Africa, so we exchanged some small talk in French. "It's beautiful here. You must be hungry . . ." Nothing too specific or committal. I ate, drank tea and smoked cigarettes. They showed me my bedroom. I wanted to take a shower but decided to lie on the bed for a few seconds and fell asleep almost instantly.

I woke up a couple of hours later in that plush bedroom with a view of the sea, constantly probing at the fishbone in my throat—that feeling of being *almost* free. I wanted to leave, but I wasn't sure where I could go, and I was worried they could easily send me back across the border and sell me to someone else. The two men tried to tell me in very broken English that I couldn't go out because I didn't have any documents and might get arrested. But I didn't believe them. I'd been to Beirut a few times and nobody ever checks documents on the street.

When I walked out of my room, the two men were still there. They asked if I'd slept well. I nodded contentedly. I noticed one was sitting near a telephone, a proper landline. So to gauge how free I was I asked them to write down the number—just in case someone wanted to call me. I didn't expect them to do it, but they wrote it down. Then they asked if I needed a cell phone. I shrugged my shoulders as if to say, *Yeah, that might come in handy*. So one of the guys went out. Twenty minutes later he was back and handed me a brand-new BlackBerry.

"Okay," he said, "now you can call your family." I said okay, I will. But I waited for a while, then went back to my room.

When I came back out the two men had left. They weren't on the balcony, so I assumed they had gone out to run some errands.

I decided to call my father. But I was worried about the BlackBerry they had given me. My paranoia kept conjuring images of Hezbollah operatives listening in. So I decided to use the landline.

"Papa, I'm in Beirut. I can't talk much," I said, hoping my tone would convey a sense of urgency. "But I'm safe. This is my number. Have someone call me."

I waited impatiently near the phone. Five minutes later I got a call from a woman named Mila Jubin, who asked me in French if I was Jonathan Alpeyrie. *"Oui, c'est moi."* She said that someone from the French embassy would call me. I told her to hurry because I didn't know how long I'd be able to answer the phone.

Immediately afterward the phone rang.

"Monsieur Alpeyrie?"

"Oui."

"This is Patrice Paoli . . . Where are you exactly? And are you okay?"

"I'm fine. I'm being held in a penthouse apartment in the Marina Towers."

"Are you able to leave? Can you make an escape?"

I looked around. The men weren't there.

"I think so."

"In twenty minutes be at the Four Seasons hotel; it's just down the street about a hundred meters to the east. Ask and you'll find it."

I knew exactly where it was. I looked around the house. The men were still out. I could have just walked out. But for some reason I felt I needed all that stuff they'd gotten me, so I went to get the suitcase. I should have just left it there, but I had nothing, and I figured it might give me some sort of protection. I moved as stealthily as I could, wheeling the suitcase behind me, through an area next to the kitchen. There was a back door leading to a service elevator. As I approached it, one of the big African maids tried to stop me.

"Où allez-vous, monsieur?" Where are you going, sir?

"Il faut que je m'en aille." I have to get out of here.

I couldn't let anything block me, so I shoved her out of the way, practically a punch, and pressed the elevator button. Fortunately she didn't raise much of a fuss and the elevator was already at the floor.

Once out of the service elevator on the ground floor, I cut through the lobby and walked out the main entrance. They were all looking at me as I shlepped that hulk of a suitcase behind me.

As soon as I was outside I walked toward the Four Seasons and even asked a passerby to make sure I was headed in the right direction. He pointed to a building within a stone's throw. I walked toward a huge area where the cars and taxis pull up. There was an overhanging glass ceiling above the revolving door of the entrance. I walked in, checked out the lobby like I was looking for someone, then walked back out through the revolving doors. I looked around again, then went in and took a seat in the lounge. In less than half a minute I felt someone put his hand on my shoulder.

"Jonathan Alpeyrie?"

"*Oui.*"

"*Venez avec nous—vite.*" Come with us, quickly.

There were two men dressed in casual polo shirts over jeans. One of them took my suitcase and put it in the trunk of the car, a bit surprised by how heavy it was. The other led me into the backseat.

We started driving. They said they were taking me to the French embassy. But first we had to stop at a passport photo shop to take some pictures of me for my documents.

After the photos they brought me to the embassy. It looked like a marvelous Ottoman palace, with arabesque motifs and arches straight out of the *Arabian Nights*. The gates opened right away and as soon as I got out of the car I was greeted by the ambassador and his staff, one of whom helped me with my suitcase. I was free.

BOOK 2

SAVING THE SCAPEGOAT

MY FATHER GOT THE PHONE CALL at around seven in the morning, eight days after I'd gone missing. He was walking down Fifth Avenue, near the synagogue on Sixty-second Street, on his way to an appointment. It was May 6, a sunny Monday morning already drawing Manhattanites into Central Park as the streets crescendoed toward a frenetic rush hour with taxis slaloming down the avenue between the cars.

From the first day I was captured, I tried to think as little about my life back home as possible—especially about my father. Whenever I was in New York, we saw each other regularly and spoke almost every day. Since his heart attack in 1997, I'd always been careful about him hearing any shocking news about me. So the thought of him getting wind of my kidnapping involved images of his heart failing him, and I couldn't afford to feel that much emotion in my situation. Later, as we spent time together, he gradually filled me in on what he went through and how he tried to get me free.

He first started worrying after four days of not hearing from me. Normally when I was in a combat zone I would send him short emails or texts, just to let him and my mother know all was well. He stopped getting texts after I'd crossed the border into Syria because my phone no longer had reception. Still, I managed to send off an email when I was filing pictures. *"Tout va bien."* All is well.

Then I dropped off the radar completely.

So when my friend Aaron called him he was already braced for bad news.

"Hello."

"Jean-Louis?"

"Yes?"

"This is Aaron. I'm calling about Jonathan. He's been captured."

"What?"

"I'm in touch with his fixer. They think he's a spy. I don't know much more than that . . ."

My father was stunned, frozen on the street, on the verge of collapsing. He described it as being hit by lightning. The traffic sailed past him and the world became strangely silent. As soon as he hung up the phone, the horns on Fifth Avenue were blaring again. All he could do for a few moments was stand on the sidewalk and look in several directions, wondering, *What do I do now?* Passersby must have thought he was lost. Then he got back on the phone, canceled his appointment, and walked back home.

AARON SCHUMM WAS my closest friend in New York. He initially started worrying after he'd sent a few WhatsApp messages and didn't see the double check mark indicating his message had been received. But he just assumed I'd lost my phone.

After a few more days, when I was supposed to be back in New York, Aaron tried to contact me via Facebook. But on my Facebook wall he saw a post from a mutual friend, a woman from Holland. "I'm in Paris. Where are you?" Below her query there was a reply from Alfarook, my fixer: "Jonathan has been kidnapped."

Aaron was in a taxi that morning going to the airport and he started messaging frantically from the backseat. Alfarook wrote that there had been four or five people in the car when it was ambushed. He said they kept me because they thought I was a spy.

Aaron told Alfarook to immediately delete the Facebook post. After that he sent a quick message to our Dutch friend not to post anything else.

AFTER AARON CALLED, it occurred to my father as he was walking home that I'd given him the phone number of Robert Doueihy, the Lebanese Christian Maronite businessman whose family had long-standing political connections. Doueihy was my contact in Lebanon and I'd given my father his number in case something happened.

But my father didn't want to call him from the street, so he waited until he got home.

"Hello, Mr. Doueihy?"

"Who is this?"

"I'm Jean-Louis Alpeyrie, the father of Jonathan, the photojournalist."

"Yes, yes, Jonathan. Has something happened?"

"Well, it seems he's been abducted. We've heard from his fixer that his car was ambushed."

"We'll find out where he is," Doueihy said. "But he should be fine."

Soon after, Doueihy called back and told my father that I was still in Yabroud as far as his people knew, but he'd try to get more information.

My father immediately called my mother, who was living in Mexico. Even after their divorce they remained friends and communicated regularly.

"Daniela," he said straightaway, "Jonathan's been kidnapped." My mother never tolerated people beating around the bush when they had something important to say, so there was never any point in preparing her.

"I sensed it. I told him not to go," she said. "I had a premonition that something wrong would happen. He never listens."

After some initial venting, my mother shifted into her more charac-teristic pragmatic mode. The one trait of hers I always tried to emulate was her ability to survive in harsh conditions. She'd overcome a lot of hardships, and I liked to think that I'd inherited some of her fierce grit in the face of adversity. Instinctively, she felt that my social media pres-ence should be wiped as clean as possible, so she called Aaron, who was very tech-savvy, to have him delete everything he could.

Several days later, Doueihy called back and told my father that I was in the hands of the Free Syrian Army, in a Christian area, so I should be okay. In one of the subsequent emails Doueihy explained to my father that my captors thought I was a spy.

I'm not sure how much Doueihy really knew at that point. I assume he got his information from the Doctor and his people.

FOR THE FIRST FOUR DAYS my father hardly slept and just stayed at home. His wife, Ann, my stepmother, was in Boston, where my sis-ter Lauren had had some surgery. My father cloistered himself in his uptown apartment alone with Sam, a pet cat who was dying of cancer. Eating was more the act of injecting fuel into his system so he could keep moving. He prepared food for Sam, feeding him twice a day and making sure he had water and took his medication.

But my father's entire routine revolved around waiting for Doueihy to call him back, respond to an email, tell him something, anything that might release him from the paralysis of uncertainty.

Sam could not walk well because of his cancer. But he seemed to take it stoically, so my father tried to absorb some of that stoicism. After a couple of days, the cat came to sleep on his bed, as if he under-stood something was amiss. During those first few days, when there was only the two of them, they communicated silently about their own pain. This was very unusual for my father, a thoroughly social animal who loves being with other people and has made a successful career out of finding the right people for the right position. The cat's presence was no doubt a comfort to him, although minute by minute, as he watched Sam struggle through his last days, it must have been hard not to project that same fate onto me.

WHEN ANN CAME HOME after four days she could see my father was very optimistic about news from Doueihy's emails—overly optimistic—and she tried to keep him on an even keel. When things took a turn for the worse, Ann kept a more cautiously optimistic tone.

At that time my father was working at Heidrick & Struggles, an executive search firm. He'd go to the office, where he tried to carry on as if everything were normal. But some of his colleagues, especially his secretary, had already noticed a change.

The H&S office was in Midtown, so he'd often go to St. Patrick's Cathedral on Fifth Avenue to pray. As he liked to say, there are no atheists in foxholes, and he felt the need to pray for me to be released. As time went by, though, it occurred to him that many had died who were just as important to their families as I was, and the modality of his prayers shifted: "Help me stay strong and all in one piece to get my son out."

SLOWLY TECHNOLOGY INVADED his private space. He slept one hour at a time, with his BlackBerry always close at hand to check if there were any messages from Doueihy. All his daily activities became consumed by events unfolding on the other side of the world, events shrouded by huge lacunas of information and muddied with the inevitable miscommunications and lies every war seems to breed like tumors. And as Sam's tumors quietly metastasized, my father's BlackBerry became the center of his life. It never left his hand and would rest on the night table while he slept. My father's entire universe was held suspended by the gentle vibration indicating a call or an email.

What kept going through his mind was: *Why? Why did I let Jonathan go? How could I have let him pursue the road he had chosen years ago?*

One of my father's many friends was the French philosopher and anthropologist René Girard, who had spent the latter part of his life teaching at Stanford University and had a significant impact on his view of the world. Girard had developed a number of ideas about the scapegoat. He theorized that all human societies began through acts of violence, and that we are defined primarily by our ability to control our violence: through religions, philosophies, ethics, and so on.

In biblical times a goat would be sent into the wilderness after the Jewish chief priest had symbolically laid the sins of the people upon it. My father tried hard not to extend that analogy to his only son, but at times he couldn't help it. In a society morbidly obsessed with the visual image and other superficial trappings, it was easy to imagine—especially in his state of near-constant anxiety—that I had been called upon to go into the wilderness with my camera as a scapegoat.

Such mental tangents would often get the best of him and start pulling him into a tailspin, so he simply went back to his BlackBerry for distraction.

FOR THE NEXT FEW WEEKS, news about my whereabouts—or lack of any—kept my parents, sister, and the few friends who knew about my kidnapping on an emotional roller coaster. Initially the information kept changing. At first they were told I'd been taken because I was assumed to be a spy. In that case everything would get cleared up. Doueihy then told my father that I was in the "Christian mountains." Over time, however, the tone of the emails changed. (Doueihy didn't want to be called on the phone unless the circumstances were exceptional. My father called him anyway.) The communication became more negative: "He was somewhere else"; "He had not listened to good advice and had gone where he shouldn't have"; "My people are looking for him."

Finally, after several weeks, Doueihy sent an email confirming their fears. I had indeed been kidnapped. It was clear that I was being held hostage. The only good news was that Doueihy said I'd been abducted by a "friendly" group of the Free Syrian Army in Yabroud.

Occasionally my father wasn't sure whether to trust Doueihy, but that only led to the harsh realization that he had no choice. His Lebanese contact was the only one with any concrete information.

At one point Doueihy told him that they could get me out by means of a humanitarian convoy on its way to a destination just a few miles from where I was being held. From there I'd be brought to Lebanon. He never really explained the details of how that would happen, but my father wanted desperately to believe it was feasible.

He waited all night, hoping to find out in the morning that I was free. But instead, he got word that it hadn't worked out.

THE GOVERNMENT CONTACTS ADDED to the roller-coaster ride. At first it was the Americans. My father and Ann were both at home when a call came from the American embassy in Jordan. The caller claimed to be an FBI agent. Ann refused to say anything. She was suspicious for any number of reasons, but especially because she assumed that the FBI only handled domestic cases.

"I don't know who you are," she said. "You say you're FBI, I don't know. If you give me your phone number I can check and then call you back."

Everything seemed legitimate, and they confirmed that yes, Jonathan had been kidnapped. Initially they didn't provide much help, but then the FBI called and came to see my father. They sent an agent, a woman who came with another female colleague. The two of them debriefed him, asking him all sorts of questions: who knew what . . . who had contacted him . . . He told them what he knew, but he was basically in the dark about so many things. And the FBI didn't propose any particular action.

My father was surprised that the State Department wasn't handling the case. As far as he could tell, the department didn't even make any effort. It was all in the hands of the FBI, and he couldn't understand why the FBI would be involved. It didn't seem logical, not even to Ann, who was born and raised in the United States and whose father had been in the military.

Then the French made contact. A woman called from the Ministry of Foreign Affairs, known more commonly as the Quai d'Orsay. Her name was Mila Jubin, the same woman who spoke to me on the phone when I was in Beirut. She got Ann on the phone, who went through the same routine as with the FBI, calling back only when she was certain it was legitimate. At that moment my father had just come back home from taking a walk outside, so he called the number and wound up talking to Jubin.

AT MORE OR LESS the same time, he started to get all kinds of calls from people who had heard about my capture, like the head of Polaris Images, the agency I was working for. There was also a well-known British journalist who wanted to help, saying he had some contacts in the area. He put my father in touch with a man in Lebanon who would regularly cross the border into Syria to bring medical supplies to the people in the war zones. But this Lebanese man seemed like the kind of person who keeps telling you what he thinks you want to hear. My father mentioned the man to Jubin and she had one of the Arab-speakers on her team call the man up, pretending to be speaking on my father's behalf. She got back to my father the same day and confirmed his intuition, "You can talk to him as much as you want, but bear in mind that he serves no purpose. He'll tell you whatever he thinks will make you happy."

The only person who seemed to have any leverage in that wasp's nest I'd fallen into was Doueihy. And Doueihy told my father not to talk too much. But he couldn't be one hundred percent sure about Doueihy, either, so he asked Jubin. The Quai d'Orsay certainly knew Doueihy—everybody knew Robert Doueihy—and agreed that if any civilian could contact and convince the people holding me, it was him.

My father also called the FBI regularly about his contacts. They acknowledged them, but nothing more—unlike the French, who were more adept at interacting with the Levantine mentality.

GRADUALLY, MY FATHER FELL into a routine: eating very little, going to the office two or three times a week (but doing nothing). Fortunately his secretary, Susan, was one of the few people who knew what was going on. She was practically telepathic and had guessed there was something horribly wrong, so he had to tell her.

Ann played a key role in forcing him to do things. She kept him optimistic whenever she sensed the dark clouds approaching. Just when my father's emotions were about to reach a critical mass that resulted in paralysis, she'd ease him back into a functional mode with dialogues that always followed the same pattern:

"Jonathan's not coming back," he'd say. "They're going to kill him. I can't take it anymore."

"No, he'll make it. He's been through difficult situations before and has always come back. He knows how to handle situations like this and find his way with people, no matter how foreign they may be."

"I'm not sure. This time it's different, much worse. He won't come out alive."

"You're wrong. And as usual you're worrying yourself sick. Take a walk, do something."

"What difference will it make?"

"Just remember, if the worst happens, you still have a wife, a daughter, family and friends who love you. If something were to happen to you, Lauren would be devastated for life."

"What about Jonathan?"

"Jonathan will survive more easily there than you will by fretting at home. Remember, he's someone who everyone likes. He naturally wins people over. It's second nature for him. His captors will inevitably like him. They'll grow attached to him. He'll make himself useful. That's how he is. And he'll make it . . . Now go for a walk. It'll do you good."

Ann's assessment, in the end, turned out to be accurate. And if there was one redeeming aspect to my experience, it was a fuller realization of that "second nature" of mine, the ability to win people over without trying, especially people capable of violence.

AFTER FIVE OR SIX WEEKS my father's world shifted again with news from Doueihy. They wanted money: $750,000. My father immediately offered to pay, but Doueihy refused out of hand. "That's not how things work here. If you accept immediately, then they'll pull back and ask for more," he said. "Let me negotiate with them. We'll start at two hundred thousand."

My father insisted he was ready to pay any sum, sell everything he owned and borrow money on top of that to pay my ransom—even stuff the cash inside a golden calf and lay it at the feet of the commander. But Doueihy was adamant; it would only make matters more difficult. "You don't know how these people think."

As usual, my father deferred.

THE NEGOTIATIONS OVER MONEY dragged on for weeks. My father moved from hope to despair on a daily basis, often within the span of minutes. He felt paralyzed and needed to do something, take an action. So he decided to fly to Lebanon on his own and see what could be done. But as soon as he floated the idea to Doueihy, the response was unequivocal: "No. You will be miserable and useless. Stuck in a hotel room. At best you'll only bother us. At worst, someone will try to kidnap you, too."

The paralysis was aggravated by the need to maintain secrecy. At one point Aaron, with whom my father had been in contact at least once a week, suggested they use an acquaintance of Aaron's who worked at a major television network to publicize my disappearance. Both my mother and father were totally against it. They'd been warned by Doue-ihy, the Quai d'Orsay, and the FBI that any kind of publicity would only disrupt the extremely delicate negotiations in progress. Another one who suggested going public was J. P. Pappis, the founder of Polaris Images. My mother practically ate him alive from her redoubt in Mexico.

It was one of the few times that she dealt directly with one of the pieces involved in the puzzle. She's a person who has always wandered through life on the margins. That's where she's most comfortable. She spoke every day to my father, but let him deal with Doueihy and the government because she knew she was incapable of being diplomatic. She was a tough woman, tempered by a difficult childhood and adoles-cence, and it instilled in her a take-no-prisoners approach to life. But that approach was a perfect counterbalance for my father. He called her almost every day and her reaction was always controlled, matter-of-fact. She absorbed everything he told her coldly, analytically. "This sounds right . . . That's unrealistic . . . It's not going to happen . . . This guy sounds crazy or dangerous . . . He's lying to you . . ."

She trusted Doueihy, and she liked the French, but she never trusted the FBI. Of course no one was telling my father everything they knew, but she felt the FBI was the least forthcoming. Still, she never asked to talk to any of them directly. That was my father's role. He interacted with people. That was his strength. My mother's strength was the abil-ity to remain cool-headed, and that helped my father get through the more difficult days. Calling her regularly helped him to think properly and not succumb to raw emotions. She became his reality check. And oddly enough, her toughness—to the point of callousness at times—was making him stronger.

Learning about this dynamic only confirmed what I was already aware of: that I had inherited a lot—maybe too much—of my mother's doggedness. Once she decided on some crazy adventure, there was no stopping her. Her tenacity could be frightening. I unconsciously tried to imitate her, pursuing an ostensibly mad path with cool precision.

MY MOTHER'S PRESENCE INCREASED as the emails back and forth with Doueihy grew more hopeful. In one he said, "We have identified the house and have it surrounded." By "we" my father assumed he meant "his people," but when he tried to imagine how many people it took to surround a house in possibly hostile territory, his concern grew. Then another email: "We have seen Jonathan and he is OK."

That was a period of daily ups and downs as the negotiations seemed to continually stall and restart. Sometimes there was no news for several days; then Doueihy would send emails saying his people could not cross the border or send news because of battles raging in the area. He seemed most concerned with Hezbollah. Then my father would get an email saying, "We are negotiating again."

So he was fairly optimistic the day when Doueihy dropped the real bad news on him: "There is another group that is negotiating to take Jonathan."

They switched from email exchanges to phone conversations because there was no time to be wasted.

"Who are these people?" my father asked.

"They're bad people. Very dangerous. Jihadists. They're close to convincing Jonathan's captors to give him to them. We can't let Jonathan fall into their hands."

"So what can we do?"

"I have one hundred fifty people ready to assault the house. But I need your agreement as Jonathan could be killed during the assault."

"I see. I'll need to talk to his mother."

"Hurry. We don't have much time."

As my father called up my mother it was impossible for him not to imagine me in the hands of some hooded fanatic posing in front of a camera, poised to slit my throat for the sake of a spectacle meant to glorify the name of his horrific god. Somehow the image steeled his will.

"This is the situation, Daniela . . . We have to make a decision."

She was quick: "We have no choice. Let's do it."

He hung up and sent an email to Doueihy giving him the green light to send his men in and rescue me.

THAT WAS SEVERAL WEEKS before I was taken to Damascus. Even though my father and I have gone over the events from our separate perspectives many times, there are still big question marks. Initially, he didn't know who the jihadists were. Later Doueihy identified them as Jabhat al-Nusra, an affiliate of al-Qaeda. The Islamic State in Iraq and Syria, aka ISIS, was still little known in Syria and operating more in the eastern part of the country at that time.

I wondered if the smuggler had anything to do with Doueihy's men. Or if the sheikh who had visited me and who seemed to hand me over to the government troops had anything to do with Jabhat al-Nusra. Things may have been clearer had I known whether the sheikh was Sunni or Shia. But I couldn't tell the difference and it didn't occur to me ask. In any case, looking for clarity in that part of world has always been a fool's errand.

Ultimately Doueihy would never publicly admit to any involvement. Moreover, he always maintained that my trip to Damascus was a fiction. And I assume he would never acknowledge connections to such high-ranking Syrian government figures as Aboud. But I've often wondered about the possibility that "Doueihy's men" were actually Aboud's men. I'll probably never know for sure.

FORTUNATELY FOR ME, the assault didn't take place. Doueihy called the following day to say that negotiations had restarted and appeared to be going well. My father became more optimistic, but by then the ordeal had taken its toll.

Finally it all seemed to come to an end with the telephone call from

Yann, after I had contacted him from Damascus. My father was visiting one of his closest friends in Los Angeles and eating at a Japanese restaurant. After the news they stayed at the restaurant and celebrated with beer after beer late into the night until the owner politely asked them to leave. He called my mother first thing in the morning and both waited for their scapegoat to return.

DEBRIEFING

I WAS FREE—MORE OR LESS. I still couldn't do anything I wanted because I was confined to the French embassy in Beirut and needed to be debriefed. But at least the pall of coercion around me had lifted.

Before my kidnapping I wasn't exactly sure what a debriefing entailed. After I was released I found out it was a lot like an interrogation—minus the subtext of threat, and conducted by ostensible friendlies who try to give you the benefit of the doubt.

Since I was one of the first hostages in Syria to be released, I was expected to be a source of unprecedented information. Almost as soon as we got to the French embassy, two casually dressed gendarmes came to debrief me; they looked like they were about to go on a leisurely Sunday stroll in the park with their families. I was put in a big room, just the three of us, and they asked me a series of questions in an attempt to piece together the timeline of my captivity. They showed me pictures of all the other people who had gone missing. They asked me if I'd seen them, if I knew who they were. I didn't recognize any of them. They especially wanted to know everything about my release period: the day and night I spent in Damascus.

I gave them a minute-by-minute account of how things had happened. They wanted to know how I was transported from one area to another, what kind of car, which roads we took, how many checkpoints.

"Do you know who paid your ransom?" they asked.

"Yes." I told them about Aboud.

"How do you know he was the one who paid?"

"He told me himself. So did Atrash and the others. From the look of his manor house it didn't seem like very much money for him."

They left me in the room alone for a while, then came back with a picture of Aboud. "Yeah, that's him."

In all, the questions took about two hours. I was psychically exhausted. I looked around me: the grounds were palatial. And yet, I wasn't sure if I was still incarcerated or not.

LATER THAT DAY I met alone with the ambassador Patrice Paoli, who was a very congenial man. We talked about the general situation in the Middle East, and specifically the Syrian War. From my scant experience with diplomats, I'd always noticed they had a remarkable capacity to say nothing substantial in a most eloquent manner. Paoli wasn't like that at all. Maybe it was because we were speaking in private. Whatever the reason, he articulated a very nuanced understanding of the Syrian situation: a multifaceted war that was evolving into an even more complicated proxy war for external players, a war in which shifting alliances were the order of the day and trust could be bought as easily with money as with blood.

He showed me the grounds of the Pine Residence, now the French embassy, which had been built during World War I in lavish Ottoman style so that the growing merchant class in Beirut could have a watering hole. Originally there was supposed to be a casino, but that never panned out as it came to be used as a military hospital during the war.

There was also a tennis court on the grounds and a horse-racing track next door.

He continually asked me if I was okay. He never used his authority to keep me at a distance, even though he could have. After all, he was the ambassador of France in Lebanon, an important position because Lebanon had been part of the French Mandate between the wars and has remained Paris's sole outpost in a very volatile region.

When I saw the swimming pool I asked if I could use it. Fortunately, among all the things Ray-Ban had bought for me and put in my roller suitcase, there was even a pair of sporty shorts that could pass as bathing trunks.

I ate dinner with the ambassador and his wife, who also went out of her way to make me feel at ease. Comfort does wonders to buttress your sense of freedom, even if you can't go where you want to.

THE NEXT MORNING I woke up with the first light and felt as if my brain had shut down. For about twenty minutes I didn't know where I was. *This must be what amnesiacs experience.* I heard some chatter down the hall in French and all sorts of memories started coming back to me, but I couldn't connect them to the palm trees and tall Mediterranean pines I saw outside the window.

I lay in bed piecing together my situation. I was free. Sort of, depending on the definition. If freedom meant doing whatever I felt like doing then I certainly wasn't free. I couldn't just walk out and take a stroll through this hilly residential neighborhood. I had to ask permission. Maybe get an escort. But my wishes would probably be indulged because I was being held by friendlies and protected by them.

By that token, I had also been held and protected by ostensible friendlies before this, in the Light House. They just weren't as friendly as the people at the French embassy. The Syrian rebels could beat me if they wanted, but they'd stopped wanting to after a certain point.

That said, they could and did sell me. It was all relative. As was my freedom. The French embassy could also beat me or sell me if they wanted to. But they wouldn't. (Or at least that was how I was putting things together in my quasi-amnesiac state.) That was the social pact. I was a citizen of La République Française, and now I was at their embassy, which is considered to be *sol français*, French soil. I was a privileged heir of the revolution whose legacy was liberty, equality and fraternity.

But it took a while for all that to sink in as I lay on my bed, unsure of which country I was in. I realized freedom—at least mine—was as precarious as the conceptual thread that held the words "I want" together. As soon as you don't know what you want, you're a prisoner. As soon as you find out you can't get what you want, you're a slave.

THE FOLLOWING DAY the same two casual gendarmes came to me and conducted another debriefing. They showed me photos of various rebel leaders, none of whom I recognized. Then there was a photo of Kamal Atrash, the Lebanese Druze who had convinced Aboud to raise his offer. After that came a series of photos of other people who had been kidnapped, journalists and aid workers, including the American photographer James Foley, who was the only one I recognized. But I'd never seen him in Syria or in person, only from the news.

They asked the same questions from slightly different angles, trying to triangulate my responses into a three-dimensional representation of truth. They wanted to know if I'd been alone. What the military situation was. How many soldiers, types of weapons. What they did during the day. Whether they drank alcohol or smoked cigarettes. How often they prayed. I spent hours answering their questions and it occurred to me that I, too, wanted to triangulate some semblance of truth that I felt had begun to slip away. In that sense our will and desire—mine and that of my debriefers—coincided. That little tinge of complicity helped me feel freer.

WHEN THE TWO MEN finished, they told me the FBI would be coming in to debrief me. Now the Americans wanted to have a go at me. And why not? I was a dual citizen and a privileged heir to *their* ideals, too—land of the free, home of the brave, and whatnot. I had to fulfill my part of *that* social pact.

The American debriefing had a very different flavor. Two men in suits walked through the French embassy and straightaway you could pick them out as G-men. They appeared to be much more serious about their work, much more in my face. The French came across as two nice guys, smart, but just some dudes you might strike up a conversation with at a café in a foreign country. The Americans were all business. They only showed me pictures of the American hostages: Jim Foley, Austin Tice, Kevin Patrick Dawes, and a few others.

The FBI debriefing was a lot shorter and felt very abrupt compared to how the French did theirs. Once they'd asked all their questions, they said thank you and left, as if they had to clock out somewhere. They kept their inquiries into my health and mental state to a perfunctory minimum—just enough to get a sense of whether my experience had unhinged me to the point where it skewed my memory.

I STILL HAD THE BLACKBERRY they'd given me at the Marina Towers and Atrash had my phone number. So he had his daughter, who spoke good English, call me. "You should meet us today outside the embassy," she said, conveying her father's suggestion. "We'll drive you and have a meeting." I told her I'd get back to them. Of course as soon as I relayed this to the French authorities, they said, "You're not leaving this embassy at all. You're staying with us. You don't have papers. We don't know what they want from you." In this case not being totally free kept me from having too much choice and wandering into another potential trap.

It was never clear what Atrash wanted. I doubt he had bad intentions. Like everyone, he was probably just concerned about his own interests and wanted to make sure his ass was covered, but I never got the chance to find out.

THE FOLLOWING DAY I did yet another major debriefing with two French intelligence officers. If this was freedom, then it was pay-as-you-go freedom, with my memory as currency. But again, they were so friendly, so pleasant, that it turned out to be therapeutic. I finally had people to talk to, and in my own language—people who listened intently and genuinely seemed to care about my well-being.

It made me look forward to going home and seeing my friends and family, even though I wasn't sure how I would react.

The rest of the day I wandered around the Pine Residence and ate delicious food. After months of simple Levantine fare I could finally indulge in the rich French cuisine I grew up with: cassoulet, gigot d'agneau, or boeuf bourguignon. The flavors brought me back to the days when my father would drive me to restaurants hidden in the middle of the French countryside.

I especially looked forward to talking to Paoli. Without going into any details he gave me a fresh sense of all the political convolutions in this part of the world. The ambassador had a very realistic assessment of the Arab Spring, which everyone had been hyperventilating over just a couple of years earlier: basically, that democracy and mob rule were cut of the same cloth. It had taken France decades to evolve the institutions that had channeled the mob rule of the Terror into a bona fide democracy. And France came from a Christian tradition that had evolved the notion of individual dignity with respect to the human person, backed moreover by a Roman juridical tradition with long-developed laws regarding property rights: fundamental elements for elaborating the idea of "human rights." It's not something you can easily overlay onto a society with another history and tradition.

I walked around the magnificent garden and watched the

groundskeepers prune the trees. It was very colonial. As I looked out from the Lebanese hills I thought about the history and tradition of where I was standing. I wondered if there had been any sacrifices to Baal on this very spot. And then my brain shut down again. I didn't want to think about it. From a wide-angle perspective this whole Syrian War struck me as a historical clusterfuck that could even help set off some global Armageddon.

Whenever such thoughts pushed too hard against my skull, and my heart started skipping, I went to the pool to cool off. There were people coming and going, and the ambassador's wife would often be relaxing there. It was a very big pool and I would just do laps back and forth to channel me into a zone somewhat loosened from all the uncertainties that had gnawed my nerves raw. I swam until the entire universe was unified in the act of inhaling and exhaling as I cut through the water. But from time to time that quasi-mystical state would be interrupted by the image of Essad floundering in the water with me teaching him the one thing that gave me a sense of peace.

Swimming gave me an appetite and I wandered toward the dining room and adjacent kitchen. The chef saw me and must have known my situation, so he invited me into the kitchen and asked if there was anything special he could prepare. He'd lay out an array of cheeses before me and offer wine and whiskey. I hadn't touched any alcohol in months and as soon as my tongue got its first taste I could feel the warmth work its way down my gullet to salve so many frayed nerves.

AFTER THE SECOND DAY I was moved to another room, downgraded because of the arrival of new guests. It didn't matter because I spent a lot of my time on the Internet trying to catch up with my life. The embassy kept a computer next to the kitchen, so I'd communicate with the outside world and take breaks for wine and gourmet snacks, maintaining a nice buzz throughout the day.

I even contacted the woman I'd made a date with in Paris for the day after I was supposed to have returned. I'd met her shortly before I left for Syria. I got kidnapped the very day after I'd set up the meeting.

She responded, "You're an asshole. I waited for you for two hours. Who does that? Now you're reaching out months later?"

I told her I'd explain if I saw her in Paris. Not even close to knowing what I had been through, she was understandably wary.

One night soon after that, there was a dinner and a concert. Robert Doueihy's wife showed up. She was French, and I'd known her for more than a year. In fact, it was through her that I met Doueihy, who set me up with the Doctor, who got me into Syria and hooked me up with Alfarook, who contacted his other fixer friend, who was probably the one who got me kidnapped. She wanted to see if I was all right and told me that her husband had been very concerned and in constant contact with my father. The subtext of the conversation was something like: *For political reasons he can't be associated with this publicly, but he's very happy you made it through alive.*

ON MY FOURTH AND LAST DAY at the embassy, the two very kind gendarmes who had picked me up at the Four Seasons came in and said, "We're having problems getting your papers. You have no documents and the Lebanese government is not happy that you went out of the country and then came back in illegally."

It was true. I'd effectively been smuggled into and out of Syria. So the French government had been negotiating for several days.

The gendarmes said, "We have an embarrassing request. We need five hundred dollars from you."

I said, "Why?"

"Well, we had to pay for the administrative fees that the government of Lebanon requires in order to get some of the documents you need to leave the country. But they weren't sufficient. They need something else, and that costs five hundred dollars."

"Can't the French government pay for it?" I asked. *I mean, it's five hundred bucks,* I thought to myself, *which is nothing for the government of one of the richest nations in the world. Who gives a shit?*

The gendarmes cringed with embarrassment. "I'm sorry, the government insists they don't want to pay for it. Bureaucracy."

There was something Kafkaesque about the whole situation. I wondered what life as an eternal prisoner of the Pine Residence would be like. I assumed the resistance stemmed from the fact that I also had a US passport; the French felt that the Americans should foot some of the bill—petty Franco-American rivalry. Or maybe they suspected I had my own money and they wanted to see if I'd break it out.

Of course I still had the four thousand dollars Aboud had given me, which I wanted to keep secret. But if it meant forgoing my freedom, then there was no question. So I told them the truth: I had four grand in my pocket; Aboud had given it to me. The gendarmes took the hundred-dollar bills to check if they were real—none of them were fake—kept five hundred, and gave the rest back.

I got my documents the next day. At least they booked the flight for me and didn't make me pay out of my own pocket. I assumed they had a deal with Air France.

THE SAME TWO GENDARMES drove me to the airport. We cut ahead of the queue and they led me through security, flashing their badges to the various authorities.

At one point we got stopped and they pulled out the official documents. The Lebanese security officer shook his head and said, "You can't leave the country." The French gendarmes started negotiating in English with the security. After five or ten minutes they agreed to let me go through their customs.

We waited together and had some coffee. I wasn't sure what the problem was exactly. Probably the fact that I had no documents, which needed to be explained. The French embassy in Lebanon wasn't equipped to make new passports, so I was without one. I got a new passport when I got back to Paris. Or maybe they wanted baksheesh—a bribe. In the end I didn't care as long as I got out of there.

When I took my seat in the plane I realized the whole crew knew about my situation. The pilot came to see me and they put me alone in a special coach area. I must have looked like a freshly cleaned homeless man with my white T-shirt and a plastic bag filled with the few belongings I'd decided to keep. (I'd left the big roller suitcase with all the other stuff behind.) The stewardesses were all very friendly and very pretty. It had been a while since I'd felt any even remotely flirtatious vibes from women. It sort of dazed me.

When we landed in Paris's Charles de Gaulle Airport the pilot told everyone over the intercom to stay put. "We have a special guest on the plane, who needs to exit first." I didn't realize they were talking about me. A stewardess came up to me and said, "Okay, Jonathan, we can go." So everyone was suddenly scowling at this tired-looking, bearded skinny guy with shitty clothes and a plastic bag, and half-wondering, *Is he famous?*

As soon as the plane's gate opened into the jet bridge I saw my uncle Claude, my father's younger brother, along with two secret service men who took me off the plane very quickly. I followed them. We went through the bridge and then to an underground passage where the VIPs go: a maze of tunnels and rooms. After about a five-minute walk there was a glass door, and I could see my best friend, Yann, along with three other friends. We all started hugging each other; it was very emotional. Mila Jubin was also there, the woman with whom I'd spoken on the phone briefly from Beirut. She was the one who had handled my case and acted as my father's liaison with the French foreign ministry.

Suddenly they had everyone leave the room. An older man came in and introduced himself as a psychologist. He asked if I wanted to talk about anything. I tried to dismiss him as quickly as possible and make him understand that his very presence was aggravating me. So he just handed me his card and said to call if I wanted to talk.

Then all the others came back in and we left the airport. Finally, I was free—at least to do whatever I wanted and go wherever I pleased.

AS SOON AS I got to Paris the government put out a press release and everything became public. The press corps got wind of it and the next thing I knew I was in a shitstorm, getting calls left and right. My email inbox was greeted with an avalanche of messages. I gave my first interview to *Paris Match* because the editor, Régis Le Sommier, was a friend of mine and I wanted him to have the scoop. Then came the radio and TV. I was getting my fifteen minutes of fame—and then some.

Jean-Fabien, one of the friends who had shown up at the airport, owned a houseboat on the Seine, near Pont de Sèvres. He was going away for a while so he gave me the keys and told me to have a party.

I invited the girl I'd made a date with two days before I got kidnapped, the one I'd stood up.

"I'm having a party on this boat. Please come. You'll understand why I wasn't able to show up." I didn't tell her why; I was, in fact, surprised that she hadn't been made aware of the media frenzy surrounding me.

She said, "No way. You must be kidding."

But she ended up coming anyway. At first she tried to give me the cold shoulder. I was standing behind the bar and she walked up to me very nonchalantly.

"Would you like a drink?" I asked, and handed her a glass of wine.

"So what the hell happened?"

"I was kidnapped."

Naturally, she thought I was lying.

"Check the Internet," I said. "It's all over the Web."

But before she had a chance to raise a doubt, one of my friends walked behind her and said it was true.

She felt bad—shocked. "I'm sorry, I had no idea."

Now I had her complete sympathy, which I could probably have parlayed to seduce her. But all I wanted was to be surrounded by people in a sympathetic but superficial setting that didn't test the limits of human interaction. I'd been debriefed so many times that I didn't want to have anyone asking too many questions if it wasn't strictly necessary.

OF COURSE, ONCE IN PARIS I needed to be officially debriefed some more. I was summoned to the Ministry of Foreign Affairs at the Quai d'Orsay, where I saw Jubin again. She was a very pleasant woman—petite, reserved and elegantly dressed.

The next day she asked me to come to her office once more. The DGSE, France's external intelligence agency, was there, with about ten people asking me all sorts of questions—mostly the same ones: How did I get out? Who and what money? Who were the rebels? How many were there? What kinds of weapons? Cities? Terrain? Fighting? Shelling? I was spilling it all out now, almost by rote, honing a narrative that helped chip away at the daze I still felt.

I SPENT A WEEK in Paris, then flew back to New York. When I got to JFK Airport my father was there with Ann. My sister Lauren couldn't make it because she had a work commitment in California, and we agreed it would be better to spend time alone as soon as things calmed down. I'd also asked my ex-girlfriend Tara and her son Kyle to be there. I wanted to be surrounded by people who knew me well. It was almost as if I needed a reality check because I sensed something had shifted.

Within a week, my friend Aaron, the one who had first gotten news of my abduction and told my father, threw a big party for me at a girlfriend's house, where he invited all my friends. My father was there, too.

Eventually my mother came to New York from Mexico and stayed with me for more than a month.

Everyone kept asking me what had happened. I appeared on CNN and Fox News. Old friends would probe me casually, or if they didn't want to be too intrusive, then I'd see the look in their eyes . . . *So? What was it like?* It was a never-ending debriefing—extending into this book even—as if by fixing the narrative of my own abduction I could plug up some gaping black hole that experience had opened in my universe.

CAUGHT IN THE RIP CURRENT

MY FATHER FELT A GETAWAY BY THE SEA would help me readjust, so he booked a hotel in Boca Raton, Florida, where he invited me along with Ann and my sister Lauren. He understood that I needed a break from all the questions posed by others. I needed to look inward and work out so many of my own questions now rising to the surface like foam in a simmering pot, or flotsam after a storm. And he knew the sea always gave me solace.

In some ways my father knows me better than I know myself. (And if my father knows who I am better than I do, then my mother knows who I *can* be—my potential—better than anyone.)

I SWAM IN THE ATLANTIC. Then, after I exhausted myself, I sat on the white sand and watched the waves from a distance, breaking gently and foaming up at my feet before they retreated. The metaphor hit me suddenly and unequivocally: History is like the ebb and flow of the ocean. The whole of it is so vast that you can only hope to fathom the surface, a little of the depths, a few specifics with respect to the life it breeds. What we understand of history from our limited human perspective can be likened to what we are able to see from the shore, or from some vessel plying its way across the surface. Hurricanes, typhoons and other tempests come and go more or less frequently, revealing themselves to be cyclical, perhaps even corresponding to some vague elaboration of chaos theory. But when you're in the middle of a storm, floating on a fragile boat, or trying to ride a wave on a surfboard, every lash and curl of water can lead to your undoing.

I'm certainly not the first to milk this metaphor. In *War and Peace* Tolstoy described the great men of history as merely riding the crests of historical waves set in motion by myriad forces beyond their control or comprehension. But it's a metaphor that springs from the core of my being.

Given my druthers there's nothing I love more than skirting that edge where the ocean licks the land—swimming and surfing much more than sailing, since you need to have your skin immersed in it.

It's the same with history. Studying it from books or even archeological digs is somewhat like sailing: enjoyable and rewarding in and of itself. But plunging into the thick of it is a qualitatively different experience.

I've always felt like my time here on earth is just a blink, and the more you study history (not to mention paleontology or geology) the more the significance of that blink tends to diminish. So when I'm in the whorl of some historic event, I feel much more alive with respect to the oceanic vastness of time itself than when I'm just an observer, studying it several times removed by mediating factors such as books or visual chronicles.

As far as my own understanding of history is concerned, the twentieth century, with its world wars, was a massive tsunami that crashed down on all our notions of civilization. Nothing of human activity's superficial mechanics remained the same. Maybe in essence people were still the same—they still fell in love and fucked as they'd done for eons—but the planet was suddenly swarming with mechanical vehicles, the magic of electricity and nocturnal light infiltrated our dreams, and we began to project our words, thoughts and images instantaneously across impossible distances through a previously unimaginable ether.

I was born into a world still sweeping up the detritus of that massive tidal wave. I'd hear stories of horror and heroism. And I've always been eager to swim through the waves, constantly on the lookout for that big one.

What happened to me in Syria, I thought as I watched the soothing Atlantic froth up on the Florida shore, was quite simple. I got caught in the rip current of history. Major changes have been occurring along one of the world's geopolitical fault lines. Jihad in the age of the Internet was crashing headlong into the tail end of the black-gold rush. The postcolonial Muslim world was experiencing an epochal upheaval and I rushed in to watch the flare-ups and capture images of them. But I got caught in a rip current and was dragged out toward that scary place where you suddenly know just how little you count.

Fortunately—whether from experience, instinct, good karma, or sheer dumb luck—I did the right thing. I didn't try to swim back to shore against the current and risk succumbing to exhaustion. I let the rip take me for a while. Then, when I felt it loosen its grip, I tried to swim parallel to the shore, out of that narrow channel that seemed to defy the oversimplified logic of ebb and flow. It worked. I'm still alive. Somewhat free.

SO NOW I KEEP asking myself: *Why me? Why was I the lucky one?* I could have been hit by a shell while captive and no one would have known anything about me or how I vanished from existence. No CNN, no Fox, no film rights, no book deal—just an untimely and messy death in some Syrian shithole. Or I could have been sold to a more fanatical group of jihadis and beheaded as propaganda fodder. My fifteen minutes of fame would have come as a poster child for Allah's wrath manifested in the blade of the faithful.

There is, of course, the karmic explanation, which I've never been fond of—even though it might offer a tidy etiology. As I watched the waves I thought of the several lives I'd saved thanks to my swimming prowess.

There was that kite surfer in Mexico whom the wind simply lifted into the sky, only to throw him back into the water. He got tangled in the parachute, and even though the edges were designed to float, he nearly suffocated under the fabric. I swam out about a half a mile and helped him back to the beach.

Then there were the two Indian girls in Puerto Rico who got caught in a current that threatened to fling them into an outcrop of rocks on the shore.

In Hawaii I helped two other teenage girls who got caught in a rip current that was dragging them out to where huge waves were poised to slam them into the rocks. One of them was holding on to me and I showed the other one how to dive into and under the wave just before it broke and curled into a roiling broth. It took about six or seven waves, but with each one we managed to get a little closer to where they could stand with their heads above water.

Once, in Panama, on an island by the Colombian border where fishing boats ran drugs, I came close to dying myself. I got caught in a wicked rip that tore the leash off my surfboard. I managed to swim back, with great difficulty, and collapse on the shore. It was already a terrifying experience for someone like me, who was trained to swim long distances competitively. It's hard for me now to imagine what someone already uncomfortable in the water must go through when that otherwise gorgeous maw of a breaking wave swallows him or her. Probably like getting eaten by a whale. And when you suddenly realize you're in the beast's belly reflecting on how to get out—like Jonah or Pinocchio—it means you're already dead.

As I treaded water just beyond the line where the waves break, the up and down of the ocean swelling serenely—like the diaphragm of some sleeping beast—burnished the meditative state that always comes over me after a long swim. I knew that evening I'd be having a pleasant, civilized meal with a family who loved me. They were all doing their best to understand how I felt. But I wasn't sure myself how I felt. As I floated I imagined myself having just been spouted out from inside a whale, where I'd gotten glimpses of mysteries I'd wind up chasing forever.

If I were inclined to think in terms of karma, I'd attribute the fact that I'm still alive to being in the black on some cosmic balance sheet. The lives I'd saved over time were like money in the bank—which helped pay my ransom. But I've never liked that sort of new-age logic and tend to shun it. I even have trouble attributing my survival to sheer luck. Somehow grace had come my way—which I can never expect to figure out. At best I can hope to carry on treading, more or less ignorant of the mechanism by which some are saved and others fucked.

OTHER HOSTAGES

WHATEVER THE METAPHYSICAL REASON behind my freedom, I owed it to those still captive to help in any way I could.

As soon as I got back to the United States I was debriefed by the FBI. They came to my father's apartment in Manhattan: two agents, both women. They helped me get some money back to cover all my lost equipment and urged me to help them track down several Americans who were still in captivity.

Syria was fast becoming the most dangerous place for journalists and aid workers in my lifetime. Reports of abductions appeared on a monthly or even weekly basis. By the time I was released there were dozens of foreign hostages still in rebel hands. Very few major media outlets were reporting directly out of Syria. The majority of reports in newspapers were being filed from Beirut or some Turkish border town.

In general, war correspondents and photographers don't elicit much sympathy when something bad happens to them. Certainly not as much as an aid worker. The prevailing attitude is: *you* choose to go into this situation, *you* put yourself at risk, and *you* are the one making a living off of war; danger comes with the territory. I've even met extreme pacifists who refuse to help war correspondents in any way because they feel by doing so they would be validating war in general. When I come back at them with the argument that allowing people to see the horror of war tends to make populations more averse to inciting war, it doesn't seem to take hold. In any case, anyone with an ideological agenda—be it pacifism or nationalism or feminism—needs to draw some rather arbitrary lines in the sand in order to placate their conscience. I was never a pacifist, and I've always felt that war is as "valid" as a hurricane or tornado. To eschew such disasters by hiding out in the Yukon, where they're less likely to happen, is no answer. In fact, the absence of eyes watching probably encourages those inclined to incite violence.

That said, war photographers are an admittedly surly breed. We're super-competitive, addicted to risk, and often become jaded after chasing death and destruction for so many years. If pacifists hold us in contempt, then soldiers tolerate us as long as we don't get into situations that force them to risk their lives for the sake of some hack who might otherwise make them look bad.

In the end, we conflict photographers and journalists are obliged to help each other out. I've made some very special friendships with colleagues over the years. As often happens with soldiers, coming under fire shoulder to shoulder with another person and surviving tends to solder a relationship that might otherwise come apart.

So, shortly after I was released, when asked by the French and US governments to help track down remaining hostages, I couldn't say no. It also gave me a concrete objective to work for and helped me process the experience I'd just come through.

I WAS APPROACHED by Fredrik Holm, a Swedish photographer trying to locate a couple of his countrymen, reporter Magnus Falkehed and photographer Niclas Hammarström, who had been captured in late

November 2013. We communicated via Skype and he asked if I could help him. I agreed.

Falkehed and Hammarström had been kidnapped in the same area as me, around Yabroud, most likely by the same unit. I got through to a Christian Syrian woman who took care of Mohammed Aboud's businesses in Canada, and put them in touch. The whole process was complicated by the fact that in Sweden it's the police who deal with hostage situations, which doesn't make much sense if the abduction takes place beyond their jurisdiction. (Similarly, neither I nor my father ever fully understood why the Americans used the FBI to follow my case rather than the State Department—although one can at least assume that the US federal police has a global reach.)

The woman agreed to get Aboud involved and act as go-between. I hadn't spoken directly to Aboud since he said goodbye to me at the Lebanese side of the border. Aboud said he was happy that I'd gotten back safely and he seemed willing to help. But after a week or so of back-and-forth through his representative, he eventually said no. Apparently, the reward he'd been expecting from the French and/or US governments— namely, to get himself and his businesses removed from the sanctions list on which he appeared in 2011, shortly after the Bashar regime had begun its crackdown—hadn't materialized yet, and he was bitter about the lack of gratitude. (This was in the late fall of 2013, but a year later, in November 2014, Aboud had been removed from the European Union's blacklist, only to be placed back on it in January 2015.)

For more than a month I was on Skype every morning, trying to connect with various people. I got in touch with Fares and other contacts on the ground who would be able to help the Swedes and French communicate with Essad (the French were involved because Falkehed was a resident of France and had family there). They wound up contacting him and sent people in from Lebanon. I don't know exactly how it came about logistically, but when Essad met these people he said, "I don't have any hostages. It's another group that has them. I can't help you." Of course, he was lying about everything. Everybody knew it. When they asked him, "What about Jonathan?" he said, "Oh, I didn't kidnap him. All we did was help him. We just kept him safe. And then we got him out." It was obvious he was full of shit, and the questioners just laughed at him.

Shortly after they were abducted, the Swedes tried to escape. Hammarström was shot in the leg as he ran away and they were caught again very quickly, brought back, and then beaten.

I went to Paris to meet Falkehed's wife and two daughters, who lived there. They were worried to the point of tears and I tried to reassure them.

In early January 2014 the two Swedes were released along with a rather opaque explanation of how they crossed the border—similar to mine. The people involved were no doubt concerned about drawing too much attention to just how fluid alliances in that part of Syria are.

Although I was very happy to help anyone, the experience left me with a slightly bitter aftertaste because I didn't get a single call from the journalists, even though I helped a lot. I'd just been released myself, and was already very raw emotionally. I took it upon myself to help them out and was harboring some hope for solidarity. In the end it only confirmed to me that, though there are those of us who feel connected by a sense of duty and respect to one another, all too many combat photographers and journalists tend to behave like mercenaries and have little sense of honor and loyalty.

I HAD A SOMEWHAT more edifying experience helping two Spanish journalists, photographer Ricardo Vilanova and Javier Espinoza, a correspondent for *El Mundo,* both of whom had been in Homs with Marie Colvin when she died. Ricardo was a friend of mine, a stand-up guy who was known for taking crazy risks, even by the standards of the profession. I met him on the Syrian border with Turkey in March 2012, the second time I went to Syria. The two of them were kidnapped in Raqqa in December 2013 and wound up hostages of ISIS, among the same group of twenty-three hostages that included the American James Foley and John Cantlie, the Brit who wound up making propaganda videos for ISIS. They were held there for about six months, under horrible conditions: tortured by Jihadi John and the other Beatles, as the four notoriously sadistic British-born jihadis were known.

The French secret service called me and asked if I could help. There wasn't much I could do, but I did know a man in France, a refugee living in Orléans who was from Raqqa. So I flew to Paris and I met with him. I also arranged for the secret service to meet with him. He didn't want to get paid and had very little money, but still he took his car all the way to Paris. They organized a meeting at a café, where he told them he had good contacts on the ground who would be able to locate what prison they were in. Eventually, through his contacts in Raqqa, he found out where they were. In return he wanted a French passport, but the French said they couldn't do it.

Since then Espinoza has said he doesn't want to cover any more wars. He's older, has kids, and he's seen his fair share of wars. But Vilanova got right back to work. Me and a few other colleagues put several thousand dollars together when he was released so he could buy some new equipment. Since then he's been to Libya, Yemen, and most recently to Iraq.

I understood both their positions. A part of me was finished with this thankless work. The romanticism and glory of a combat photographer has diminished significantly in the age of smartphones and digital photography. In addition, the type of wars going on today—with asymmetrical battles in which jihadis rely as much on propaganda as on military prowess—encourage visual terror, with beheadings of innocents broadcast over the Internet. Journalists make for tempting targets, especially since by definition they know people in the media, which amplifies the effect.

An ancillary issue is whether governments should pay ransoms for their citizens taken hostage. The United States and Great Britain are adamant about not paying ransoms or even negotiating with hostage takers. The United States went so far as to make it illegal for families of hostages to pay ransoms to terrorists, though they have since recognized the cruelty of such a law and now make allowances.

On the other hand, the French, Italian, Japanese, and other governments—although they refuse to admit it—are well known for paying out substantial sums of money for the return of their citizens. Of course, the hostage takers know this, and as a result they prefer to target citizens of spendthrift countries with deep pockets.

THIS BRINGS UP ANOTHER very relevant dilemma with respect to all the hostages still being held captive: should the family and friends go public or not?

From the beginning, my family felt it best to keep my situation out of the press. My father was advised by Robert Doueihy to keep a low profile and let him negotiate in the shark-infested waters of the Levantine hostage souk. French and US government officials concurred. At one point, when all hope seemed to be fading, my friend Aaron in New York suggested contacting a friend who worked for a broadcasting network, but my father forbade him. In another instance J. P. Pappis, the founder and president of Polaris Images, my photo agency, wanted to go public and my mother effectively threatened him. In fact, as soon as she got word of my abduction, my mother had the foresight to have Aaron, who was very tech savvy, erase as much as he could of my online profile.

Her concerns were justified later when James Foley's family went public and the news that his brother was an officer in the US Air Force became known to his ISIS captors.

As I've explained, as soon as I was released, I was asked to appear on TV shows and do interviews for magazines. On the one hand, this offered me a vehicle for telling my story and, let's face it, raised my quota professionally. (It's absurd how surviving capture and torture adds to your credibility, but that's how it works.) On the other hand, I had very strange people coming out of the woodwork to get a hold of me.

One particularly unpleasant experience involved an American photojournalist who had also been held captive in Syria. He lived on the east coast of the United States and contacted me. He seemed like a decent enough guy, but there was something unhinged about him— which was no surprise. He had found out that the US government had given me about ten thousand dollars to help me buy the equipment I'd lost. This had happened mostly thanks to the good graces of the FBI officers who were handling my case.

This photojournalist, however, was very outspoken and had begun to do the speaker circuit, often criticizing the US government for its policies. He was also hounding me to help him get money from the feds. I politely tried to keep him at a safe distance, but the more aloof I was the more belligerent he became, calling me names like "the Four-Hundred-Fifty-Thousand-Dollar Man," sending me pictures of terrorist beheadings, and eventually threatening me with "I'm gonna kick your ass" or "I'm gonna kill you."

Rather than deal with this whacko one-on-one, which would have been a lose-lose situation, I just referred it to the FBI officers, and they said he'd been threatening them, too, accusing them of having stolen money from him. Finally the district attorney called me in for questions so they could build a case against him.

For a while, though, I was looking over my shoulder. Then somehow the wind was taken out of his sails and it all seemed to die down.

ANOTHER AFTEREFFECT of my captivity was that I was suddenly considered a Syria expert and my opinion was requested by other journalists. I appeared on CNN with Anderson Cooper and Christiane Amanpour. I also appeared on Fox News's *Hannity*, though Sean Hannity was sick or on vacation that day. It was late August, shortly after the Syrian government was accused of launching sarin gas missiles into the Ghouta district of Damascus. In order to punish the Syrian government, Obama was preparing to bomb the Bashar regime—but was hoping to avoid it by first asking for congressional approval, and then cutting a deal with Russian president Vladimir Putin to pressure Bashar to eliminate his chemical weapons.

On that episode of *Hannity* I said flat-out that I suspected the opposition rebels of using chemical weapons, that the Ghouta episode may have been a false flag operation. I'd heard such rumors even before I was captured; United Nations representative Carla Del Ponte had already raised such suspicions in March of that year.

In various other interviews I basically said what I'd always thought: that the Bashar regime, despite its brutality, was the only thing keeping Syria from disintegrating into chaos that both fed and was fed by radical Islam. No matter how much aid the rebels got from the West, they would only become further radicalized, and this would spell disaster for a heterogeneous society like Syria, especially for the Alawite and Christian minorities. Essentially it was a choice between two evils, and Bashar's secular Baathists were the lesser evil. The alternative was either a long, drawn-out civil war if Bashar's troops managed to hold out, or widespread massacres of Alawites and Christians at the hands of Sunni radicals if Bashar was defeated.

After these public appearances a number of my colleagues reproached me, calling me a traitor (though what cause I was betraying, they couldn't say). The progressives and lefties who constituted the majority in the US and French media still believed that a neoliberal democracy with respect for human rights was a viable alternative for areas of the world that not only had no democratic tradition, but were advocating a return to a tradition that was antithetical to democracy as we knew it in the West.

I had nothing against the opposition rebels, even though they were my captors. I always respected their struggle and understood it. But I also always knew that the fall of the Bashar regime would inevitably lead to the rise of ISIS or something similar, and to the persecution of Shiites and Christians. It was basic realism I was expressing.

But realism isn't always the goal of journalists covering wars. The agenda of many combat photographers is either ideological (an attempt to save the world by bringing to light the suffering of war's victims) or aesthetic (getting that perfect combination of composition and content so that a specific moment in history is captured in iconic form). I admit to being guilty of both to some degree. Ideologically I have no pretensions about saving the world or making it a better place, but I would definitely like to see European and Western culture survive, if not prevail. And aesthetically, I'd like those who encounter my work to see history unfold at least partially through my eyes.

So the more I thought about it after my release, the more I was itching to hone my vision again.

LOSERS

HISTORY IS WRITTEN BY THE WINNERS: it's a tired and easily forgotten truism. But what about the losers? How does a nation or civilization that has been either swept away, devastated, or simply marginalized by the waves of history come to terms with a narrative that presents an existential threat to its identity? How does a nation come to terms with the evil it has perpetrated?

There's no easy answer to these questions because historical events are rarely so black-and-white as to even remotely allow for a good-guy/bad-guy dichotomy. That only happens in Hollywood, crap novels, and high school history books. The deeper you go into the minutiae of trying to figure out the infinitely complex fabric of what exactly happened in the past, the more you get tangled in a universe of loose threads.

A few months after I'd returned from Syria I was invited to Minneapolis by the city's Oromo diaspora community to take part in a conference. As one of the few photojournalists who had ever bothered to chronicle their plight I was held in high regard. They opened themselves up to me, invited me into their homes, and thanked me for helping their identity become known beyond their little community.

The Oromo were a perfect example of a group that had been marginalized by history. When I first set out to follow them through the savanna of southern Ethiopia, only a handful of my colleagues (in theory people who should be well acquainted with history, politics and geography) had even heard of them. Since the Oromo Liberation Front is outlawed and considered a terrorist organization by the Ethiopian government, and the Ethiopian government is friendly with the United States government, there is little sympathy for the OLF in Washington.

But like so many small nations struggling against oblivion in the age of globalization, the Oromo do everything they can to keep their narrative alive. My photos of the Oromo Liberation Army were very important to them, and they went out of their way to show their gratitude. Despite their graciousness, or perhaps because of it, I felt a tinge of sadness for these people because I sensed how much they feared having their identity erased from the "book of life" that history is supposed to offer us. This is almost impossible to imagine for an American or Frenchman, whose historical narrative is still in flower. But the Oromo seriously risk becoming like the Dacians or Vandals or Sarmatians or any number of now-nameless nations who mingle inseparably with the rubble and dust of history.

In our age of nuclear superpowers, massive campaigns to conquer territory or subjugate other nations are rare (the US-led invasion of Iraq being a notable exception). Usually the nations who take up arms are already, in a sense, losers. That's why they fight to begin with. They've already been either subjugated or oppressed or forced to assimilate, and they've taken up arms to forestall what is perceived as imminent annihilation.

These are the fighters that fascinate me most. And over the years I've come to appreciate the notion of loss and sacrifice that such soldiers embody. Progressive liberal culture in the United States and Europe often tends to disparage as foolish the ideas of honor, duty and national pride that drive men and women to fight, but that's only because they can afford to be dismissive: other fools in the not-too-distant past have fought and died so they can be comfortably smug in their positions of power.

MY ATTRACTION TO LOSERS grew in the course of a project I started in 2003: photographing World War II veterans. I was based in Santa Barbara, California, where I'd moved after graduating from the University of Chicago. I'd just started working professionally as a photojournalist two years earlier. I had an old Rollei Rolleicord 1956 medium format camera—a real antique. While in Santa Barbara I got to know some World War II vets and took very classic portraits of them. By then, of course, they were old men and it wasn't always easy to imagine them storming a beachhead or jumping out of a plane. But I had them pose in their rooms, or wherever they felt comfortable. Some of them brought out memorabilia from their war years: medals, photos, uniforms, flags.

Originally it was just something to do, but I quickly grew enthusiastic about the project because these men had incredible stories and we all knew their time on earth was running out. In California I pretty much only had access to American or Canadian vets, and I wanted to get the stories of other nationalities. So I started reaching out to French and Belgians who had fought in the war.

Inevitably, as the scope of the project grew, I felt I had to get the Axis point of view. Then the idea of a book came about, with interviews and photographs. Covering both sides was much more interesting—at least for me. Around 2006 and 2007 I started traveling all around the world, particularly to central Europe and Japan, in order to find Axis veterans.

Compared to Allied veterans, meeting the Germans was much harder, especially those who had fought with the Waffen SS, an elite corps of troops who were not fully integrated into the Wehrmacht or Luftwaffe. When the Germans began losing the war, the Waffen SS was opened to non-Germans, so many Norwegians, Belgians, Finns, Yugoslavs, Ukrainians, and even French and Americans fought in SS divisions. It was always more of a prize for me to find Waffen SS men, because they were the elite corps of one of the most formidable armies ever put together. And the interviews were always fascinating because these troops had been repeatedly thrown into the most difficult situations and most intense battles.

Most of them were fiercely proud of their service to their country. But the fact that Germany was so tarnished by Nazi ideology—with its anti-Semitism and the attempted genocide—forced them to keep their pride quiet, expressing it only to those they felt would understand the complexity of the circumstances. So when they opened up to me, I took it as affirmation that all those years of studying history had trained me to grasp the nuances that rarely come through in films and books.

ONE VETERAN IN PARTICULAR, Ernst Gottstein, left an impression. He was a short, compact man, about five feet four, who participated in many of the most crucial battles that the Wehrmacht had to fight.

Gottstein (God-stone in German) was an ethnic German born in 1922 in the Sudetenland, the swath of Czechoslovakian territory that Hitler invaded and annexed in 1938 under the pretext that it was majority German. As a German, unsurprisingly, Gottstein supported the annexation. His father was in charge of storage facilities for the farmers in the region, and they owned their own farmland. He graduated in 1941, volunteered for the German Wehrmacht, and decided to join a tank outfit. He trained for six months on armored cars, from March 1941 to September of the same year. After his training he was transferred as a first-class private into the Third Infantry Division and was part of a reconnaissance unit, which used armored cars and sidecars as well. The Third Division was already on the Russian front; so, ten days after the end of his training he moved eastward by railroad, then had to walk about sixty miles to Vitebsk, in what's now northeastern

Belarus. As soon as he arrived at the front he started fighting. While driving to the front with the sidecar, he and his comrades were ordered to stop and unload their weapons. At that moment a comrade from the same training school was hit in the head by a sniper. It was his first moment facing death. He wanted to get revenge on the Soviets who had just killed his friend, so he strafed the enemy position in anger with an MG 42 machine gun.

He continued fighting with the division in Smolensk, where he saw heavy action in the neighboring countryside. The division got as close as twelve miles to the capital district of Moscow. He spent the entire winter there, enduring the subzero conditions. The Germans hadn't anticipated fighting through the winter, so they didn't have the proper clothes. When the temperature got down to minus 41 degrees, vehicles froze up in the cold and wouldn't start unless a fire was built under the motor. On top of that, there were constant Soviet counterattacks in November and December 1941. Mass infantry assaults came their way, and with only a few tanks they had to defend their positions with knives or shovels since they were usually running out of ammunition. During that time Gottstein was also used as a courier for neighboring divisions.

In November 1941, he was promoted to *unteroffizier*, and in early 1942 he fought a Soviet unit mixed with partisans along the porous front. In April 1942 he was wounded in the shoulder on the Russian front about two hundred miles west of Moscow when an artillery shell burst near him. He was sent by railroad to Germany; about 20 percent of the wounded soldiers in the train died. At each stop soldiers who had just died would be dragged out of the wagons. Gottstein finally arrived in Vienna to be treated. It was a beautiful spring day, which he considered the best day of his life.

At the beginning of the war he was very motivated and, like most Wehrmacht soldiers, very confident about Germany's final victory. When he returned to Austria, though, that confidence was gone. He felt like an old man.

He didn't want to return to Russia, or anywhere near the eastern front, where what at first had looked like a rout was by that time turning into a very hard slog. He found out that the German army needed troops for Africa, so he volunteered for the Afrika Korps. He went through a physical to make sure he was in good shape for the difficult desert conditions and went through further training in Berlin. In July he was transported to Greece by train, then took a plane in August 1942 to Derna, in what's now eastern Libya, sixty miles west of El Alamein. He fought in El Alamein in an armored car platoon unit as part of the Third Panzer Division, a recon unit, the only such unit in Africa, since the rest had been sent to the Russian front. He was under the direct command of the legendary field marshal Erwin Rommel.

By late August 1942, he saw heavy combat. After the defeat of El Alamein he participated in the entire retreat until they reached Tunisia. He told me that he still remembered the differences in climate between Russia and the North African desert. He also gave me his impressions regarding the difference between Soviet soldiers and British soldiers. Soviet officers didn't seem to care about their soldiers much, he said. The British soldiers were more independent and better taken care of. The Brits were also more conventional, sporty, and fair, while the Russians would disregard conventions and even fight at night. During his first Christmas in Russia there was fighting, whereas in North Africa the war was put on pause for the holiday.

He described to me an incident in Cyrenaica, a region of Libya: One night they were hiding in a wadi to keep cool and it started raining hard. The wadi overflowed and four soldiers died. He only managed to survive because his tank was at a slightly higher elevation.

The old man still had a sense of humor. He described to me how in Tunisia he'd fought against the British Eighth Army. During the battle for Tunisia, as they retreated, they would often be strafed by British aircraft. One time all the soldiers started running to the side of the road and dove for cover, but there was no plane; the panic had started because one German soldier needed to go to the bathroom and the others followed suit.

While defending Tunis from the British in May 1943, Gottstein was wounded on the right side of his belly when an artillery shell landed nearby—a flesh wound. He was sent by plane to Sicily, from where he took another plane to Berlin. There he was treated for his wound, after which he went to Denmark for a few weeks. After further training at an officer academy for three months he was promoted to lieutenant.

He had the choice of unit, so he chose one in Vienna. Then he got his orders to go with the Second Panzer Division, based in the Pripet Marches of Belarus—a one-way ticket to the front. He was promoted to company commander of armored cars. He fought for two months, and by late summer the tank division was sent to northern France to be refitted and to prepare for the imminent Allied invasion.

They were based in Cambrai, where they got new equipment. In June 1944, with everyone expecting the invasion at any moment, his unit was put on alarm, but they didn't get any orders. On the sixth they heard that a large contingent of Allied troops had just landed, and only then did they realize that this was the main invasion force. On the seventh they got an order at night, but it was too late. They had to go through Paris to reach the front lines in Normandy, and as they got closer to the front, they were subjected to more and more attacks from Allied fighter bombers, so they got an order that small units had to go alone to reach the front at a special location.

They finally got to the front on June 10. Gottstein saw heavy action in Avranches against American troops; he was under constant bombardment from artillery and aircraft. "I've never seen so much firepower," he said.

He recounted how lucky he was when, after placing his unit near a bocage to ambush Allied troops, they were bombed heavily by a barrage from ship artillery. The bocages in front of them and behind them were completely destroyed, whereas the barrage had missed their line completely. Soon afterward they captured American maps and he saw that the line his men were holding was not on the map. The oversight saved their lives.

During the last days of the battle at the Falaise Pocket, his unit got lucky because it was based on the division's perimeter; he was driving with his men and the Americans closed the pocket soon after. Then suddenly a small convoy was coming toward him—Americans. He kept driving and as he passed by threw a grenade into a halftrack, which blew up because it contained an ammo crate. He managed to escape because the Americans were in shock. By the end of the battle he had only 25 percent of his men left. He arrived at the Seine but all of the bridges had been destroyed.

With the reorganization of the German forces, he saw heavy action on the Siegfried Line to defend Germany. Allied aircraft often bombed them. No activity was possible during the day. He also fought in the Ardennes Offensive with the same division in December 1944 and saw heavy action in Bastogne against American troops. His units were in the farthest point of the offensive between Marche and Dinan.

At one point he got the special order near Rochefort to go through a forest to a restaurant near a crossroad. He went inside to ask for directions because he'd heard a lot of noise. When he opened the door he saw the restaurant filled with American soldiers, so he pointed his machine gun. Some of them fled; three American officers who were studying a map were taken prisoner. The map they'd captured was very important.

Despite such an exploit, he didn't get the Iron Cross, because instead of carrying on further in the offensive (which could have been accomplished by shooting the prisoners and moving on), the units waited half a day, wasting too much time. His commanding officer did all he could to ensure that instead of a medal he got a court-martial. Fortunately one of his friends saved him by lying and saying that he was not in the area during that time. Eventually they ran out of fuel and walked back to the division.

After the failed offensive Gottstein fought in Prague. By late January 1945 his unit had only three officers left. After a two-week leave he was sent to the village of Oberlauringen, near Schweinfurt; defending this village was his last operation. American tanks and soldiers closed in on him. Gottstein's unit shot at the tanks, killing some of the soldiers, but there was a wall behind him and he was wounded by his own weapon's backblast. He was then taken prisoner by American troops, who treated him, and that was the end of his extremely eventful war.

All wars and violent insurrections have their share of horrors, but compared to the two world wars of the twentieth century, today's conflicts seem like brushfires. Gottstein fought in almost every major campaign of Germany's epic defeat. But he fought for the losing side, and any heroism his fight may have entailed will always come with an asterisk for the average Joe fed on Hollywood films full of Nazi villains.

AS I WAS GATHERING material for a book, I'd accumulated enough for a one-man show in a SoHo gallery. My portraits were well received, but I caught a lot of flak for including photos of Waffen SS veterans.

"Don't you have ethical problems glorifying Nazis?" I was asked.

"I don't think I'm glorifying them," I responded. "And I'm not sure these people were Nazis. In any case, that's irrelevant. They all fought in the same war, each for their own reasons. I wanted to get both sides."

I was accused of hiding behind objectivity.

"You give them the same degree of honor," another person said.

"Well, I give them all a minimum of honor in this project. They all fought, they all risked their lives, and they've all survived to this day. I'm out to honor at least that—survival. I don't know enough about them to judge them. And even if I did, it's not so clear-cut."

I tried not to pursue the polemic, but such criticisms made me realize how little people really knew about World War II. The Waffen SS veterans were elite troops; the foreigners who joined them were usually fighting for their own nation. They believed, rightly or wrongly, that communism was the greater evil. Someone like Gottstein, on the other hand, was simply a patriotic German. All of them must have witnessed horrors, and many, I assume, have had to reconcile themselves with their own conscience.

My project was primarily meant to extol survival—like taking photos of people who've been pulled out from the rubble of a collapsed building during an earthquake. Some survivors just happened to be nearer to the fault line. They were born male and in a year that required their entire generation to be mobilized for a struggle presented to them as good versus evil. And the ones I find most interesting are those who fought valiantly and lost, then had to spend the rest of their lives reassessing the notions of good and evil according to which they fought.

Such views weren't very appreciated among the press community. Many journalists consider themselves champions of justice and truth—which is why they feel they're required to plumb the depths of injustice and bullshit. I recognize that there must be some absolute truth and justice out there, but it would be presumptuous of me to try to advocate for it through my pictures.

As far as I'm concerned, discrete events happen in the ebb and flow of history, and I try to record them. I often choose to portray soldiers because they embody ideas of honor and valor that have lost much of their meaning in our society. At a minimum, I'm looking for the faces that reflect those notions—much like looking for artifacts in a living, breathing archeological site.

PLAN B

My father would casually insert that question into a conversation consisting mainly of anecdotes about what we'd seen and done since the last time we were together.

"I'm not sure" or something equally vague was usually my response.

My father is a very reasonable man. He assesses situations and goals, then determines how to achieve a desired goal with the given resources. And he's honed his intuition and skill over the course of a decades-long career in recruitment. It's inevitable that a professional headhunter will try to find a perfect slot for his son.

I was thirty-four years old. Many of my friends had already veered down the path of marriage and children. Yann, with whom I'd attended the Lycée Français in New York, had settled in Paris, where he'd landed a steady job with a French government energy utility, using his preternatural math skills to come up with pricing strategies. He was now married, with a kid on the way. Aaron was also settling down with a beautiful girlfriend, and they wanted to build a family. He was in the planning stages of launching an IT business and was looking to buy an apartment in Manhattan.

The other direction for me could be to just slip off the grid, like my friend David, who disappeared after I moved to New York. I couldn't trace him the few times I tried, and I assumed his violence had gotten him killed or institutionalized. Given my own fatal attraction I wondered if that was an ineluctable fate for me as well.

I hadn't been in a long-term relationship since Tara, the woman who had met me at the airport and with whom I've remained dear friends. She was a bit older than I was, with a young boy from a previous relationship, and as I mentioned earlier, she wanted to have a child with me. But I simply wasn't ready to have children. Also, I didn't feel I could commit to any kind of stable situation as long as I constantly kept a bag packed in my closet while I scoured the Internet for conflicts to shoot. No matter who I was with, I was always itching to get on a plane and leave Manhattan behind, with all its hipsters, fashionistas, rooftop club denizens, and success addicts.

I went about my business. Helping other hostages helped me adjust. I was invited to conferences. The US government asked me to attend seminars meant to prepare State Department workers for situations in which they might be abducted and held for ransom—like during the Iranian hostage crisis. I did some fashion shoots, made appearances on TV. Speaking in public came easy to me.

"You can't keep working freelance much longer. You need to start considering a plan B," my father said. "Why don't you teach?"

I always gave my father's suggestions their due consideration. They were reasonable, pragmatic. And he's a wise man.

At times he would relay a message from his old friend Gerard, a larger-than-life character I'd always admired. He'd led a regiment during the Algerian War, which kept France busy in the late 1950s up until 1962. When I was released he said, "Good. I hope he learned his lesson and never goes back. I know that part of the world and I know war. There's nothing you can say or show that we don't already know. Human beings will never change."

I continued making contacts in the world of photography and journalism. People became interested in making a film of my experience. I was alive, healthy, free.

All the same, I'd get off my motorcycle as I went from appointment to appointment in Manhattan, park it in some illegal spot, taking off the license plate so the meter maids couldn't track the bike to my name, slip off my helmet, and simply zone out as I went to where I needed to be. I'd find myself in the middle of some small talk at a social event and images of destruction would pop up in front of me as I spoke, truncating the conversation in midsentence. I listened to people explaining potential projects. I pitched a host of stories I was only half-interested in shooting. And all the while my mind was in some space between the captivity of the dark room in Syria, wondering if I'd get beaten or torn to pieces by a mortar, and that near-palpable glory beaming out of young soldiers' eyes before the grind of war numbed them to the myths that had incited them to take up a weapon.

"You need a plan B," my father said.

But most plan Bs looked very unappetizing—like a hot breakfast that's been sitting on the table for hours. I couldn't see myself in any kind of office situation where I had to show up every day and follow a protocol that was tantamount to being handcuffed to a bedpost by the window. It struck me that that was how most people lived—and *wanted* to live—chained to a comfortable bed with decent company, next to a window from which they could watch the drama of the world unfold. I still needed to break out and plunge into that drama. I'd been spoiled by the chance to make a living doing this work straight out of college, and now certain situations were hard to accept. Maybe if I found the right woman, settled down, had children. Many conflict reporters and photographers give up the edgier aspects of their trade with the arrival of kids. But I wasn't there yet. That edge still beckoned. Something was still roiling inside me and I suspected it was connected to a wave of history poised to come crashing down. Whatever it was, it was keeping me from committing to anything that didn't feed that sense of imminent peril I'd developed antennas for.

MY MOTHER WAS LESS DIPLOMATIC, more brutal with her advice. "You're crazy if you want to go back. An idiot." I didn't even have to tell her. She could often sense what was churning inside me before even I was fully aware of it.

She came to New York and stayed with me for about six weeks. She'd helped me find the one-bedroom apartment I was living in. But if I ever intended to settle into a *bobo* existence (French slang for "bourgeois-bohemian"), I'd need more space. I started thinking about selling the apartment and finding something bigger for the same price, farther uptown in Harlem, or even the Bronx.

My mother had a knack for entering unknown territory and sussing the ins and outs immediately. She'd spent her youth on the road, traveling through Asia and the Americas. One time she had even cropped her hair short and traveled through Anatolian Turkey as a man.

If from my father I inherited a pragmatic analytical side, my mother passed on to me an uncontainable passion for life and adventure. So it was a bit contradictory that she was telling me to stop chasing wars. If anyone understood the rush I felt, it was her.

She liked to kid me about how lazy I was as a baby. I didn't walk until I was about eighteen months. "You just reached up with your arms waiting for someone to pick you up . . . And just like now you wouldn't listen to anyone. You were deaf then, and you still pretend to be deaf."

It was true. I was almost totally deaf as a child. The teachers in nursery school noticed I didn't interact with the others. I just sat in the corner and drew pictures. They called in my mother to tell her, and she said, "Maybe he's deaf?" Sure enough, my parents took me to the doctor and I was deaf. I had to have four operations over the course of the years. Now I can hear almost perfectly—although a few times when I was too close to an RPG going off, I had a ringing in my ears for weeks and my hearing got damaged.

EVEN THOUGH MY MOTHER told me I was crazy to go back and my father tried to corral me with reason into a safer career, they both understood my compulsion. Each of my parents in his or her own way enjoyed the thrill of taking calculated risks that required a certain amount of skill and savvy. My mother traveled solo to places most women would avoid altogether, and she was fearless in confrontations with anyone that crossed her. My father, too, liked to push himself in certain areas. When he was younger he would often have to drive from Brussels to Paris, office to office, as fast as he could in his BMW. This was in the days before accurate photo controls for speeding, which are now ubiquitous on European highways. He and his friends would compete to see who was fastest. My father managed the two-hundred-mile trip in two hours and three minutes. Only his business partner managed a faster time with one hour and fifty-seven minutes.

For sure there was a deep strain of risk-taking embedded in my DNA. But on a more superficial level, I can't deny that was I still caught up in the mystique of the combat photographer, the romanticism. There's an element of freedom that inevitably forces you to push your limits and confront your fears. You have to be both quick and cool, right in the middle of things and totally invisible. You move through a theater in which the laws of society are upended or annulled altogether, and you need to figure out what the code of behavior is in any given context and adapt your own code to it instantly.

I grew up with images of Steve McQueen in *The Great Escape* fleeing from the Germans toward Switzerland and finishing with that classic-yet-futile motorcycle jump. The combat photographer has a lot in common with someone who rides a motorcycle. There's a willingness to be exposed to danger, and the sense of freedom involved in reaching a destination—or just riding for the sake of it—often becomes an end in itself.

Combining the two—riding a bike through the world's no-go zones—seemed to me the ultimate adrenaline rush. I had images of Sean Flynn (the actor Errol Flynn's son) and Dana Stone riding their motorbikes into Cambodia just before they vanished forever in 1970.

So even though there are always nobler reasons for living the life of the combat photographer—like showing the world ignored pockets of injustice or chronicling history for posterity—you can't deny the simple fact that it's cool. Never have I felt so alive and free and grateful and in touch with the cosmic forces jostling for power as when I've been photographing soldiers fighting for their lives and those of their compatriots. And I know most of my colleagues feel the same.

SO AS I READJUSTED to my previous life in New York, I kept one eye glued to the news. While I was being held captive in Syria, Egypt's democratically elected Muslim Brotherhood government, led by Mohamed Morsi, was overthrown by popular protests that led to a military coup. Now a new general, Abdel Fattah el-Sisi, was playing pharaoh—and he was determined to root out any opposition. Two years of turmoil since the Egyptian revolution had been enough.

Obviously the Muslim Brotherhood was not happy about its brief and incompetent rule getting cut short, so they tried to protest. They set up camps in squares all over the country, hoping to ignite another uprising like Tahrir Square. The biggest one was in Cairo's Rabaa al-Adawiya Square. But Sisi would have none of it. On August 14, 2013, after half-hearted negotiations failed, Sisi sent the military into the camps, where an estimated six hundred to a thousand protesters were killed in what's come to be known as the Rabaa Massacre.

In November of the same year, protests started in Ukraine after their corrupt president backed out of an association agreement with the European Union. Tens of thousands of people gathered in Kyiv's Independence Square, known as the Maidan.

Something was brewing. Something's always brewing somewhere in the world: oppression, discontent, revolt, basic bloodlust.

As I've noted before, my mother named me after Jonathan Harker, the character in Bram Stoker's *Dracula* who travels to Transylvania and meets the fearsome count determined to wreak havoc throughout England. Harker has no pretensions of being a hero, but in the end he is instrumental in killing the vampire who is the embodiment in human form of all that is evil.

Today's real vampires, in my limited experience, are fat warlords and clerics commanding God-addled kids who wield Kalashnikovs and RPGs, convincing them to don explosive vests with promises of heaven. The warlords feed off these boys' blood and the light beaming from their eyes as they all get drunk on mere motes of Allah's omnipotence.

Usually there's no visible Dracula out there to zero in on. At most some camouflaged movement behind buildings or trees, or a human form imagined as the source of a whistling mortar, a helicopter rotor's high-speed throb in the distance, a plane shrieking by to blast out your little rabbit warren. Still, we all need to personify evil and exalt our devils. And the real personification starts inside each of us—in the first nervous twitch, in the frustration that comes of self-righteous indignation left unrectified.

In our struggle with evil we deal less with vampire fangs than with absence—a vast free-floating void, which our nature abhors even as we are secretly sucked into it. You really feel it when things are calm in a war situation. You see it in the soldiers' various tics, their commanders' anxious laughter. It hums beneath the calm as pure potentiality. A compulsion to act, defend—in short, to kill—that is almost palpable.

By most ethical standards that compulsion to act is evil. But it's a very attractive evil. There's also a more banal evil born of absence— when nobody acts, nobody says this is not right, not good. This type of evil is often confused with ignorance or stupidity—and too often justified as tolerance.

I keep wondering how long I can sit back and observe so much human folly without acting. My worst times in captivity were when I felt powerless. Now that I was free, the prospect of inaction, like nothing else, carried me back to that sense of impotence.

THE SIREN CALL OF VIOLENCE

YOU FOLLOW THE NEWS. You know something is happening in some far-flung place, an event or upheaval that could alter the tide of history—or at least your blindered vision of it—and you wish you were there. You come from a society in which the only thing people still hold sacred is the right to have fun, to be entertained. Our only value is to have the means—usually money or fame—required to obtain the consumer goods and services that will enable such fun. All other rights are negotiable, contingent on the freedom to amuse ourselves.

Those who would destroy our society hold an angry idol sacred. And as things stand now, they will defeat us because they are willing to die for their idol. We won't die *for* fun—only *of* it.

FOR SEVERAL MONTHS AFTER I was released, I watched videos of combat from Syria almost every day. I'd watch the rebels open fire with their AK-47s and RPGs, screaming *"Allahu Akbar,"* and I could practically smell the gunpowder wafting through my well-lit uptown apartment. I kept following the rapid rise of Daesh, or ISIS as it's called in the Anglo world (I don't like calling them by the name of a goddess). I knew something like that would happen. Even the rebels who had kidnapped me, who were ostensibly moderate, were becoming more radicalized by the day. Before the uprising many of them were clean-shaven and drank alcohol, veterans of Bashar's army or police force, or simple students looking to get a foothold in an increasingly globalized world. By the time this war is over, many of those still alive will probably make Osama bin Laden look like a libertine.

A few of my closest friends kept asking if I was okay, if I needed help. I was zoning out a lot, losing the train of conversations as my thoughts kept wandering back to the images I'd been watching on my computer, which brought me back to the images I'd been trying to capture for years.

But I needed to watch those videos. I needed the adrenaline I'd had there when everything I did was a matter of life and death, from the way I cut a tomato to how I took a shower and shit.

Oddly enough, even though I'd just been as close to hell as most humans ever get, I missed it. I'd sit at my desk in the evenings after having spent the day Skyping with others involved in some hostage situation and I'd surf back and forth from combat videos to the news. Arab Spring gone awry. Democracy in Iraq a bloody farce. Waves of migrants capsizing in the Mediterranean, washing up on Europe's shores. I'd play with a pen as I watched the images and doodle shapes that reminded me of the maps I'd chip out from the peeling paint in the Light House, conquering the world in my mind while I was cuffed to the bed. Everywhere I went I'd see those shapes: half-torn posters in the subway, the last bits of guacamole in a bowl at a taco joint, even in a piece of skin scraped off from a spill on my motorbike. That's what happens: you start to miss some of your captors. They even have a name for it, a "syndrome," the Stockholm syndrome. Those guys were in my life almost every minute, 24/7 for eighty-one days. I missed Mej, Fares and Noor. Crazy as it sounds, I even missed Abu Talal, even though I hated him. You spend so much time with them in a state of heightened awareness, and suddenly they're not there anymore. You even start to miss your very captivity.

EGYPT IN THE ARAB WINTER

DURING THE TIME I was a hostage I made a lot of promises, vows: *Oh, if I ever get out I'll never be a war photographer again, I'll become a sort of peacenik, a better person, more patient, less judgmental, more forgiving, patch things up with that cousin I fell out with, help the infirm and crippled cross the street . . .* These vows took on religious overtones. Vows that might help me get out alive, be reborn.

I actually fulfilled many of the vows. But as for changing jobs, it wasn't that easy.

My first forays back into journalism came in collaboration with a writer, Dorothée Moisan, who had interviewed me for a book she was writing on political abductions for ransom. She was very smart and hardworking. When I went to Minneapolis, she came along and we did an article about the Somali community there and how terrorist elements find fertile ground for recruitment in various Muslim diasporas.

Later, toward the end of January 2014, Dorothée and I went to Egypt for *Paris Match* to cover the third anniversary of the revolution, which fell on the twenty-fifth; we also hoped to do a human interest story about children living in the streets. Egypt was a good place for me to get back in the saddle. It wasn't a war zone like Syria, but it was very volatile and could blow up from one minute to the next. Despite Sisi's crackdown and arrests, the Muslim Brotherhood still had strong popular support, and those with any connection to the thousands arrested were even more supportive. It was a complex place domestically and a crucial piece in the Middle East geopolitical puzzle.

We first explored the Coptic Christian community in Old Cairo. There were very few Westerners in that part of the city, and we were already drawing attention to ourselves. After three years of turmoil, Western powers, especially the United States, were blamed for everything by all sides. The secularists blamed Obama for throwing their longtime president and ally, Hosni Mubarak, under the bus during the protests and for supporting the Morsi government when it was elected; the Islamists blamed America for undermining their legitimacy by blackmailing Morsi into continued support for peace with Israel. It was typical of the whole Arab world after the collapse of the Ottoman Empire. The knee-jerk reaction to anything that didn't work was to blame it on outsiders: Western colonialism, Zionists, communists, capitalists. The only ones who actually seemed to be addressing the real problem of radical jihadis were the dictators, who preferred to crush opposition quietly rather than advertise a growing problem and thereby exacerbate it.

The day before the anniversary of the revolution was a Friday, the day of the week when Muslims gather at their mosques and the imams give sermons intended to rouse the faithful to action. We were woken up by a powerful explosion. Our hotel room was on the fifteenth floor. We went out onto the balcony and saw a plume of black smoke about five hundred yards away as the crow flies. I grabbed my camera and started shooting.

We jumped into a taxi immediately and went to the site of the explosion: the headquarters of the Cairo police. There was a corpse at our feet, wounded scattered around, ambulances, firemen, soldiers. Normally I wouldn't have hesitated to pull out my camera and start taking pictures, but right away I sensed the atmosphere was electric and the Egyptians were already giving us wary looks.

Dorothée didn't dare film anything except for a few brief videos with her smartphone, as did many of the onlookers. Interviewing the Egyptians on-site was impossible. I managed to steal a few images without being noticed but couldn't get to the crater. They wouldn't let journalists anywhere near the explosion, so we pretended to move around like a couple of tourists who had wound up there by accident. At one point, a woman a few feet away from us started shouting. Dorothée was fluent enough in Arabic to understand that the woman was accusing Americans of every evil imaginable.

We decided it was time to slip away. A few minutes later, three German journalists working for ARD television were attacked by the crowd. Two of them were stabbed and wound up with serious injuries.

If it hadn't been for an undercover police officer who fired his weapon into the air, they might have gotten torn apart by the crowd.

Three other explosions rocked Cairo shortly after that one. They were claimed by a jihadist group based in the Sinai, which would later declare allegiance to Daesh.

Rather than try to get to the explosion sites and be kept away, we went to the Mohandessin neighborhood, near a bridge where every Friday the Muslim Brotherhood had been clashing with police. Tanks, rifles, tear gas launchers, and a lot of heavy weapons all came out in preparation for the worst. Everyone was extremely nervous.

During that time, we heard sporadic gunfire from the other side of the bridge, where the Muslim Brothers were supposed to be demonstrating. We asked some Egyptian journalists why they hadn't tried to cover the conflict from the Islamist side, and they said they used to, but then stopped because they would be systematically attacked with knives and stripped of their equipment.

Suddenly a minibus drove through the crowd and hit one of the officers on the bridge, adding to the confusion and raising the tension. Dozens of people started to gather and police responded with tear gas. Everyone ran away, and following the advice of our Egyptian colleagues we ran with them. Then a young Egyptian took me and Dorothée and pushed us into a taxi, saying the street might suddenly turn against us.

The following day, January 25, was the third anniversary of the revolution that led to Mubarak's fall. All our Egyptian contacts were telling us to lie low and stay away from crowds celebrating. At midday, we decided to try our luck at Tahrir Square, which was like a fortress surrounded by soldiers. We passed through the identity check and pretended to be tourists. I had taken care to bring a discreet backpack that didn't make me look all kitted out like most photographers.

The square wasn't that crowded yet, so we took the opportunity to shoot some pictures, schmooze with a few people, shake hands, and let them ham it up in front of the camera. But as soon as we felt we were being observed by an undercover police officer we bailed out.

Later that afternoon, we decided to cover a demonstration organized by the Third Square movement—youth advocating a third way, opposed to both the Islamists and the military, who feel the need to continue the initial Tahrir Square protests that had brought down Mubarak. I took pictures freely there. As the demonstrators were trying to reach Tahrir Square, they were immediately chased away by the police, who caught them in a pincer, firing tear gas at the rear and causing panic.

Up ahead a police van barreled full steam into the crowd and let loose with more tear gas. The demonstrators dispersed in all directions and I ran away with Dorothée, trying to protect her from getting stampeded. We finally followed a group into an alleyway and escaped between the buildings. Later we heard that one of the protesters had been killed by police at that spot.

After returning to the hotel to send the photos, we went back out into the streets and came by chance upon a new skirmish between Sisi supporters and those of the Third Square. We had to duck down to keep from getting hit by flying objects. As I approached the heart of the riot, an Egyptian grabbed me by the arm, obviously unhappy with my presence. It was time to bail. I signaled to Dorothée that we needed to leave immediately. One of the rioters followed us for a few seconds before giving up.

The next morning we decided to leave our press cards and radio recorder at the hotel. We went to Heliopolis with a friend, Paul, to attend a Coptic Christian mass. Everything went well, but as we were having tea with Paul in a coffee shop, two plainclothes policemen, armed and holding handcuffs, approached us and asked why we were there. We explained that we were tourists. They took Paul off to the side to check his identity card and even checked what images I had in my camera. Luckily for us they bought our story and didn't hassle us any further.

On the twenty-seventh, Paul called and informed us that three journalists, an Egyptian, an American and a Brit, had been arrested in the apartment where they were working. Another American journalist friend said her cameraman had disappeared. A French colleague told us there had been several arrests on the twenty-fifth of journalists in Tahrir Square. She summed up the situation this way: "Watch out, because today, as soon as someone starts filming, they'll suspect it's someone who works for Al Jazeera and they'll start chasing him." Since late December, four Al Jazeera reporters—an Australian, a Canadian and two Egyptians—had been arrested. The army suspected them of complicity with the Muslim Brotherhood, because the television channel was funded by Qatar, which was known to bankroll the Muslim Brotherhood all across the Middle East.

Finally Dorothée and I came to the conclusion that there was no way we could do the story on the street kids we'd originally set out to do.

In all likelihood, before my capture in Syria, I would have been more reckless. I probably would have decided to stay, get a bit closer to the crowd, catch the wild look in the demonstrators' eyes. But the thought of rotting in an Egyptian prison dissuaded me.

On top of that, Egypt was Arab and Muslim. Everything about the people around me—their voices, the harsh guttural sounds of their language, the way they gesticulated and screamed at you when there was an issue—reminded me of everything I'd just been through. It brought me back to Syria and I had a lot of trouble keeping cool.

I also sensed an underlying menace to everything about Islam: the submission and conformity it exacted, the heavy-handed metaphors of violence. As someone who is drawn to violence, I understand its attraction and feel that most people who would accuse me of being an Islamophobe don't appreciate just how powerful and appealing those metaphors of violence and conquest—which permeate the Quran and so much of Islamic culture—can be.

As a European and American—proud of the Western culture grounded in that refined weave of Greek philosophy, Roman law, and Judeo-Christian ethics—I see today's expression of Salafi Islam as a threat, a real existential threat. Europeans have become so soft, so complacent, so absorbed by their own hedonism that they can't even recognize the violence directed at them until there's an explosion or a puddle of blood at their feet. They rally behind ideals whose sources they've forgotten, if not rejected outright. And their defense of those ideals rarely goes beyond rhetoric—or worse, smug offensive satire. Since so few are willing to act violently in defense of their ideals, they keep themselves in a state of denial with respect to those who have long ago declared war on those ideals and have readily backed their declarations by shedding blood.

Now Europeans are beginning to wake up. But this will probably lead to conflict among Europeans before the real threat is dealt with.

I've traveled through more Islamic countries and spent more time shoulder to shoulder with Muslims than most Westerners, often risking my life with them and coming to their aid. And there is a beauty to Islam that is unique. It's a sublime expression of belief in God.

But I do not want it in Europe. And that's because I doubt today's Europeans have the mettle it takes to stave off a force that would, in the name of God, raze the foundations of what we Europeans cherish. Anyone who's spent any time with a jihadi in combat knows what his ultimate concern is. And in the jihadi's eyes, that ultimate concern will not tolerate the commitment to reason, freedom and universal love that has painstakingly informed Europe over the course of millennia. It's so simple and so clear that most Europeans have lost the ability to see it.

UKRAINE: EUROPE'S FAULT LINE

WHILE I WAS IN EGYPT, Europe had begun to crack along one of its historical fault lines. In late November, Ukrainian president Viktor Yanukovych backed out of the long-negotiated European Union Association Agreement, encouraged by pressure from Russia and a $15 billion incentive loan. The pro-European Ukrainians started protests in the heart of Kyiv and the Yanukovych government tried clumsily to prevent a repeat of the 2004 Orange Revolution, when his electoral victory was deemed fraudulent. Initially the protests were small, but within a week he had the Interior Ministry's special riot police, known as the Berkut, crack down violently on what was mostly young people and students. This only caused the protests to grow.

Thousands of protesters set up a tent city in the middle of Independence Square, known as the Maidan, in frigid temperatures. It was immediately dubbed "the Euromaidan" and garnered the support of the international community, which infuriated Moscow. I followed the events closely in the news, and by early January it seemed as if the protests would peter out. Then, on January 16, the Yanukovych government hastily rammed a bill through the parliament that would have severely limited freedom of expression and right to assembly. Over the next three days the demonstrations gathered momentum and turned violent, with protesters attacking the Berkut and other Interior Ministry troops, using cobblestones, Molotov cocktails, even makeshift catapults. Protest leaders began disappearing; one even turned up several days later, badly beaten and with half his ear cut off.

Dorothée and I decided to go to Kyiv a few days after we got back to Paris from Cairo. We wandered around the vast tent city in temperatures that dropped down to minus 28 Celsius (minus 18 Fahrenheit) and published a piece in *Elle* about the women on the Maidan. But the atmosphere had settled into a stalemate, with Interior Ministry troops on one side of the barricades made of sandbags filled with snow and protesters on the other huddled around burning trash bins. At times it felt like there was more conflict among the hordes of photojournalists trying to get a shot from the top of the barricades than on either side of them.

We decided to go to the eastern part of the country, which most journalists ignored. With respect to the EU Association Agreement, Ukraine was divided virtually fifty-fifty, along geographic lines. The west of Ukraine, closer to Europe, wanted to be part of the EU and have that vast market open for their products. They also felt that setting themselves on an EU membership track would expedite Ukraine's perennial battle against the corruption poisoning its politics and society. It would also make it harder for Russia to carry out its revanchist designs: that is, turning Ukraine into a client state it could fully control. In the east, however, where ties to Russia were much closer, they felt that moving away from Moscow would adversely affect their primary trading relationship. They also had more of a historical distrust of Western capitalism, Catholicism, and Atlanticism—viewing the EU as a stalking horse for a Western occupation that would force its decadent consumerism and gay marriage on them.

We went to Kharkiv and Dnipropetrovsk, both Russophone cities where you would seldom hear any Ukrainian spoken on the street. There you could see that the Soviet Union had not entirely vanished. Many people were wary of the protesters in Kyiv, seeing them as pawns for violent nationalists. They also didn't trust the opposition politicians, who they assumed were almost as corrupt as Yanukovych. Perhaps the one thing that everyone had in common was a loathing for the corrupt Yanukovych government and his "Family," a close group of cronies that included his sons, who had become fantastically wealthy in just three years of his presidency. The only place where Yanukovych still had support was in his hometown of Donetsk and in the coal-mining and steel towns of the Donbas region that surround it.

Shortly after we returned to Europe, the Maidan exploded. Protesters tried to reach the nearby parliament buildings to force Yanukovych's resignation. Pressure was building on him from Russia to crush the demonstrations. On February 18 the Berkut broke through the barricades and took back nearly half the square. Protesters piled up new barricades of tires and wood, then set them on fire, feeding the flames with anything that would burn.

Things settled down the next day, with the Maidan divided practically down the middle. The standoff couldn't last and opposition leaders, who were always a step behind the street, were frantically negotiating with the government, which wanted to relinquish as little power as late as possible, offering early elections and other concessions. But it was too late.

Just before dawn on the twentieth, shots rang out and several Berkut soldiers were hit. They were sitting ducks there in the square surrounded by tall buildings, so they decided to retreat up a hill and regroup. The protesters followed, and that's when the massacre started in earnest. As the protesters climbed the hill on Institutska Street, which led from the Maidan past the Ukraina Hotel and up to the cluster of government buildings, Berkut shooters began picking them off one by one. By the end of the day around seventy people had been killed and many others wounded.

I watched much of this from New York, streaming live from various Ukrainian news outlets. It was incredibly frustrating not being able to be there and move around. I rarely trusted other people's eyes. The media always needed to trim most of the chaos. When you're there in the flesh, the full sensorial impact makes you aware of just how complex any given event is. If you're attuned to the complexity of all the inputs, you can draw conclusions that benefit from both intellect *and* intuition.

Within two days the government had fallen. Yanukovych left Kyiv and eventually turned up in Russia. A new interim government was in place—mostly full of familiar faces from Ukraine's parliament.

The country was still in shock when less than a week later Russia launched its operation to take over Crimea. On the twenty-seventh Russian special forces broke into the Supreme Council building in Simferopol. A puppet government was installed, Ukrainian airports and military bases were surrounded, ships were blockaded, and by March 16 a referendum was held.

Not only did the Ukrainians not put up any resistance, but many troops defected to the Russian side—which, due to a long-standing treaty from the fall of the Soviet Union, had an important naval base in Crimea, with at least twenty thousand troops stationed there permanently.

As soon as the pro-Russian population in eastern Ukraine saw how easy it was to divorce from Kyiv with a little help from Moscow, protests began flaring up in Donetsk, Kharkiv, and other cities with high concentrations of ethnic Russians. The country was rapidly splitting apart and unless the new government in Kyiv could mobilize its lame army, the revolution would fizzle out and Russia, which had amassed upwards of a hundred thousand troops along its border with Ukraine, would march into Kyiv and install a Moscow-friendly puppet the way it did in Crimea. Later, interviews with and intercepts of key Russians involved in fomenting the uprisings confirmed that the revolts in the Donbas as well as in Kharkiv, Zaporizhia and Odessa were part of a coordinated Kremlin plan. At the very least, the new Ukrainian government would have to crush the growing rebellion in the east. In other words, a war was practically inevitable.

NOTWITHSTANDING ANY VOWS I may have made to myself while captive, I never had any reservations about going to Ukraine. My father didn't seem very pleased, but he understood. My mother told me I was out of my mind. But this was something I needed to see up close because many of my ideas about Europe and the direction in which it was headed were being played out on the ground in real time.

In Syria I'd gotten an intimate sense of how complicated the geopolitical situation was—much more intimate than I'd bargained for. I got to see how jihadism grows and festers on its own soil. Now that Europe seemed to be cracking, with a sclerotic NATO alliance trying to keep a resurgent Russia down, I needed to immerse myself in the oncoming waves, even at the risk of getting caught in a rip again.

This was the first time in my adult life that a war seemed imminent in Europe. I'd covered the war in Georgia, but that always felt like the periphery of Europe. And during the Yugoslav wars, where many of my older colleagues had cut their teeth, I was just an adolescent. The resurgence of nationalism in Europe was something I'd been watching and predicting for many years.

In the context of Ukraine, the initial conflict was ostensibly between half the country who wanted to be part of a supranational European Union and half the country who wanted to remain in a neo-Soviet Union, which by definition implied a sort of internationalism. Both these movements were part of the fabric of a globalization process that dates back to long before the term became a buzzword, back to mercantilism and the rise of colonial empires. But on a deeper level, notwithstanding the chants of "Ukraine is Europe," the Ukrainians were not willing to die for the sake of a bureaucracy in Brussels. Very early in the Maidan protests, anyone with any knowledge of Ukrainian history could see that regardless of the calls for an association with Europe, the country's ultranationalists were poised to hijack the movement. And most of those nationalists didn't care much for the EU. What they wanted was to get rid of the pro-Russian Yanukovych and break further away from Moscow's influence. The more moderate protesters were largely aware of this fact. Indeed, with all the posters of Stepan Bandera, the leader of the Organization of Ukrainian Nationalists during World War II (who was vilified by Soviet historians as a Nazi collaborator and lionized by Ukrainian nationalists as a hero who opposed both Soviets and Nazis), it was impossible not to be aware. But the moderate protesters also knew that if Yanukovych decided to crush the Maidan with force, these nationalists were the ones who would put up a fight. They were the ones throwing cobblestones and Molotov cocktails, and they were openly recruiting young men for what they understood would degenerate into a war once Russia decided to intervene with force.

Meanwhile, the coal miners around Donetsk, who were protest-
ing against Kyiv, harbored only a lukewarm allegiance to any notion of
an international workers' movement or Soviet glory. They simply felt
more Russian than Ukrainian and hoped Putin would march in at their
request to rid them of the fascist junta full of faggots and American
agents who had taken over in Kyiv.

In Ukraine, all of Europe's ivory-tower illusions of transnational solidarity would swiftly be trumped by good old-fashioned nationalism—
just as in Syria the rebels' hopes for liberal democracy ceded to good
old-fashioned sharia law.

For years I've been gradually ostracized by colleagues when I talk
about statism in Europe. Basically, this view considers the European
Union to be an untenable overlay on European nations, one that will
ultimately paralyze if not destroy Europe as a political and cultural
force. Whether we like it or not, the nation-state is still far and away
the most viable form of political organization. The European Union,
though it may have originated as a noble measure to keep European
countries from starting more wars, has in effect reduced Western
Europe to a place where maintaining the neoliberal free market system
is the overriding concern. All its high-minded ideas of four freedoms—
the free movement of goods, capital, services and people—were originally aimed at creating a single market, at making money. Today Euro-
crats justify these developments with the assumption that if everyone
is making money and there is widespread prosperity, then we will have
a quasi-utopia in which rational self-interest will prevent different
nations from trying to destroy or subjugate each other.

But this assumption has always been patently false. Prosperity and
interdependence among nations during the Belle Époque in no way
prevented World War I. The European Union has given more power to
multinational corporations that—unlike the state—are not beholden to
ensuring the well-being of the nation and its people. Multinational corporations are beholden to their shareholders, and in a very limited way:
they have to make profit, and make it quickly, in the short term, calibrat-

ing all their decisions to make the quarterly earnings reports look good. The single market erodes the individual state's capacity to mitigate the deleterious effects of elementary capitalist greed. Hence the EU, as it has developed, is complicit in the gradual breakdown of cultural and ethical values that have been subsumed by rampant consumerism. The ideal citizen of the EU is not someone willing to fight for European values, but rather a good consumer who can drive domestic demand and production so that we can pay for the cradle-to-grave social welfare system cracking as a result of the baby boomers getting old. By reversing the priorities (that is, profit and economic indicators become more important than the people) the free market has come to be seen as a virtuous end in itself rather than just the means of ensuring cradle-to-grave health care and the continuation of a millennial tradition of agriculture and food production. It gets to the point where what Big Pharma, insurance companies, and Monsanto want becomes more important than what new mothers, cancer patients, or struggling farmers need. The EU, for all its politically correct rhetoric, willingly collaborates in this process.

Now, with the Syrian tragedy coming to a head, the United States has been looking more and more like the "great and powerful" Wizard of Oz, who's just had the curtain behind him drawn open by Dorothy's dog Toto. They are no longer willing to play the world's policeman— and probably not even capable of doing so without unleashing other catastrophes, such as Iraq and Libya have demonstrated. The Syrian rebels never counted much on US help, and the Ukrainians would rapidly be disabused as well. The rule of thumb has become every nation— every faction even—fights for itself. European nations' recent retrenchment into self-interest is yet another symptom of a new historical wave welling up.

THE STEPPES OF UKRAINE, extending into endless Asia, have been a stage for human conflict since the prehistoric Aryans first swept across them on horses, and even before. Everything Europe is and has become can be traced to movements across this flat grassland, where the cultures that occupied it preferred mobility to the trappings of civilization, and where scorched earth was more than a tactic, it was a metaphysical rite.

Several times in the twentieth century the events in Ukraine had a huge impact on the course of European history. Battles there during World War I and the Russian Civil War laid the foundation for the rise of Bolshevism. During World War II, the Germans' biggest mistake, according to many historians, was to antagonize the initially welcoming Ukrainian population. Moreover, the vast majority of Jews killed in the Holocaust died in the forests of Ukraine and Belarus, with bullets to the head or suffocated in a truck full of carbon monoxide, rather than in the extermination camps farther to the west.

There was no way I would miss what was about to unfold in Ukraine, because I felt it was just a prelude to a greater upheaval throughout Europe. Despite the trauma of my kidnapping being still undigested, the thrill of witnessing history was too attractive. As soon as I tied up some loose ends back home, I flew to Ukraine in April and settled in Donetsk, where the protests were already gaining traction.

By early April many government buildings in eastern cities were being taken over by anti-Kyiv protesters. I called Jean-Claude Galli, a French journalist I'd met during the 2008 war in Georgia and become friends with, who now worked for Swiss television. I asked if he wanted to come join me in the Donbas and cover the rebellion. He was short, quick, and had a deeper, more nuanced understanding of geopolitics than most reporters. About fifteen years older than me, he'd made his reputation covering the Yugoslav wars in the 1990s. I liked his approach because while all the other journalists were covering the war from Croatia, Sarajevo, or other parts of Bosnia, he based himself in Belgrade to get a better look at the putative "bad guys." Now a similar situation was developing. As far as most of the Western press was concerned, the violent revolution in Kyiv was a great achievement for freedom and democracy, while the violent protests simmering in the Donbas were fomented by Russia's revanchist ambitions. While this may have been true, I've always been curious to see why the "bad guys" were considered as such. It gives you more insight into the "good guys'" darker places.

We rented a car and drove around the Donbas region. By April 9 the Ukrainian government had launched its Anti-Terrorist Operation, or ATO, which was a rather bureaucratic euphemism for war. Meanwhile ultranationalist volunteer battalions were being spawned every day.

On April 6 demonstrators stormed the Regional State Administration building in Donetsk and demanded a referendum be held, like the one in Crimea. There were a few clashes in the main square, and if there were any pro-Ukrainians there, they were forced to keep a low profile.

I traveled with Jean-Claude to the various cities under rebel control. The landscape outside the smoke-charred and rusting Soviet industrial towns was flat, a gently rolling steppe sown with wheat or sunflowers. It was perfect tank country, especially as the soggy spring ground hardened with the warmer weather. Some of the most intense battles of World War II took place here, particularly in the late summer and fall of 1943, when the Soviet army, having gained momentum after the Battle of Kursk, pushed on to the Dnieper River, where the German army had established dense fortifications. In the course of a few months around two million soldiers died on those steppes during the Battle of the Dnieper. (My friend Yann and I—both of us World War II buffs—had always wanted to travel to Russia, Belarus and Ukraine to visit the sites of many of World War II's epic battles.)

The separatists were a ragtag bunch, but the Ukrainian army they faced was still in shambles from two decades of neglect and corruption. Checkpoints cropped up along the roads every day. In order to dislodge the separatists, the Ukrainians resorted to heavy artillery and shelled the separatists until they scattered. Volunteers from Russia started coming into Donetsk.

The Ukrainian strategy relied on artillery, so much of my work involved going to target sites and photographing the damage. At one point photographer Scott Olson and I got caught in a firefight in the town of Kramatorsk, which at the time was controlled by rebels. Ambushes were also common, but unless you were embedded with the rebels (who were not that organized yet) it was hard to get access.

I RETURNED TO THE UNITED STATES in May to take care of prior commitments. The Balkans were hit with severe flooding so I went to Serbia to cover that for my agency. Meanwhile, I followed the news from Ukraine closely. In May referendums were held and the rebels declared the establishment of the Donetsk People's Republic (DPR), the same for the neighboring Luhansk People's Republic (LPR). By July, though, the separatists were getting pushed out of many cities they'd taken control of. Then they shot down the Malaysia Airlines plane, which was big news all over the world and attracted even more journalists to the Donbas. There was a mass retreat from Sloviansk and much of the border with Russia was back in government hands. Kyiv was optimistic that it would soon crush the rebellion, and it looked as if the Ukrainian forces would try to surround Donetsk and lay siege to it.

As soon as I settled my business in New York I went back to Ukraine. I flew into Kyiv and took a train to Donetsk. The city's population, about two million before the war, was less than half that now, and it was thinning out by the day. Surprisingly, the trains were still running in and out of the city, though some of them had to take alternate routes when bridges or tracks were blown up.

Donetsk was preparing for a siege. When we journalists got our accreditation at the government offices, along with a list of dos and don'ts about what we could cover and photograph, the authorities handed us a single-page, double-sided how-to manual in Russian about preparing for urban resistance: setting up sniper nests, blowing up holes between apartments for safe passage, communication strategies, and so forth. Every day the city emptied out. Those who had relatives in parts of Ukraine that were quiet went there. Others had contacts in Russia and went there. A stealthy process of ethnic cleansing was under way.

All around the city, especially near the airport, shells would land, and I'd instruct a fixer to take us to the site. One day I had the opportunity to go a funeral of rebel soldiers killed in action. At the time no one seemed to mind my taking pictures, but when they got published the DPR authorities were not happy at all and I knew I probably wouldn't be allowed back if I applied for accreditation in the future—that is, if the DPR even existed in the future.

EASTERN UKRAINE BECAME a magnet for every combat photographer and journalist in the West. I met colleagues whose work I knew, and I traveled together with some of the better-known ones, in particular, Scott Olson, Spencer Platt and Jérôme Sessini. All of them were older and more experienced than me, so I learned a few things about the trade from them.

But on the whole, combat photographers and journalists are a cantankerous bunch, with big egos, and they don't often get along with each other. To top it off, there were hordes of younger freelance photographers and reporters crawling around Kyiv and Donetsk, trying to make a name for themselves in a business that was less and less forgiving every year. Many of them came on their own dime with little hope of making money. They were there just to establish their reputations.

Still, in Ukraine, hunkered down in a city with diminishing food supplies, ATM machines running out of cash, and the few inhabitants still left gearing up for a siege as they got shelled from three directions, I felt in my element. It was as if I could only appreciate the feeling of freedom in a context in which that freedom was either curtailed or so at risk that it was impossible to take for granted.

My experience in Syria no doubt had a lot to do with it. In retrospect, a little crumb of freedom in captivity—whether sunbathing by the empty pool or sneaking a glimpse at a note hidden in the cuff of my trousers—had more specific gravity than any mind-boggling array of drinks and scantily clad women at a Manhattan club. Thanks to my captors I was beginning to experience freedom less as choice per se than as some power that exacts a sacrifice as prerequisite.

BY AUGUST, EVERYONE—the press, the people in Donetsk, even the rebels—was expecting Ukrainian army soldiers to enter the suburbs at any moment. Either the city would capitulate suddenly or the Ukrainians would have to begin the hard slog of urban warfare: house-to-house battles mixed with intermittent artillery barrages. And if the remaining citizens of Donetsk hated the Kyiv government already for the bombs they dropped on their town, it would only get worse.

The first signs of a possible reversal came in reports as early as mid-July that the Russians were launching artillery strikes from Russian territory itself. Then there were humanitarian convoys coming in from Russia suspected of bringing in weapons and reinforcements. By late August the counteroffensive was under way and many Ukrainian troops got caught overextended, especially in the town of Ilovaisk, about six miles east of Donetsk, where hundreds of Ukrainian volunteers from the Donbas Battalion got surrounded in a pocket and were cut down in an attempted breakout.

At about the same time, while a host of other journalists and I were holed up in a Donetsk hotel, trying to keep up with the very fluid situation on the ground, we got word that James Foley had been beheaded by Daesh, which had posted the gruesome scene online. Many of the journalists knew Foley personally. I knew of him through my friend Giorgos Moutafis. I was very conscious of the fact that Foley had been abducted first in Libya (where Giorgos had met him) and then again in Syria, where he was executed. I took it as a cautionary tale. He'd pressed his luck, and maybe I was doing the same with mine. There was no telling what could happen in Donetsk, so I started to plan an escape route.

BY SEPTEMBER THE TIDE had turned and Ukrainian president Petro Poroshenko was suing for peace. Russian forces were obviously helping the previously demoralized rebels and the world was witnessing an invasion of Ukraine, with all eyes focused on the scenario of a land bridge connecting Crimea to Russian territory along the northern shore of the Sea of Azov. The main obstacle for the Russian forces would be the major port city of Mariupol, which had been under Kyiv's control throughout the summer.

I joined up with Spencer Platt and we drove across the front lines to Mariupol, under Ukrainian control. We waited for Russian forces to lay siege to that city of a million inhabitants. By September 5 a shaky truce was agreed upon, the first of the Minsk Accords. Neither side trusted the other, so Spencer, Jean-Claude and I stayed in Mariupol, waiting for hostilities to flare up again.

FOR THE FIRST TIME in the conflict I got a look at the new Ukrainian volunteer battalions. Mariupol was the base of the Azov Battalion, an ultranationalist bunch that caught international attention because their symbol—a stylized *I* and *N* (for "Idea of Nation")—looked very much like a Nazi Wolfsangel. The ones I had contact with, however, seemed like very typical young men fighting for a cause—in this case against a Russian invasion. Just as the ones on the other side were fighting against what they deemed to be a "Banderite" coup (in Kremlin-speak, Stepan Bandera was a synecdoche for all manner of Nazi sympathizers) that wanted to nullify the Soviet glory of their parents and grandparents, especially those who had lived through World War II.

And yet, to an outside observer, especially one like myself who can barely make out the difference between the sounds of spoken Russian and Ukrainian, this looked like a civil war. On top of that, I was told by my fixers that practically all the Azov Battalion members spoke Russian among themselves rather than Ukrainian. The only fighters who spoke Ukrainian were the ones from the western part of the country.

Granted, academics are in disagreement about the extent to which this is a civil war, but to the untrained eye, these were the same people. They spoke the same language, went to the same schools, and worshipped in the same churches. They were neighbors before the war and married each other without any thoughts about nationality. Families were torn apart by having to take sides. And on a military level, the officers from opposite sides all knew each other. The older ones had served together in the Soviet army, and many of them were Afghan vets. The younger ones had served in the Ukrainian army. They were taught from the same manuals, using the same weapons.

There's something about a civil war that makes it even more malign than a conventional war of self-defense or territorial conquest. There's an element of self-loathing involved. You look at the "other" and it's impossible not to recognize a facet of yourself. Often it's some part of yourself you admire or at least indulge in. Acting out violently is almost like cutting off one of your own limbs. This is why in civil wars all sorts of taboos tend to be broken: rape, disfigurement, torture. The enemy, rather than being some "other" who can be subjugated or chased away, is considered an internal element that needs to be purged, excised.

I often thought of David, the childhood friend who would lose control and turn on me violently. I knew he never consciously wanted to hurt me, but when he exploded, it was as if he were trying to exorcise some demon within himself, and I, having become an extension of his own being, was the straw man. Over time I came to understand the dynamic, and I eventually forgave David. His violence taught me a lot about people, how easily they can succumb to irrational forces. But it also left an indelible mark within me, a stain that seems to spread with every war. I would often watch fighters coldly, trying to understand why they felt they needed to kill. Usually their reasons seemed more than valid—self-defense or retaliation for violence or injustice they'd been subjected to. Sometimes it was a question of honor or glory. I've never come across the stereotype of a sadist who killed for the sake of killing, someone who worshipped murder. I've tried to observe soldiers with the detached compassion of a therapist, feeling I needed to remain above the fray. But the more I watched them, the more I recognized how much of that violence was just the flip side of a familiarity that was growing too uncomfortable. And watching wars was surely a way for me to process the violence that left its mark on me as kid—violence that can be terrifyingly seductive.

AMONG UKRAINIANS, THERE WAS no shortage of skeletons in either side's closet, skeletons of men and women who had died a violent death. All those bones elicited the compulsion to purge the nation of its horrors. But as the irony of history would have it, the purges themselves became horrors to forget and/or remember . . . again and again, in a vicious circle going back to those first burial mounds on the steppes.

After the Minsk agreement, the Ukrainians managed to hold the cease-fire line just east of Mariupol. The fighting subsided so I went back to New York.

Nobody really expected the cease-fire to last, and in December, the continual battle (despite the Minsk cease-fire) for the Donetsk airport, which the Ukrainians controlled, flared up again. The rebels launched an offensive with the help of Russian regular army troops. In January there was a significant uptick in the fighting all along the front.

I went to Ukraine again, only this time I was on the Ukrainian army side because I'd become a wanted man for the Donetsk rebels, who didn't take kindly to my photos of their funeral. In any case, I felt it was important for an observer to see both sides of the equation, something that is not always easy to do for a war reporter. I'd managed to do it during my several trips to Nepal in 2005, first moving with the Maoist rebels, and subsequently with the Gurkhas in the regular army. Covering both sides helps to confirm the fact that soldiers are very similar all over the world, acting mainly as vehicles for less visible powers and principalities.

I traveled to cities like Kramatorsk, which had been shelled by rebels with powerful Grad rockets from nearly twenty miles away.

Then I did a piece together with Ukrainian journalist Elena Savchuk about female fighters in the Aidar Battalion, based near Luhansk. The photos caught a lot of flak when they appeared in the *Guardian* because one of the vans in the background had some neo-Nazi markings stenciled on it. Obviously the fair-skinned female volunteers in the Aidar Battalion had some white supremacist comrades-in-arms.

The presence of far-right neo-Nazis on both sides of the cease-fire line is well documented. Ukraine's other source of twentieth-century horror came from the Stalinist legacy. Although the ultranationalists were still a minority in Ukrainian society, and the Nazi collaborators tended to be concentrated in western Ukraine, which had only been absorbed into the Soviet Union in 1939, no one in contemporary Ukraine above a certain age could escape having to deal with the communist regime in one form or another. Almost everyone worked the system as best they could; only a tiny minority were dissidents, and they tended to pay a steep price for their dissent. When the Soviet Union disintegrated and the full extent of Stalinist malfeasance became common knowledge, Ukrainian society underwent a radical examination of conscience. In a sense, the only people who were clean of conceptual complicity in the crimes that took place in these bloodlands were the utterly indifferent, the lobotomized proles. Then, in the post-Soviet era, these indifferent innocents were the first to fall prey to aspiring oligarchs whose overriding concern was to make money.

So when the neo-Nazi junta in Kyiv bombed the neo-Stalinist Muscovite terrorists—or when the bloodthirsty dictator Assad bombed the radical jihadist terrorists, for that matter—it was not unlike a desperate cancer patient letting loose on a tumor with radiation or chemotherapy. By killing cells that have run amok they hope to preserve the rest of the body.

CANCER IS AN APT METAPHOR for the wars I've witnessed in my little bracket of time alive. When I was cuffed to the bed in Syria, chipping paint off the wall and imagining maps of conquest, I was just eking out my own survival, trying to stay afloat through the process of metastasis. I felt like a healthy cell observing all the other cells around me becoming irreparably damaged. And I knew the longer I was there, the harder it would be for me to avoid getting altered within or engulfed entirely.

Nations at war and rebels fighting oppression tend to imagine their adversaries as tumors to be kept at bay, controlled, eliminated. In Syria I got caught in the rip current of a Sunni-Shia struggle that had ramified beyond any easy distinctions and was now braiding into the broader Muslim-Christian struggles ebbing and flowing through a history of caliphates, crusades and colonialism. I was watching the process play out at the microscopic level, but at the time I was too preoccupied with survival, too scared to see it in perspective.

Whether it's dictatorship versus democracy, communism versus capitalism, Christianity versus Islam, or any confrontation among the countless subsets of nested identities, civilizations have a way of keeping healthy by recognizing the "other" as a potential menace. All those who would dismiss the idea of "clash of civilizations" seem to be denying the obvious. For my own part, I needed to accommodate my behavior to the "others" who had taken me hostage. But I never denied that they were a threat to my life. Had I done so and dismissed the clash aspect of civilization, I may have wound up with an AK-47 in my hands fighting alongside my captors. Paradoxically, my dismissal of the clash in order to embrace the other could have ultimately turned me into a jihadi, out to destroy the very stuff I was made of.

For anyone who wants peace in the world, preventing cells from running amok would seem to be the solution (at least in this admittedly reductive metaphor), just as prevention may be the best way to stave off cancer. Unfortunately, anyone with a cursory understanding of history cannot but be aware of the fact that we are still at a point in human evolution in which the most effective means of dealing with these perceived tumors are violent: neutralization and excision.

It's hard to imagine an alternative healing solution for the world's ills that doesn't smack of the Kingdom of Heaven on earth. Prevention is an ideal to shoot for. Alas, human civilization has millennia of momentum behind it in which mutual antagonisms have informed our cultures and consciousness, and the damage cannot be undone by simply wishing it away. We're living in an age of metastasis, an age in which miracles are hard to imagine.

ENTER THE KESSEL

THE CEASE-FIRE LINE after the first Minsk agreement was an unruly series of twists and turns that formed natural salients. A common military tactic is to close in on the base of a salient from two flanks, creating what's known as a pincer movement. Once the pincer is closed and the troops within the salient are surrounded, it's known as a pocket. In Russian, these pockets are called *kotyol,* from the German *kessel,* which means cauldron. The metaphor is apt because the troops inside are still numerous enough to be boiling with activity and capable of engaging in heated battle, at least in the beginning. After the pincer closes and the troops become surrounded, either they surrender, they break out, or the contents boil to death—civilians as well as soldiers.

This part of Ukraine saw one of the most successful kessels in history. In September 1941, during the First Battle of Kiev, the Germans surrounded nearly the entire Southwest Front of the Red Army, encircling 450,000 Soviet soldiers. Casualties—killed, missing and wounded—ran up to 700,000 during the monthlong battle. And that was only on the Soviet side.

Such numbers are unimaginable today. Five years of the current Syrian War hasn't produced as many casualties as just that single battle. In my lifetime, only the various Congo Wars, where I actually got my first experience in combat photography, approach those numbers: estimates range from two to five million excess deaths due to a decade of sporadic fighting. But in that largely ignored war it was a question of militias destroying remote jungle villages and civilian casualties. You didn't have mechanized forces and millions of infantrymen arrayed against each other.

To the east of the Donbas, in Stalingrad, the most significant kessel of World War II took place, which proved to be the turning point in Europe. In September 1942 the German army cornered the Soviets in the city named after Stalin himself, against the banks of the Volga River. The battle degenerated into house-to-house warfare. Both sides poured in reinforcements. Then, in November 1942, the Soviets launched Operation Uranus and encircled the entire German Sixth Army. The cauldron boiled for months. By February 1943 General Friedrich Paulus of the Sixth Army had surrendered. All told, the five-month battle saw nearly two million casualties.

No matter how I tried, I simply couldn't imagine such numbers. Already what I'd seen in my career was horrific enough. And when I looked at all the young Ukrainian and Russian soldiers at the checkpoints or riding armored personnel carriers and tanks, I couldn't help thinking that their grandparents had lived through those million-casualty battles.

The most prominent salient on the front line established by the Minsk Accords was in Debaltseve, a city with a strategic rail hub about halfway between Donetsk and Luhansk. The Ukrainian army controlled it and the rebels needed it so they could transport goods and arms more easily from Russia. Without Debaltseve, large rail shipments going from Russia to Donetsk had to pass through Rostov-on-Don, to the southeast.

THE BATTLE FOR DEBALTSEVE started in earnest around January 16, 2015, when heavy shelling on the part of rebels, flush with matériel brought in from Russia via "humanitarian convoys," started pounding the Ukrainians' flanks along the road from Debaltseve to Artemivsk, about twenty miles to the northwest.

I based myself in Artemivsk, which was controlled by the Ukrainian army, at the home of an evangelical Christian family (a rarity in this overwhelmingly Orthodox part of Ukraine). The road between Artemivsk and Debaltseve was still open and being used by the Ukrainians to bring in reinforcements and ammunition, and bring out the wounded. I found a driver who would take me into Debaltseve to photograph the remaining civilians.

On my first day there, I met Yevgeny, a short man in his thirties who worked for the Red Cross. Like the family that put me up, he was also an evangelical Christian. He drove a Red Cross SUV and handed out plastic bags full of food and supplies to a long line of people, mostly elderly, who were very disciplined as they waited for the humanitarian aid. There was constant shelling all around. He smiled at me as he paused to take a deep drag from his cigarette, so I walked up to him. He spoke some English and I asked him what he was doing.

"Every day I come here to distribute aid packages. I drive on that road, an hour and a half. Very dangerous. The Ukrainian army is being compressed on all sides."

A few of the locals realized I was a foreigner and they had Yevgeny translate. "Tell him Poroshenko is a bastard," they said. Most of the remaining inhabitants, Yevgeny told me, were just waiting for the Russians to come. But the Red Cross driver struck me as someone mainly concerned with helping his people. He considered anyone from the outside with weapons—whether Ukrainians from the west or Russians from the east—as undesirable elements in his native Donbas.

On the whole, I saw very few Ukrainian soldiers in the middle of Debaltseve. They were mostly concentrated on the outskirts, trying to put up a defense and keep the pincer from closing. I knew there had been heavy fighting in the nearby towns of Yenakiyeve and Vuhlehirsk, and that the rebels were gaining ground with the help of the Russian regular army, almost closing the road several times. There had been reports of troops with very Asiatic features, no doubt from Siberia.

I asked Yevgeny if I could come with him the following day and he agreed.

IN THE MORNING I had my driver drop me off in the center of Artemivsk. Yevgeny was already there. I was nervous. It was gray, with low cloud cover; the temperature was unseasonably warm—which for Ukraine in February meant right around the freezing point. Very grim, but perfect light for taking photos outdoors.

I rode shotgun in Yevgeny's SUV. The back was crammed with about a hundred plastic bags full of pasta and other nonperishable food. We drove down the only highway, through checkpoint after checkpoint. The Ukrainian army knew Yevgeny well, so they let him pass with a nod or a wave. A couple of times he stopped and exchanged a few words with soldiers who were obviously friends. Most of the soldiers looked at him like he was crazy, but they respected and admired him because he was selfless when it came to helping people.

About fifteen klicks from Debaltseve we got to the last Ukrainian checkpoint. The soldiers told us, "We can't do anything for you beyond this point." But they waved us on anyway.

As we were driving down the road we heard continual whistling right over us. One shell landed a mile away, the next five hundred yards away, then a few only a couple of hundred yards off the road. Yevgeny kept barreling straight ahead. Not far from the last checkpoint we went over a mangled bridge. From there the road went downhill and passed between two small lakes. To the right was Svitlodarsk, a town with a huge power station that was constantly getting shelled, seemingly from every direction.

After the lakes we passed through an almost abandoned checkpoint. All you could see were the antitank guns right out in the open, manned and ready for a major assault. The road beyond was littered with destroyed vehicles still smoking, ammo dumps, trucks whizzing by back and forth with bullet and shrapnel scars—and mud everywhere. Some of the trucks had flak jackets hanging off the doors for protection in case someone tried to gun them down from the side of the road.

A couple of klicks before we hit Debaltseve, on our left, I could see a tank hidden behind a small house. It looked like a DPR tank, waiting for an ambush. Yevgeny saw the tank, too, and eyed it carefully as he continued down the road.

The deeper we drove into this apocalyptic scene, the more nervous I became. The shelling was much more intense than the day before. We got to the northern edge of Debaltseve and it was completely destroyed, rubble everywhere. Yevgeny knew exactly where people were hiding in their cellars. He parked beside a series of long Soviet-type buildings and honked his horn a few times. When I stepped out of the car it was dead silent except for incoming or outgoing shells. Then all of a sudden people started popping out of doorways and climbing out of holes in the ground. Within a few minutes there were about two or three hundred people emerging from every nook and cranny of that shattered neighborhood. They were mostly elderly, shrouded in layer upon layer of clothes to fend off the damp cold at night. The gas and electricity had been out for days. They all waited in line with remarkable patience. Yevgeny opened the hatchback of his vehicle so he could distribute the food. He took the names of the people one by one so he could know who was there and keep people from trying to get double rations. Even though the locals were well disciplined, a few of them started shoving each other at one point. Then the shelling picked up. A mortar landed on the next block over, but everyone just shrugged it off.

We'd been exposed for an hour and a half and I was already eager to get out of Dodge. Yevgeny saw it in my expression and told me we weren't finished yet. He distributed more packages, took more names, had a few brief conversations, then finally said we could go. But first we had to go to the center of town, to the city hall, which had been converted into a refugee center.

He parked in front of a typical Soviet government building: both grandiose and functional, always looking old and decrepit before its time. People were pressing around him desperately. I had a bad feeling, like a shell was going to land on us any second, like we'd pushed our luck too far. All I wanted to do was leave immediately. Yevgeny packed about a dozen desperate elderly people into the back of the SUV so tight that they were practically standing. Finally he hopped into the driver's seat and gunned the throttle, and we were bouncing through the shredded streets out of town.

The shelling on the road was much heavier. That bad feeling was amplified with every explosion. We were no more than a couple of

miles north of the town when Yevgeny got a phone call. We needed to
go back. Now I was sure we were going to get hit. The laws of probability
were simply against us. He made a U-turn and said, "We have to pick
someone up, or try to."

Fortunately where we needed to go was on the outskirts of the
town. Yevgeny parked the car right on the side of the road, which was
getting shelled regularly. He told everybody to just stay inside and not
move, as if they could possibly move in the back. I went with him and
ran across the road to a row of houses; most of them were destroyed.
We slipped through a shattered wall that partitioned the backyards of
two typical Ukrainian houses with their corrugated metal roofs. One of
the houses must have taken a direct hit a few hours ago, right in front.
It was freezing and there was a dusting of snow on the ground. I was
walking behind Yevgeny and he pointed downward, as if telling me to
watch out. There, at my feet, was a dead body, a man. Out of instinct
I took a picture of him. He looked stiff already. Yevgeny said he was
the grandfather who owned the house. The direct hit had killed him. I
stepped over the body but there was debris everywhere and I was try
ing not to fall on it. Toward the main entrance I saw an old lady sitting
motionless next to three plastic bags full of her belongings, everything
covered in debris. She was staring at her husband lying there stiff in the
snow. Staring at him for hours no doubt. They'd been trying to leave.
Two younger men, who were now talking to Yevgeny, had called him
on the phone and asked him to please pick her up. But she wouldn't
move. She refused to go anywhere without her husband. Yevgeny tried
to convince her but she was practically catatonic. He shrugged his
shoulders and looked back at the crowd of people crammed into his
car. There was probably no room anyway. So we just left her and let her
keep watching her husband. Maybe she saw something happening to
his soul that we couldn't.

In any case, we went back to the car, where everybody was in a
panic, and we started driving.

Not more than a few miles out of town, right where we'd spotted the DPR tank on the way in, we came to an overturned truck on the side of the road and another one trying to stop. Dead bodies were strewn all around. Yevgeny pulled over and a few DPR soldiers came out with their weapons trained on us. They'd just cut off the road with an ambush. The kessel was officially closed and we were caught inside. They'd just killed about a half a dozen Ukrainian soldiers who were now lying in the middle of the road, so there was blood everywhere, ammunition everywhere, and on the side of the road four or five prisoners were crouched down and looking up at us.

Three DPR soldiers came toward our car. From the glow in their eyes and their numb, slack-jawed expressions you could tell that they had just killed. I hid all my cameras as soon as I saw them coming. One soldier grabbed me and pulled me out of the car with Yevgeny. I looked around; there were about ten of them. They must have been waiting with the tank to ambush reinforcements going into the town. Up till that point the Ukrainians had managed to keep the road open.

There was an officer with them, and I was fairly certain he was Russian. A very handsome man, with blue eyes and a short beard, he had a professional bearing that all the other soldiers naturally deferred to. I pulled out my French passport. He took it and said, "*Oh, Frantsuz.*" He looked at me, opened the passport, and compared faces. One of his soldiers came up to us holding a helmet filled with all sorts of ammunition. They were scavenging everything they could get their hands on. With Yevgeny translating, the officer said, "So, do you have a problem with the DPR?" "No," I said, "do you have a problem with the French?" He started laughing. I pulled out my cigarettes and offered him and the others a smoke. They all came around to get my cigarettes and we started smoking to cut the tension. The officer had a good smile and he asked me, "Why are you here?" I told him I was helping Yevgeny. He looked into the back of the car, which the other soldiers had already checked out, and saw the poor old people. For them it was their people, too. So they just let us go and started fighting again.

The front line was only about a hundred yards away, over a slight rise. There was a checkpoint full of Ukrainian army and their armored personnel carriers. Everyone there was extremely nervous and ready to shoot anything that moved. Now the Ukrainians stopped us and came toward the car. Suddenly they recognized Yevgeny, who gave them all the information. "You just lost half a dozen guys. Another half a dozen are prisoners. Three trucks got stopped." Yevgeny told them there was infantry and tanks. They were literally a hundred yards away, but you couldn't see them because they were in a dip beyond the slight rise.

From there we went back to Artemivsk, checkpoint to checkpoint, all the way. Yevgeny stopped each time to talk to the commander and fill him in on the details of the ambush and the rebel positions. Now the Ukrainians would try desperately to reopen the road and help their troops break out of the kessel. Meanwhile the refugees were taken to what looked like it used to be a school, and Yevgeny dropped me off at New York Street Pizza, a restaurant that had a Wi-Fi connection fast enough for me to file my photos.

I SAT IN THE RESTAURANT with a beer editing a photo selection . . . these good, these no . . . To my left there was a poster of Frank Sinatra, behind me Led Zeppelin at Madison Square Garden; across the room Marilyn Monroe was giving me the eye. These yes, these no. Some photos were good in terms of composition, but unfortunately I was the only one who would get the context. Others had context, but I didn't get the frame right, or the light was off. The gun-gray sky of a dreary Donbas winter, though, was perfect.

Just as I was sending the selection of photos to my agency, the pizza came, served to me by a young blond girl who looked like she was trying to imitate the seductive pout in the Marilyn portrait watching her all day long.

I ate the pizza with my hands and mentally went over the photos I'd just filed. The one with the old man stiff in the snow stayed with me. In my mind I also went over all the photos I'd missed, hundreds of them: the ones of dead Ukrainian soldiers after the ambush, the prisoners crouched down and staring at me with their hollow eyes as they braced themselves for a very bad day. But the one missed photo that remained indelible was the old lady—we'll call her Masha (she deserves a name)—staring at her husband, plastic bags full of her possessions, ready to get out of town. Only she refused to go without him. All she could do was watch . . . and wait.

As I stared into my computer at the image of her husband, Ivan (he deserves a name, too), I wondered, *Why him, why not me? Why was I deemed worthy of survival, of getting out of Syria, of breaking out of the kessel? Was it just dumb luck? Or some sort of grace?* And in my staring I entered Masha, still in Debaltseve no doubt—entered her mind, or soul, or whatever—and I felt like I knew how she felt to be stuck watching and waiting, numbed by flights of hope and despair. Seems all I've ever trained myself to do in my short life is wander and watch such dramatic flights and falls, then freeze them in images that will wait for someone in the future to figure out how they happened, and why.

EPILOGUE

SINCE MY RELEASE I'VE MANAGED TO KEEP TRACK of some of the people who played a role in my abduction and captivity. Their fates are indicative of just how convoluted the war in Syria has become.

Alfarook, my fixer, left Syria and was in Turkey the last time we made contact. We communicate from time to time via Facebook and emails. Still, something inside me has always harbored the suspicion that he may have facilitated my abduction somehow, if even unwittingly.

In June 2016 Alfarook sent me a message that Essad had been assassinated. The commander and two of his men had been killed in Rankous, within a few miles of the place where I was kidnapped. Apparently Essad, like many of the Free Syrian Army commanders, had been running various illegal rackets to raise money. In effect, he had become as much a gangster as a freedom fighter. There were rumors that he had been talking to the government to gain some opportunistic advantage.

Fares, last I heard, was where he'd always been, back at the family house in the Qalamoun Mountains, near where I was kidnapped, surrounded by fruit trees and cultivating honey.

In one of the last messages from Fares he said that Essad, Abu Talal, and Noor had all been fighting in the northern Homs region. Fares also told me that Baby Donkey had joined Daesh and was fighting for them in Raqqa. It didn't surprise me because he was the type who could easily be brainwashed. I found Abu Talal on Facebook and he accepted my friend request, but we haven't exchanged any messages.

I asked Fares about Mej and he told me that Mej had migrated to Germany.

Fares also told me that Rabiyah had been captured, almost certainly tortured, and killed in prison by the Assad government's troops.

Ray-Ban is now a refugee in Lebanon.

The only time I got in touch with Kamal Atrash was when I was in the French embassy. He tried to meet with me outside, but I was forbidden from leaving. He is still a very active pro-Syrian figure in Lebanese politics.

The only time I had any communication with Mohamed Aboud since my release was indirectly. While I was helping with the release of two Swedish journalists captured in the same area, potentially by the same group, I helped put the Swedish and French governments in touch with one of his representatives in Canada. He wasn't very cooperative. Later I found out it was because he and his company still hadn't been taken off the European Union's sanctions list. Eventually he was taken off the list, but then he was reinstated again, as far as I could find out.

I emailed Robert Doueihy for Christmas 2013 and he very politely replied to me. He maintained that the Damascus part of my story was made up, that I had gone straight to Lebanon. He had even said as much to my father. But in private he was always very nice to me and my father, very happy everything worked out. I just assumed there were certain connections he couldn't acknowledge.

As for me, I keep doing this work. Most recently I covered the Battle of Mosul in March 2017. I've also returned to Ukraine several more times. On one occasion I was photographing a soldier from Ukraine's Donbas Battalion as he shot an RPG at separatists during a firefight in Shyrokyne, not far from Mariupol. The building we were in took a direct hit. The blast affected my hearing and later tests revealed some brain trauma. Maybe that explains why I still haven't figured out any plan B— even though I'm working on it.

ACKNOWLEDGMENTS

Every day I try to be as grateful as possible, especially given the risks I continue to take. First of all I'd like to thank my parents, who went through the ordeal with me and have always been there when I needed them. With respect to this book, Stash, Bonnie, and I would like to thank my father, Jean-Louis, in particular for his contribution; Atria's publisher, Judith Curr, for seeing the story in book form before anyone else; Rakesh Satyal for his deft editing; Jack Kliger and Steve Millington for playing matchmaker at Michael's; and John Connor and Caterina Zaccaroni for their support. We would also like to thank all the editors and graphic artists who worked on this book or have ever helped get my pictures out into the world. Of course, I am especially grateful to those of my captors who were kind and to the people who negotiated my release and paid my ransom.

INDEX

ABOUT THE AUTHORS

Born in Paris in 1979, **Jonathan Alpeyrie** moved to the United States in 1993. He graduated from the Lycée Français de New York in 1998, and went on to study medieval history at the University of Chicago, from which he graduated in 2003. Alpeyrie started his career in photojournalism shooting for local Chicago newspapers during his undergraduate years. In 2009, Jonathan became a photographer for Polaris images. His photography career stretches well over a decade, and has taken him to more than twenty-five countries, covering thirteen war zones throughout the Middle East, Africa, Europe, the Caucasus, and Asia.

Alpeyrie has worked as a freelancer for various publications and websites such as the *Sunday Times*, *Le Figaro* magazine, *ELLE*, *American Photo*, *Glamour*, *Aftenposten* (Norway), *Le Monde*, and BBC. His photographs have been published in *Vanity Fair*, *Paris Match*, *La Stampa*, CNN, *Bild Zeit*, *Der Speigel*, the *Guardian*, and the *Atlantic*. A future photography book about World War II veterans is in the works (Verve Editions).

Stash Luczkiw is a poet, novelist, translator and journalist. He works as an editor for *Longitude*, an English-language magazine of international affairs published in Italy. Stash met Jonathan Alpeyrie in Donetsk while covering the war in the Donbas region of Ukraine. They have returned to Ukraine several times and produced reports together on the war there.

Bonnie Timmermann is a producer and casting director who has worked on more than ninety movies, including such classics as *Black Hawk Down*, *Quiz Show*, and *Amadeus*. Film projects currently in development include a recounting of Jonathan Alpeyrie's experiences as a prisoner in Syria and *In Violet* written by John Connor with Mathieu Amalric to direct and star. For television, Bonnie is preparing a series based on nineteen of Andy McNab's Nick Stone novels, and *Framed*, based on Tod Volpe's memoir about the high-end art market.